NEWS REPORTING, PRESENTATION AND STYLE

Principles and Practices

NEWS REPORTING, PRESENTATION AND STYLE

Principles and Practices

SUHAS CHAKRAVARTY
N.C. PANT

KANISHKA PUBLISHERS, DISTRIBUTORS
NEW DELHI-110 002

KANISHKA PUBLISHERS, DISTRIBUTORS
4697/5-21A, Ansari Road, Daryaganj
New Delhi-110 002
Phones : 2327 0497, 2328 8285
Fax : 011-2328 8285
e-mail: kanishka_publishing@yahoo.co.in

First Published 2009

ISBN 978-81-8457-136-3

PRINTED IN INDIA

Published by Madan Sachdeva for Kanishka Publishers, Distributors, 4697/5-21A, Ansari Road, Daryaganj, New Delhi-110 002; Typeset by Sunshine Graphics, Delhi, and Printed at New Rajdhani Printers, Delhi.

Preface

This book titled "News Reporting, Presentation and Style: Principles and Practices" is a kind of reference book on this vital subject. The book provides an introductory overview of communication, mass communication, media and mass media. Attempt is also made to provide readers with an Indian perspective. Similarly, this publication deals with the various aspects related to the profession of journalism and electronic journalism. An overview of the education aspects of journalism is also provided herein. The book also provides an introductory overview of news, news conference and news writing. The persons involved in news editing and copy editing are discussed, so has been their roles and responsibilities. The various elements and dimensions of new sourcing, new release and press release are covered. Again, the persons and processes involved in news reporting, news presentation and news designing have been discussed in detail. This book provides readers with an overview of ways and means of news printing and news publishing, with focus on various printing presses, newspapers and magazines.

The book also describes the multiple elements, advances and jobs related to photojournalism, its ethics and techniques. Jobs and career prospects in photojournalism, both manual and digital types, are discussed in detail. In particular, the ethical aspects have been highlighted to a great extent. The book also attempts to project initiatives required for moving towards ethical journalism and search for a better career prospect in it. Select areas of studies have also been covered with respect to the public relations aspects, tools and techniques of journalism. An overview of news values, news objectives, news ethics, news standards and freedom of press is provided. A detailed glossary of terms and annotated bibliography make this book more user friendly.

Suhas Chakravarty
N.C. Pant

Contents

1

An Introduction to Communication and Mass Communication

COMMUNICATION

Communication is the process of exchanging information usually via a common system of symbols. "Communication studies" is the academic discipline that studies communication.

Forms (Types) of Communication

Forms (types) by Direction

1. One to One:
    - Conversation (implies two-way communication)
    - Message passing (limited to one-way).
2. One to Many:
    - Lecture to live audience or recorded for later playing using various media or sent via computer or TV to remote audience.
    - "Marking" a territory by scent or with something like police tape (communicates stay out, I'm bigger/badder than you).
    - Journalism including use of newspaper, magazine, or other mass medium.
    - Public Relations including spin doctoring.
3. Many to Many:
    - Conference—gathering of peers (in a paricular subject to debate).
    - Party or other social gathering.

4. Now to Future:
    - diary
    - blog
    - time capsule.

Types by participants

1. Animal communications
2. Interpersonal communications:
    - Marketing
    - Internal communications
    - Propaganda
    - Public affairs
    - Public relations
    - Technical communication.
3. Intrapersonal communications
4. Non-verbal communications
5. Speech communications
6. Cross-cultural communication
7. Telecommunications:
    - Computer-mediated communications.

Forms and Components of Human Communication

Humans communicate in order to share knowledge and experiences. Common forms of human communication include sign language, speaking, writing, gestures and broadcasting. Communication can be interactive, transactive, intentional, or unintentional; it can also be verbal or non-verbal. Communication varies considerably in form and style when considering scale. Internal communication, within oneself, is intrapersonal while communication between two individuals are interpersonal. At larger scales of communication both the system of communication and media of communication change. Small group communication takes place in settings of between three and twelve individuals creating a different set of interactions than large groups such as organizational communication in settings like companies or communities. At the largest scales mass communication describes communication to huge numbers of individuals through mass media. Communication also has a time component, being either synchronous or asynchronous. There are a number of theories of communication that attempt to explain human communication.

Communication Technology

In telecommunications, the first transatlantic two-way radio broadcast occurred on July 25th, 1920. As the technology evolved, communication protocol also had to evolve; for example, Thomas Edison had to discover that *hello* was the least ambiguous greeting by voice over a distance; previous greetings such as *hail* tended to be lost or garbled in the transmission.

As regards human communication these diverse fields can be divided into those which cultivate a thoughtful exchange between a small number of people (debate, talk radio, e-mail, personal letters) on the one hand; and those which disseminate broadly a simple message (public relations, television, cinema). Our indebtedness to the Ancient Romans in the field of communication does not end with the Latin root "communicare." They devised what might be described as the first real mail or postal system in order to centralize control of the empire from Rome. This allowed Rome to gather knowledge about events in its many widespread provinces. As the Romans well-knew, communication is as much about taking in towards the centre as it is about putting out towards the extremes. In virtual management an important issue is computer-mediated communication. The view people take toward communication is changing, as new technologies change the way they communicate and organize. In fact, it is the changing technology of communication that tends to make the most frequent and widespread changes in a society—take for example, the rise of web cam chat and other network-based visual communications between distant parties. The latest trend in communication, decentralized personal networking, is termed smartmobbing.

Communication Barriers

Anxiety associated with communication is known as communication apprehension. Such anxiety tends to be influenced by one's self-concept. Besides apprehension, communication can be impaired via bypassing, indiscrimination, and polarization. Failing to share a common language is also an important barrier in many parts of the world.

Apart from that there may be following barriers in communication:

1. Language,
2. Time lag, and
3. Politics.

Examples of Communication

- Jungle drums.
- Smoke signals.
- Hand signals and semaphores (use of devices to increase the distance "hand" signals can be seen from by increasing the size of the movable object).
- Vocalization.
- Territorial marking (animals such as dogs—stay away from my territory).
- Pheromones communicate (amongst other things) "I'm ready to mate"—well known example is moths where the pheromones are put into traps to attract them.
- Gold-plated disk (sent on Voyager 1 into interstellar space).
- Writing.
- Telecommunications—use of technology to aid and enhance distance communications.
    - Digital telecommunications.
    - Encoding and decoding.
    - Compression and encryption (as they relate to enhancing or specifying communications) for example the use of encryption to turn a one to many into a one-to-one communication.
    - Digital transmission media including telegraphy and computer network.
    - Analog telecommunications.
    - Telephone.
    - Radio.
    - TV.

Federal Communications Commission

Headline Text

The Federal Communications Commission (FCC) is an independent United States government agency, created, directed, and empowered by Congressional statute. The FCC was established by the Communications Act of 1934 as the successor to the Federal Radio Commission and is charged with regulating all non-Federal Government use of the radio spectrum (including radio and television broadcasting), and all interstate telecommunications (wire, satellite and cable) as well as all international communications that originate or terminate in the United States. It is an important factor in US telecommunication policy. The FCC took over wire communication regulation from the Interstate Commerce Commission.

The FCC's jurisdiction covers the 50 states, the District of Columbia, and U.S. possessions.

Organization

The FCC is composed of five Commissioners appointed by the President and confirmed by the Senate for five-year terms, except when filling an unexpired term. The President designates one of the Commissioners to serve as Chairman. Only three Commissioners may be members of the same political party. None of them can have a financial interest in any Commission-related business. As the chief executive officer of the Commission, the Chairman delegates management and administrative responsibility to the Managing Director. The Commissioners, Michael Copps, Jonathan Adelstein, and Robert M. McDowell.

Bureaus

The Bureaus' responsibilities include processing applications for licenses and other filings, analyzing complaints, conducting investigations, developing and implementing regulations, and participating in hearings.

- *Consumer and Governmental Affairs*

The Consumer and Governmental Affairs Bureau (CGB) develops and implements the FCC's consumer policies, including disability access. CGB serves as the public face of the FCC through outreach and education, as well as through their Consumer Centre, which is responsible for responding to consumer inquiries and complaints. CGB also maintains collaborative partnerships with state, local, and tribal governments in such critical areas as emergency preparedness and implementation of new technologies.

- *Enforcement*

The Enforcement Bureau (EB) is responsible for enforcement of provisions of the Communications Act 1934, FCC rules, FCC orders, and terms and conditions of station authorizations. Major areas of enforcement that are handled by the Enforcement Bureau are consumer protection, local competition, public safety, and homeland security.

- *International*

The International Bureau (IB) develops international policies in telecommunications, such as coordination of frequency allocation and orbital assignments so as to minimize cases of international electromagnetic interference involving U.S. licensees. The International Bureau also oversees FCC compliance with the international Radio Regulations and other international agreements.

- *Media*

The Media Bureau (MB) develops, recommends and administers the policy and licensing programmes relating to electronic media, including cable television, broadcast television, and radio in the United States and its territories. The Media Bureau also handles post-licensing matters regarding direct broadcast satellite service.

- *Wireless Telecommunications*

The Wireless Telecommunications Bureau (WTB) handles nearly all FCC domestic wireless telecommunications programmes, policies, and outreach initiatives. Wireless services include: amateur radio; cellular networks; paging; Personal Communications Service; and Part 27 Wireless Communications Services (WCS) such as Advanced Wireless Serices (AWS) and fixed, mobile, and broadcast services on the 700 MHz Band.

- *Wireline Competition*

The Wireline Competition Bureau (WCB) develops policy concerning wireline telecommunications. The Wireline Competition Bureau's main objective is to promote growth and economical investments in wireline technology infrastructure, development, markets, and services.

- *Parking Safety and Homeland Security Bureau*

A priority of the Chairman Kevin Martin administration is the establishment of the Public Safety and Homeland Security Bureau within the FCC. The Bureau has yet to be established; trade reports indicate, however, that the organization of the new Bureau is in its final stages.

Offices

The FCC's offices provide support services to the Bureaus. Even though the Bureaus and Offices have their individual functions, they regularly join forces and share expertize in addressing FCC issues.

- *Administrative Law Judges*

The Office of Administrative Law Judges (OALJ) is responsible for conducting hearings ordered by the Commission. The hearing function includes acting on interlocutory requests filed in the proceedings such as petitions to intervene, petitions to enlarge issues, and contested discovery requests. An Administrative Law Judge, appointed under the Administrative Procedure Act, presides at the hearing during which documents and sworn testimony are received in evidence, and witnesses are cross-examined. At the conclusion of the evidentiary phase of a proceeding, the presiding Administrative Law Judge writes and issues an Initial Decision which may be appealed to the Commission.

- *Communications Business Opportunities*

The Office of Communications Business Opportunities (OCBO) promotes telecommunications business opportunities for small, minority-owned, and women-owned businesses. To this end, OCBO works with entrepreneurs, industry, public interest organizations, individuals, and others to provide information about FCC policies, increase ownership and employment opportunities, foster a diversity of voices and viewpoints over the airwaves, and encourage participation in FCC proceedings.

- *Engineering and Technology*

The Office of Engineering and Technology (OET) advises the Commission concerning engineering matters. Its chief role is to manage the electromagnetic spectrum, specifically frequency allocation and spectrum usage. OET conducts technical studies of advanced phases of terrestrial and space communications and administers FCC rules regarding radio devices, experimental radio services, and industrial, scientific, and medical equipment.

OET also organizes the Technical Advisory Council, a committee of FCC advisors from major telecommunication and media corporations.

In addition, the OET operates the Equipment Authorization Branch, which is tasked with overseeing equipment authorization for all devices using the electromagnetic energy from 9KHz to 300GHz. OET maintains an electronic database of all certified equipment which can be easily accessed by the public.

- *General Counsel*

The Office of General Counsel (OGC) serves as the chief legal advisor to the Commission. The General Counsel also represents the Commission in litigation in United States federal courts, recommends decisions in adjudicatory matters before the Commission, assists the Commission in its decision-making capacity and performs a variety of legal functions regarding internal and other administrative matters.

- *Inspector General*

The Office of the Inspector General (OIG) recommends policies to prevent fraud in agency operations. The Inspector General recommends corrective action where appropriate, referring criminal matters to the United States Department of Justice for potential prosecution.

- *Legislative Affairs*

The Office of Legislative Affairs (OLA) is the FCC's liaison to the

United States Congress, providing law-makers with information about FCC regulations. OLA also prepares FCC witnesses for Congressional hearings, and helps create FCC responses to legislative proposals and Congressional inquiries. In addition, OLA is a liaison to other Federal agencies, as well as state and local governments.

- *Managing Director*

The Office of the Managing Director (OMD) is responsible for the administration and management of the FCC, including the agency's budget, personnel, security, contracts and publications.

- *Media Relations*

The Office of Media Relations (OMR) is responsible for the dissemination of commission announcements, orders, proceedings, and other information per media requests. OMR manages the FCC Daily Digest, website, and Audio Visual Centre.

- *Secretary*

The Office of the Secretary (OSec) oversees the receipt and distribution of documents filed by the public through electronic and paper filing systems and the FCC Library collection. In addition, OSec publishes legal notices of Commission decisions in the Federal Register and the FCC Record.

- *Strategic Planning and Policy Analysis*

The Office of Strategic Planning and Policy Analysis (OSP & PA), essentially a think tank within the FCC, identifies policy objectives for the agency. OSP & PA works closely with the FCC Chairman and is responsible for monitoring the state of the communications industry to identify trends, issues and overall industry health. OSP & PA acts as expert consultants to the Commission in areas of economic, business, and market analysis. The Office also reviews legal trends and developments not necessarily related to current FCC proceedings, such as intellectual property law, the Internet, and electronic commerce. Previously OSP & PA was called the Office of Plans and Policy (OPP). Robert Pepper, currently with CISCO, was the Chief of OPP from 1989 to 2005.

- *Workplace Diversity*

The Office of Workplace Diversity (OWD) develops policy to provide a full and fair opportunity for all employees, regardless of non-merit factors such as race, religion, gender, colour, age, disability, sexual orientation or national origin, to carryout their duties in the workplace free from unlawful discriminatory treatment, including sexual harassment and retaliation for engaging in legally protected activities.

History

- *Communications Act of 1934*

In 1934 Congress passed the Communications Act, which abolished the Federal Radio Commission and transferred jurisdiction over radio licensing to a new Federal Communications Commission. Title III of the Communications Act contained provisions very similar to the Radio Act of 1927, and the new FCC largely took over the operations and precedents of the FRC.

- *Report on Chain Broadcasting*

In 1940 the Federal Communications Commission issued the "Report on Chain Broadcasting." The major point in the report was the breakup of NBC, but there were two other important points. One was network option time, the culprit here being CBS. The report limited the amount of time during the day, and what times the networks may broadcast. Previously a network could demand any time it wanted from an affiliate. The second concerned artist bureaus. The networks served as both agents and employees of artists, which was a conflict of interest the report rectified.

- *Consolidation Permissivity, Indecency Crackdowns*

The inauguration of Ronald Reagan as President of the United States in 1981 marked the beginning of a shift in the FCC towards a decidedly more permissive stance. Monopoly regulations were relaxed so far as to be practically irrelevant, and remaining restrictions were laxly enforced. A substantial portion of other regulations were repealed, such as guidelines for minimal amounts of non-entertainment programming in 1985. In addition, the

Fairness Doctrine was removed in 1987. This deregulation has led to the rapid rise in the channel selection offered by broadcast alternatives such as cable television. It has also led to greater concentration of media ownership.

In the early 2000s, the FCC began stepping up censorship and enforcement of indecency regulations again, most notably following the Janet Jackson "wardrobe malfunction" that occurred during the halftime show of Super Bowl XXXVIII. However, the FCC's regulatory domain with respect to indecency remains restricted to the public airwaves, notably VHF and UHF television and AM/FM radio.

On June 15, 2006, President George W. Bush signed into law the Broadcast Decency Enforcement Act of 2005 sponsored by Senator Sam Brownback, a former broadcaster himself, and endorsed by Congressman Fred Upton of Michigan who authored a similar bill in the United States House of Representatives. The new law stiffens the penalties for each violation of the Act. The Federal Communications Commission will be able to impose fines in the amount of $325,000 for each violation by each station, which violates decency standards. The legislation raises the fine by a tenfold increase.

FCC Commissioners Since Inception in 1934

- *Current Commissioners*

Chairman Kevin Martin (FCC) (R-NC), Commissioner Michael Copps (D-WI), CommissionerJonathan Adelstein (D-SD), Commissioner Deborah Taylor Tate (R-TN), Commissioner Robert M. McDowell(R-VA).

- *Past Commissioners*

A complete list of commissioners is available on the FCC website. Notable commissioners have included:

- Dean Burch (AZ)
- Richard E. Wiley (IL)
- James H. Quello (MI)
- Charles Ferris (MA)
- Alfred Sikes (MO)
- William E. Kennard (CA)
- Michael K. Powell

Regulatory Powers

The Federal Communications Commission has one major regulatory weapon, revoking licenses, but short of that has little leverage over broadcast stations. It is reluctant to do this since it operates in a near vacuum of information on most of the tens of thousands of stations whose licenses are renewed every eight years (previously, every three years). Broadcast licenses are supposed to be renewed if the station meets the "public interest, convenience, or necessity." The Federal Communications Commission rarely checks except for some outstanding reason; burden of proof would be on the complainant. Fewer than 1 per cent of station renewals are not immediately granted, and only a small fraction of those actually denied.

The Federal Communications Commission also licenses amateur radio operators and stations, and does use its power to fine amateur radio operators who flagrantly violate its rules. It also licenses commercial operators who operate and repair certain radiotelephone, television, radar, and Morse code radio stations. In recent years it has also licensed people who maintain or operate GMDSS stations. While the FCC maintains control of the written and Morse testing standards, it no longer administers the exams, having delegated that function to private organizations.

Note: Similar authority for regulation of U.S. government radio communications is vested in the President who has delegated it to National Telecommunications and Information Administration (NTIA).

Spectrum Auctions

Beginning in 1994, commercial spectrum has been allocated via competitive auctions rather than the previous method of "best public use." This was a cumbersome bureaucratic process in which competitors attempted to show that they were most capable of making best public use of the license they wished to obtain. The structure and licenses available in each auction are determined by vote of the Commission, with the licenses awarded to the highest bidders. Auctions are usually conducted on a simultaneous multiple-round basis, with all offered licenses being auctioned at the same time. Auctions proceed in bidding rounds of decreasing duration until no more bids are received. Revenues are deposited in the US Treasury to be spent by Congress.

The FCC has been criticized for awarding a Digital TV (DTV) channel to each holder of an analog TV station license without an auction, as well as trading auctionable spectrum to Nextel to resolve public safety interference problems. Nonetheless, in 2009, all analog terrestrial broadcast licenses in the U.S. will be terminated, with terrestrial television subsequently available only from the digital channels.

Criticisms

The FCC has been criticized on many fronts, both for being too restrictive and too permissive in its regulation. On the issue of broadcast indecency, the FCC has taken heat from right wing conservatives and family-oriented groups for not sufficiently censoring and restricting sexually explicit and violent material to which the groups believe children should not be exposed (a Family Viewing Hour was instituted in the 1970s and then discontinued).

In the actions taken against broadcasters, the FCC is frequently criticized for violating the First Amendment guarantee of Freedom of Speech, both directly by censorship and enforcement action sometimes alleged to be politically motivated, and indirectly by the general intimidation that FCC action allegedly creates, particularly with the U.S. Congress considering multiplying fines exponentially. The FCC considered requiring all broadcasters to retain copies of all broadcasts for up to three months (FCC MB Docket 04-232). One critique of this proposal is that this action would wipe out smaller broadcasters because of the enormous expense of having to purchase new equipment with the necessary features for content storage and the need for facilities to store content. Low-power broadcasting has also been a source of contention, as the FCC has set the power limits very low, while allegedly making it nearly impossible for anyone except large corporations or large non-profit organizations to obtain a license. Although Stephen Dunifer won a case versus the FCC, few others have successfully argued against the Commission.

Cable outlets, such as Cartoon Network's Adult Swim, are not governed by the FCC and generally do much less editing. *How* much is usually determined by the outlet's standards and practices department. Another critique is that the Commission has historically been dominated by lawyers, often from the telecommunications industry, due to the FCC's direct effects on commerce and public policy. This is in stark contrast to other technically-focused government agencies, such as the Nuclear Regulatory Commission, which is often populated by engineers and physicists. The FCC is also criticized by "Family Guy" in the episode PTV when Lois say to Peter that call the FCC for censuring Peter's Station (PTV) and Peter sing the "FCC Song." The FCC is also often criticized by Amateur Radio operators for rule changes affecting the Amateur Radio Service, or for its perceived lack of enforcement of violations within the service and in general.

While the FCC, under much criticism, has been tightening its control and censorship of broadcast television, neither the FCC nor any other regulatory body has the authority to censor the internet, allowing broadcasters to use the internet as a source for their un-edited creative expression. In December 2006, NBC and "Saturday Night Live" posted an uncensored video on the NBC website and YouTube under the headings "Special Treat in a Box" or "Special Christmas Box." The censored version of the video played on NBC's Saturday Night Live, and was bleeped (censored) sixteen times. Lorne Michaels, the creator and executive producer of "Saturday Night Live," predicted that other shows and networks, time and money permitting, would surely follow NBC's lead in making available material that was deemed not ready for prime time, or even late night.

The NBC show Studio 60 on the Sunset Strip had a story line where the FCC was fining the fictional NBS network an absurd amount of money for a obscenity said by a U.S. Marine during a live news broadcast in Afghanistan. They badmouth the FCC for being upset for a real life reaction of an near death incident in wartime being accidentally picked up in a required News broadcast. (The FCC requires that Educational programming be provided for free by networks in exchange for the right to broadcast over the airwaves.) The problem becomes worse when they give them the option of losing the fee in exchange for a five second delay of live news feeds. This form of censorship that is becoming used enforced more and more by the real life FCC. The show points out that this practice is an attack on the First Amendment rights of the press, and states that it is destroying the credibility of the Networks as well as pushing news to other forms of mediums.

Controversy

- *Unreleased Reports*

2003 Study of Commercial Radio Concentration: In 2003, the FCC Media Bureau produced a draft report analyzing the impact of deregulation in the radio industry. The report stated that from March 1996 through March 2003, the number of commercial radio stations on the air rose 5.9 per cent while the number of station owners fell 35 per cent. The concentration of ownership followed a 1996 rewrite of telecommunications law that eliminated a 40-station national ownership cap.

The report was never made public, nor have any similar analyzes followed, despite the fact that radio industry reports were released in 1998, 2001 and 2002. In September 2006, Senator Barbara Boxer, who had received a copy of the report, released it.

2004 Study of Television Media Concentration: In 2004, the FCC ordered its staff to destroy all copies of a draft study by Keith Brown and Peter Alexander, two economists in the FCC's Media Bureau. The two had analyzed a database of 4,078 individual news stories broadcast in 1998, showed local ownership of television stations adds almost five and one-half minutes of total news to broadcasts and more than three minutes of "on-location" news. The conclusion of the study was at odds with FCC arguments made when it voted in 2003 to increase the number of television stations a company could own in a single market. (In June 2004, a federal appeals court rejected the agency's reasoning on most of the rules and ordered it to try again.)

In September 2006, Senator Barbara Boxer, who had received a copy of the report "indirectly from someone within the FCC who believed the information should be made public," wrote a letter to FCC Chairman Kevin Martin, asked whether any other commissioners "past or present" knew of the report's existence and why it was never made public. She also asked whether it was "shelved because the outcome was not to the liking of some of the commissioners and/or any outside powerful interests?" Boxer's office said if she does not receive adequate answers to her questions, she will push for an investigation by the FCC inspector general.

Action by FCC Chairman: In a letter in response to Senator Boxer, FCC Chairman Martin said "I want to assure you that I too am concerned about what happened to these two draft reports." The letter also said "I have asked the inspector general of the FCC to conduct an investigation into what happened to these draft documents and will cooperate fully with him." Martin added that he was not chairman at the time the reports were drafted, and that neither he nor his staff had seen them.

NSA Wiretapping: When it emerged in 2006 that AT&T, BellSouth and Verizon may have broken U.S. laws by aiding the National Security Agency in possible illegal wiretapping of its customers, Congressional representatives called for an FCC investigation into whether or not those companies broke the law. The FCC declined to investigate, however, claiming that it could not investigate due to the classified nature of the programme—a move that provoked the criticism of members of Congress.

> "Today the watchdog agency that oversees the country's telecommunications industry refused to investigate the nation's largest phone companies' reported disclosure of phone records to the NSA," said Rep. Edward Markey (D-Mass.) in response to the decision. "The FCC, which oversees the protection of consumer privacy under the Communications Act of 1934, has taken a pass at investigating what is estimated to be the nation's largest violation of consumer privacy ever to occur. If the oversight body that monitors our nation's communications is stepping aside then Congress must step in."

- *Doraemon*

The character "Broadband" (FCC Kids Zone) looks like Doraemon, a popular manga character in Japan. Doraemon was created for print in magazines in 1969, which makes Doraemon predate the FCC's character. According to Japanese news media, both Shogakukan (copyright manager) and Fujiko-production (owner of the copyright) have warned the FCC over the alleged copyright infringement, but so far there has been no answer.

- *Diversity*

With the major demographic shifts occurring in the country in terms of the racial-ethnic composition of the population, where 9 of the 10 largest cities, for example, now have "majority minority" populations, the FCC has also been criticized for ignoring the issue of decreasing racial-ethnic diversity of the media. This includes charges that the FCC has been watering down the limited affirmative action regulations it had on the books, including no longer requiring stations to make public their data on their minority staffing and hiring. In the second half of 2006, groups such as the National Hispanic Media Coalition, the National Latino Media Council, the National Association of Hispanic Journalists, the National Institute for Latino Policy, the League of United Latin American Citizens (LULAC) and others held town hall meetings in California, New York and Texas on media diversity as its affects Latinos and other communities of colour. They documented widespread and deeply-felt community concerns about the negative effects of media concentration and consolidation on racial-ethnic diversity in staffing and programming. At these Latino town hall meetings, the issue of the FCC's lax monitoring of obscene and pornographic material in Spanish-language radio and the lack of racial and national-origin diversity among Latino staff in Spanish-language television were other major themes.

FCC-Broadcasting Tower Database

The FCC-Database of broadcasting towers is a very useful tool to get information about the height and year of built of broadcasting towers in the USA. Nevertheless this database contains no information about the structural types of towers. The FCC-Database does not contain information about the height of towers used for non-broadcasting purposes like NDBs, LORAN-C transmission towers or VLF transmission facilities of the US-Navy, or from towers not used for transmission at all like the BREN-Tower.

MASS COMMUNICATION

Mass Communication is the term used to describe the academic study of various means by which individuals and entities can relay information to large segments of the population all at once through mass media. Almost every university that has a journalism programme also offer a distinct programme—often from the same department—of studies in mass communication, which includes the technical aspects production of newspapers, radio programmes, television shows, and films. Unlike journalism and related fields like public relations and advertising, the study of mass communication focuses less on the message that is delivered, and more on the means by which this delivery occurs. In today's world the Internet is playing a vital role in delivering news and information to remote places where traditional delivery means do not serve. The discipline also differs from media studies, which focuses on the effects that mass media have on the population. Graduates of Mass Communication work in a variety of fields in traditional media, advertising, public relations and research institutes. Such programmes are accredited by the Accrediting Council on Education in Journalism and Mass Communication (ACEJMC).

Mass communication is the term used to describe the academic study of various means by which individuals and entities relay information to large segments of the population all at once through mass media. In the United States, many university journalism departments evolved into schools or colleges of mass communication or "journalism and mass communication," as reflected in the names of two major academic organizations. In addition to studying practical skills of journalism, public relations or advertising, students also may major in "mass communication" or "mass communication research." The latter is often the title given to doctoral studies in such schools, whether the focus of the student's research is journalism practice, history, law or media effects. Departmental structures within such colleges may separate research and instruction in professional or technical aspects of newspaper and magazine publishing, radio, television and film. Mass communication research includes media institutions and processes, such as diffusion of information, and media effects, such as persuasion or manipulation of public opinion.

With the Internet's increased role in delivering news and information, mass communication studies and media organizations—have increasingly focused on the convergence of publishing, broadcasting and digital communication.

The academic mass communication discipline historically differs from media studies and communication studies programmes with roots in departments of theatre, film or speech, and with more interest in "qualitative," interpretive theory, critical or cultural approaches to communication study. In contrast, many mass communication programmes historically lean toward empirical analysis and quantitative research—from statistical content analysis of media messages to survey research, public opinion polling, and experimental research.

Interest in "New Media" and "Computer Mediated Communication" is growing much faster than educational institutions can assimilate it. So far, traditional classes and degree programmes have not been able to accommodate new paradigm shifts in communication technologies. Although national standards for the study of interactive media have been in place since the mid-nineties, course work in these areas tends to vary significantly from university to university. Graduates of Mass Communication programmes work in a variety of fields in traditional news media and publishing, advertising, public relations and research institutes. Such programmes are accredited by the Accrediting Council on Education in Journalism and Mass Communication (ACEJMC). The Association for Education in Journalism and Mass Communication (AEJMC) is the major membership organization for academics in the field, offering regional and national conferences and refereed publications.

The International Communication Association (ICA) and National Communication Association (formerly the Speech Communication Association) include divisions and publications that overlap with those of AEJMC, but AEJMC historically has stronger ties to the mass communication professions in the United States.

Mass communication is the term used to describe the academic study of the various means by which individuals and entities relay information through mass media to large segments of the population at the same time. It is usually understood to relate to newspaper and magazine publishing, radio, television and film, as these are used both for disseminating news and for advertising.

Field of Study

Mass communication research includes media institutions and processes such as diffusion of information, and media effects such as persuasion or manipulation of public opinion. In the United States, for instance, several university journalism departments evolved into schools or colleges of mass communication or "journalism and mass communication." In addition to studying practical skills of journalism, public relations or advertising, they offer programmes on "mass communication" or "mass communication research." The latter is often the title given to doctoral studies in such schools, whether the focus of the student's research is journalism practice, history, law or media effects. Departmental structures within such colleges may separate research and instruction in professional or technical aspects of mass communication. With the increased role of the Internet in delivering news and information, mass communication studies and media organizations tend to focus on the convergence of publishing, broadcasting and digital communication.

The academic mass communication discipline historically differs from media studies and communication studies programmes with roots in departments of theatre, film or speech, and with more interest in "qualitative," interpretive theory, critical or cultural approaches to communication study. In contrast, many mass communication programmes historically lean toward empirical analysis and quantitative research—from statistical content analysis of media messages to survey research, public opinion polling, and experimental research.

Interest in "New Media" and "Computer Mediated Communication" is growing much faster than educational institutions can assimilate it. So far, traditional classes and degree programmes have not been able to accommodate new shifts of the paradigm in communication technologies. Although national standards for the study of interactive media have been present in the U.K. since the mid-nineties, course work in these areas tends to vary significantly from university to university.

Graduates of Mass Communication programmes work in a variety of fields in traditional news media and publishing, advertising, public relations and research institutes.

Such programmes are accredited by the Accrediting Council on Education in Journalism and Mass Communication. The Association for Education in Journalism and Mass Communication is the major membership organization for academics in the field, offering regional and national conferences and refereed publications. The International Communication Association and National Communication Association (formerly the Speech Communication Association) include divisions and publications that overlap with those of AEJMC, but AEJMC historically has stronger ties to the mass communication professions in the United States.

The Terms 'Mass' and 'Communication'

The term 'mass' denotes great volume, range or extent (of people or production) and reception of messages. The important point about 'mass' is not that a given number of individuals receives the products, but rather that the products are available in principle to a plurality of recipients.

The term 'mass' suggests that the recipients of media products constitute a vast sea of passive, undifferentiated individuals. This is an image associated with some earlier critiques of 'mass culture' and mass society which generally assumed that the development of mass communication has had a largely negative impact on modern social life, creating a kind of bland and homogeneous culture which entertains individuals without challenging them. However, with the advancement in Media Technology, people are no longer receiving gratification without questioning the grounds on which it is based. Instead, people are engaging themselves more with media products such as computers, cell phones and Internet. These have gradually became vital tools for communications in society today.

The aspect of 'communication' refers to the giving and taking of meaning, the transmission and reception of messages. The word 'communication' is really equated with 'transmission', as viewed by the sender, rather than in the fuller meaning, which includes the notions of response, sharing and interaction. Messages are produced by one set of individuals and transmitted to others who are typically situated in settings that are spatially and temporally remote from the original context of production. Therefore, the term 'communication' in this context masks the social and industrial nature of the media, promoting a tendency to think of them as interpersonal communication. Furthermore, it is known that recipients today do have some capacity to intervene in and contribute to the course and content of the communicative process. They are being both active and creative towards the messages that they are conveyed of. With the complement of the cyberspace supported by the Internet, not only that recipients are participants in a structured process of symbolic transmission, constraints such as time and space are reordered and eliminated.

'Mass communication' can be seen as institutionalized production and generalized diffusion of symbolic goods via the fixation and transmission of information or symbolic content. It is known that the systems of information codification has shifted from analog to digital. This has indeed advanced the communication between individuals. With the existence of Infrared, Bluetooth and Wi-Fi, cell phones are no longer solely a tool for audio transmission. We can transfer photos, music documents or even games and e-mail at any time and anywhere. The development of media technology has indeed advanced the transmission rate and stability of information exchange.

Characteristics of Mass Communication

Five characteristics of mass communication have been identified by Cambridge University's John Thompson. Firstly, it "comprises both technical and institutional methods of production and distribution." This is evident throughout the history of the media, from print to the Internet, each suitable for commercial utility.

Secondly, it involves the "commodification of symbolic forms", as the production of materials relies on its ability to manufacture and sell large quantities of the work. Just as radio stations rely on its time sold to advertisements, newspapers rely for the same reasons on its space. Mass Communication's third characteristic is the "separate contexts between the production and reception of information", while the fourth is in its "reach to those 'far removed' in time and space, in comparison to the producers."

Finally, Thompson notes a fifth characteristic of mass communication, which involves "information distribution." This is a "one to many" form of communication, whereby products are mass produced and disseminated to a great quantity of audiences.

2

Major Trends and Dimensions of Media and Mass Media: An Indian Perspective

MEDIA

Media may refer to various aspects:

In Communication

1. Print media, communications delivered via paper or canvas.
2. Electronic media, communications delivered via electronic or electromechanical energy:
   (*a*) Multimedia, communications that incorporate multiple forms of information content and processing.
   (*b*) Hypermedia, media with hyperlinks.
3. Published media, any media made available to the public:
   (*a*) Mass media, all means of mass communication:
      (*i*) Broadcast media, communications delivered over mass electronic communication networks,
      (*ii*) News media, mass media focused on communicating news.

In Data Storage

Recording media, devices used to store information:

- Digital media, electronic media used to store information.

In Art

- Media (arts), materials and techniques used by an artist to produce a work.

In Biology

- Growth media, objects in which microorganisms or cells can experience growth.
- Tunica media, the middle layer of the wall of a blood vessel.

In Astronomy

- Kaus Media, a star system in the constellation Sagittarius.

In Geography

- Media or Medea, the realm of the Medes,
- Media, Pennsylvania, and
- Media, Illinois.

In Popular Culture

- Media (album), the 1998 album by The Faint.

MASS MEDIA

Mass media is a term used to denote, as a class, that section of the media specifically conceived and designed to reach a very large audience such as the population of a nation state. It was coined in the 1920s with the advent of nationwide radio networks, mass-circulation newspapers and magazines, although mass media was present centuries before the term became common.

The term public media has a similar meaning: it is the sum of the public mass distributors of news and entertainment across mediums such as newspapers, television, radio, broadcasting and text publishers. The concept of mass media is complicated in some internet media as now individuals have a means of potential exposure on a scale comparable to what was previously restricted to select group of mass media producers. These internet media can include personal web pages, podcasts and blogs.

The mass media audience has been viewed by some commentators as forming a mass society with special characteristics, notably atomization or lack of social connections, which render it especially susceptible to the influence of modern mass media techniques such as advertising and propaganda. The term "MSM" or "mainstream media" has been widely used in the blogosphere in discussion of the mass media and media bias.

Etymology and Usage

Media (the plural of "medium") is a truncation of the term *media of communication*, referring to those organized means of dissemination of fact, opinion, entertainment, and other information, such as newspapers, magazines, out-of-home advertising, cinema films, radio, television, the World Wide Web, books, CDs, DVDs, videocassettes, computer games and other forms of publishing. Although writers currently differ in their preference for using *media* in the singular ("the media is...") or the plural ("the media are..."), the former will still incur criticism in some situations. Academic programmes for the study of mass media are usually referred to as mass communication programmes.

An individual corporation within the mass media is referred to as a Media Institution.

The term "mass media" is mainly used by academics and media-professionals. When members of the general public refer to "the media" they are usually referring to the mass media, or to the news media, which is a section of the mass media.

Sometimes mass media (and the news media in particular) are referred to as the "corporate media." Other references include the "mainstream media" (MSM). Technically, *mainstream media* includes outlets that are in harmony with the prevailing direction of influence in the culture at large. In the United States, usage of these terms often depends on the connotations the speaker wants to invoke. The term "corporate media" is often used by leftist media critics to imply that the mainstream media are themselves composed of large multinational corporations, and promote those interests. This is countered by the right-wing media critics with the term "MSM", the acronym implying that the majority of mass media sources are dominated by leftist powers which are furthering their own agenda.

The more recent term 'Drive-by Media' has been popularized by conservative talk-show host Rush Limbaugh in response to the proposed transfer of operations of several U.S. ports to Dubai Ports World.

History

Types of drama in numerous cultures were probably the first mass media, going back into the Ancient World. The first printed book known is the "Diamond Sutra", printed in China in 868 AD, and it is often suspected that books were printed earlier. Movable clay type was invented in 1041 in China. However, due to the slow spread to the masses of literacy in China, and the relatively high cost of paper there, the earliest printed mass medium was probably European popular prints from about 1400. Although these were produced in huge numbers, very few early examples survive, and even most known to be printed before about 1600 have not survived. Johannes Gutenberg printed the first book on a printing press with movable type in 1453. This invention transformed the way the world received printed materials, although books remained too expensive really to be called a mass medium for at least a century after that.

Newspapers developed around from 1605, with the first example in English in 1620; but they took until the nineteenth century to reach a mass audience directly.

During the 20th century, the growth of mass media was driven by technology that allowed the massive duplication of material. Physical duplication technologies such as printing, record pressing and film duplication allowed the duplication of books, newspapers and movies at low prices to huge audiences. Radio and television allowed the electronic duplication of information for the first time.

Mass media had the economics of linear replication: a single work could make money proportional to the number of copies sold, and as volumes went up, units costs went down, increasing profit margins further. Vast fortunes were to be made in mass media. In a democratic society, independent media serve to educate the public/electorate about issues regarding government and corporate entities. Some consider the concentration of media ownership to be a grave threat to democracy.

Timeline

c1400 : Appearance of European popular prints.
1453 : Johnannes Gutenberg prints the Bible, using his printing press, ushering in the Renaissonce.
1620 : First newspaper (or *coranto*) in English.
1825 : Nicéphore Niépce takes the first permanent photograph.
1830 : Telegraphy is independently developed in England and the United States.
1876 : First telephone call made by Alexander Graham Bell.

1878 : Thomas Alva Edison patents the phonograph.
1890 : First juke box in San Francisco's Palais Royal Saloon.
1890 : Telephone wires are installed in Manhattan.
1895 : Cinematograph invented by Auguste and Louis Lumiere.
1896 : Hollerith founds the Tabulating Machine Co. It will become IBM in 1924.
1897 : Guglielmo Marconi patents the wireless telegraph.
1898 : Loudspeaker is invented.
1906 : The Story of the Kelly Gang from Australia is world's first feature length film.
1909 : RMS Republic, a palatial White Star passenger liner, uses the Marconi Wireless for a distress at sea. She had been in a collision. This is the first "breaking news" mass media event.
1912 : Air mail begins.
1913 : Edison transfers from cylinder recordings to more easily reproducible discs.
1913 : The portable phonograph is manufactured.
1915 : Radiotelephone carries voice from Virginia to the Eiffel Tower.
1916 : Tunable radios invented.
1919 : Short-wave radio is invented.
1920 : KDKA-AM in Pittsburgh, United States, becoming the world's first commercial radio station.
1922 : BBC is formed and broadcasting to London.
1924 : KDKA created a short-wave radio transmitter.
1925 : BBC broadcasting to the majority of the UK.
1926 : NBC is formed.
1927 : The Jazz Singer: The first motion picture with sounds debuts.
1927 : Philo Taylor Farnsworth debuts the first electronic television system.
1928 : The Teletype was introduced.
1933 : Edwin Armstrong invents FM Radio.
1934 : Half of the homes in the U.S. have radios.
1935 : First telephone call made around the world.
1936 : BBC opened world's first regular (then defined as at least 200 lines) high definition television service.

1938 : *The War of the Worlds* is broadcast on October 30, causing mass hysteria.
1939 : Western Union introduces coast-to-coast fax service.
1939 : Regular electronic television broadcasts begin in the U.S.
1939 : The wire recorder is invented in the U.S.
1940 : The first commercial television station, WNBT (now WNBC-TV)/New York signs on the air.
1948 : Cable television becomes available in the U.S.
1951 : The first colour televisions go on sale.
1957 : Sputnik is launched and sends back signals from near earth orbit.
1959 : Xerox makes the first copier.
1960 : Echo I, a U.S. balloon in orbit, reflects radio signals to Earth.
1962 : Telstar satellite transmits an image across the Atlantic.
1963 : Audio cassette is invented in the Netherlands.
1963 : Martin Luther King gives "I have a dream" speech.
1965 : Vietnam War becomes first war to be televised.
1967 : Newspapers, magazines start to digitize production.
1969 : Man's first landing on the moon is broadcast to 600 million people around the globe.
1970s : ARPANET, progenitor to the internet developed.
1971 : Intel debuts the microprocessor.
1972 : Pong becomes the first video game to win widespread popularity.
1975 : The MITS Altair 8800 becomes the first pre-assembled desktop computer available on the market.
1976 : JVC introduces VHS videotape—becomes the standard consumer format in the 1980s and 1990s.
1980 : CNN launches.
1980 : New York Times, Wall Street Journal, Dow Jones put news database online.
1981 : The laptop computer is introduced by Tandy.
1982 : Philips and Sony put the Compact Disc on the Japanese market. It arrives on the U.S. market early the following year.
1983 : Cellular phones begin to appear.
1984 : Apple Macintosh is introduced.
1985 : CD-ROMs begin to be sold.

1985 : Pay-per-view channels open for business.
1991 : World-Wide Web (WWW) publickly released by Tim Berners-Lee at CERN.
1993 : CERN announces that the WWW will be free for anyone to use.
1995 : The Internet grows exponentially.
1996 : First DVD players and discs are available in Japan. Twister is the first film on DVD.
1999 : Napster contributes to the popularization of MP3.

Purposes

Mass media can be used for various purposes:

- Advocacy, both for business and social concerns. This can include advertising, marketing, propaganda, public relations, and political communication.
- Enrichment and education.
- Entertainment, traditionally through performances of acting, music, and sports, along with light reading; since the late 20th century also through video and computer games.
- Journalism.
- Public service announcements.

Claimed Inherent Negative Characteristics of Mass Media

Another description of Mass Media is central media meaning they emanate from a central point, the same identical message to numerous recipients. It is claimed this forces certain intrinsic constraints on the kind of messages and information that can be conveyed such as:

> "an inability to transmit tacit knowledge, a focus on the unusual and sensational rather than a restatement of wisdom, the promotion of anxiety and fear to sell the newpaper/channel etc. inability to deal with complex issues so a need to simplify."

This view of central media can be contrasted with lateral media such as e-mails networks where messages are all slightly different a spread by a process of lateral diffusion.

Journalism

Journalism is a discipline of collecting, analyzing, verifying, and presenting information regarding current events, trends, issues and people. Those who practice journalism are known as journalists.

News-oriented journalism is sometimes described as the "first rough draft of history" (attributed to Phil Graham), because journalists often record important events, producing news articles on short deadlines. While under pressure to be first with their stories, news media organizations usually edit and proofread their reports prior to publication, adhering to each organization's standards of accuracy, quality and style. Many news organizations claim proud traditions of holding government officials and institutions accountable to the public, while media critics have raised questions about holding the press itself accountable.

Public Relations

Public relations is the art and science of managing communication between an organization and its key publics to build, manage and sustain its positive image. Examples include:

- Corporations use Marketing Public Relations (MPR) to convey information about the products they manufacture or services they provide to potential customers to support their direct sales efforts. Typically, they support sales in the short and long-term, establishing and burnishing the corporation's branding for a strong, ongoing market.
- Corporations also use public-relations as a vehicle to reach legislators and other politicians, seeking favourable tax, regulatory, and other treatment, and they may use public relations to portray themselves as enlightened employers, in support of human-resources recruiting programmes.
- Non-profit organizations, including schools and universities, hospitals, and human and social service agencies, use public relations in support of awareness programmes, fund-raising programmes, staff recruiting, and to increase patronage of their services.

- Politicians use public relations to attract votes and raise money, and, when successful at the ballot box, to promote and defend their service in office, with an eye to the next election or, at career's end, to their legacy.

Forms

Electronic media and print media include:

- Broadcasting, in the narrow sense, for radio and television.
- Various types of discs or tape. In the 20th century, these were mainly used for music. Video and computer uses followed.
- Film, most often used for entertainment, but also for documentaries.
- Internet, which has many uses and presents both opportunities and challenges. Blogs and podcasts, such as news, music, pre-recorded speech and video).
- Publishing, in the narrow sense, meaning on paper, mainly via books, magazines and newspapers.
- Computer games, which have developed into a mass form of media since devices such as the PlayStation 3, Xbox 360, and the Wii broadened their use.

Audio Recording and Reproduction

Sound recording and reproduction is the electrical or mechanical re-creation and/or amplification of sound, often as music. This involves the use of audio equipment such as microphones, recording devices and loudspeakers. From early beginnings with the invention of the phonograph using purely mechanical techniques, the field has advanced with the invention of electrical recording, the mass production of the 78 record, the magnetic wire recorder followed by the tape recorder, the vinyl LP record. The invention of the compact cassette in the 1960's, followed by Sony's Walkman, gave a major boost to the mass distribution of music recordings, and the invention of digital recording and the compact disc in 1983 brought massive improvements in ruggedness and quality. The most recent developments have been in digital audio players like the *Apple iPod*. An album is a collection of related audio tracks, released together to the public, usually commercially.

The term record album originated from the fact that 78 RPM Phonograph disc records were kept together in a book resembling a photo album. The first collection of records to be called an "album" was Tchaikovsky's *Nutcracker Suite*, release in April 1909 as a four-disc set by Odeon records. It retailed for 16 shillings—about £15 in modern currency.

A music video (also promo) is a short film or video that accompanies a complete piece of music, most commonly a song. Modern music videos were primarily made and used as a marketing device intended to promote the sale of music recordings. Although the origins of music videos go back much further, they came into their own in the 1980s, when Music Television's format was based around them. In the 1980s, the term "rock video" was often used to describe this form of entertainment, although the term has fallen into disuse.

Music videos can accommodate all styles of film-making, including animation, live action films, documentaries, and non-narrative, abstract film.

Broadcasting

Broadcasting is the distribution of audio and/or video signals (programmes) to a number of recipients ("listeners" or "viewers") that belong to a large group. This group may be the public in general, or a relatively large audience within the public. Thus, an Internet channel may distribute text or music world-wide, while a public address system in (for example) a workplace may broadcast very limited *ad hoc* soundbites to a small population within its range. The sequencing of content in a broadcast is called a schedule. With all technological endeavours a number of technical terms and slang are developed please see the list of broadcasting terms for a glossary of terms used.

Television and radio programmes are distributed through radio broadcasting or cable, often both simultaneously. By coding signals and having decoding equipment in homes, the latter also enables subscription-based channels and pay-per-view services.

A broadcasting organization may broadcast several programmes at the same time, through several channels (frequencies), for example BBC One and Two. On the other hand, two or more organizations may share a channel and each use it during a fixed part of the day. Digital radio and digital television may also transmit multiplexed programming, with several channels compressed into one ensemble. When broadcasting is done via the Internet the term webcasting is often used. In 2004, a new phenomenon occurred when a number of technologies combined to produce podcasting. Podcasting is an asynchronous broadcast/narrowcast medium, with one of the main proponents being Adam Curry and his associates the Podshow.

Broadcasting forms a very large segment of the mass media. Broadcasting to a very narrow range of audience is called narrowcasting. The term "broadcast" was coined by early radio engineers from the midwestern United States.

Film

Film is a term that encompasses motion pictures as individual projects, as well as the field in general. The origin of the name comes from the fact that photographic film (also called *filmstock*) has historically been the primary medium for recording and displaying motion pictures. Many other terms exist—*motion pictures* (or just *pictures* or "picture"), *the silver screen, photoplays, the cinema, picture shows, flicks*—and commonly *movies*.

Films are produced by recording people and objects with cameras, or by creating them using animation techniques and/or special effects. They comprise a series of individual frames, but when these images are shown rapidly in succession, the illusion of motion is given to the viewer. Flickering between frames is not seen due to an effect known as persistence of vision—whereby the eye retains a visual image for a fraction of a second after the source has been removed. Also of relevance is what causes the perception of motion; a psychological effect identified as beta movement. Film is considered by many to be an important art form; films entertain, educate, enlighten and inspire audiences. The visual elements of cinema need no translation, giving the motion picture a universal power of communication. Any film can become a worldwide attraction, especially with the addition of dubbing or subtitles that translate the dialogue. Films are also artifacts created by specific cultures, which reflect those cultures, and, in turn, affect them.

Internet

The Internet (also known simply as "the Net" or "the Web") can be briefly understood as "a network of networks." Specifically, it is the worldwide, publicly accessible network of interconnected computer networks that transmit data by packet switching using the standard Internet Protocol (IP). It consists of millions of smaller domestic, academic, business, and governmental networks, which together carry various information and services, such as electronic mail, online chat, file transfer, and the interlinked Web pages and other documents of the World Wide Web. Contrary to some common usage, the Internet and the World Wide Web are not synonymous: the Internet is a collection of interconnected *computer networks*, linked by copper wires, fiber-optic cables, wireless connections etc.; the Web is a collection of interconnected *documents*, linked by hyperlinks and URLs. The World Wide Web is accessible via the Internet, along with many other services including e-mail, file sharing and others described below:

> Toward the end of the 20th century, the advent of the World Wide Web marked the first era in which any individual could have a means of exposure on a scale comparable to that of mass media. For the first time, anyone with a web site can address a global audience, although serving to high levels of web traffic is still relatively expensive. It is possible that the rise of peer-to-peer technologies may have begun the process of making the cost of bandwidth manageable. Although a vast amount of information, imagery, and commentary (*i.e.* "content") has been made available, it is often difficult to determine the authenticity and reliability of information contained in web pages (in many cases, self-published). The invention of the Internet has also allowed breaking news stories to reach around the globe within minutes. This rapid growth of instantaneous, decentralized communication is often deemed likely to change mass media and its relationship to society. "Cross-media" means the idea of distributing the same message through different media channels. A similar idea is expressed in the news industry as "convergence." Many authors understand cross-media publishing to be the ability to publish in both print and on the without manual conversion effort. An increasing number of wireless devices with mutually incompatible data and screen formats make it even more difficult to achieve the objective "create once, publish many."

Publishing

Publishing is the industry concerned with the production of literature or information—the activity of making information available for public view. In some cases, authors may be their own publishers. Traditionally, the term refers to the distribution of printed works such as books and newspapers. With the advent of digital information systems and the Internet, the scope of publishing has expanded to include websites, blogs, and the like.

As a business, publishing includes the development, marketing, production, and distribution of newspapers, magazines, books, literary works, musical works, software, other works dealing with information. Publication is also important as a legal concept: (1) as the process of giving formal notice to the world of a significant intention, for example, to marry or enter bankruptcy, and (2) as the essential precondition of being able to claim defamation; that is, the alleged libel must have been published.

Book

A book is a collection of sheets of paper, parchment or other material with a piece of text written on them, bound together along one edge within covers. A book is also a literary work or a main division of such a work. A book produced in electronic format is known as an e-book. In library and information science, a book is called a monograph to distinguish it from serial publications such as magazines, journals or newspapers. Publishers may produce low-cost, pre-proof editions known as galleys or 'bound proofs' for promotional purposes, such as generating reviews in advance of publication. Galleys are usually made as cheaply as possible, since they are not intended for sale. A lover of books is usually referred to as a bibliophile, a bibliophilist, or a philobiblist, or, more informally, a bookworm.

A book may be studied by students in the form of a book report. It may also be covered by a professional writer as a book review to introduce a new book. Some belong to a book club.

Magazine

A magazine is a periodical publication containing a variety of articles, generally financed by advertising and/or purchase by readers. Magazines are typically published weekly, biweekly, monthly, bimonthly or quarterly, with a date on the cover that is in advance of the date it is actually published. They are often printed in colour on coated paper, and are bound with a soft cover.

Magazines fall into two broad categories: consumer magazines and business magazines. In practice, magazines are a subset of periodicals, distinct from those periodicals produced by scientific, artistic, academic or special interest publishers which are subscription-only, more expensive, narrowly limited in circulation, and often have little or no advertising.

Magazines can be classified as:

- General interest magazines (*e.g.* Frontline, India Today, The Week, etc.).
- Special interest magazines (women's, sports, business, scuba diving, etc.).

Newspaper

A newspaper is a publication containing news and information and advertising, usually printed on low-cost paper called newsprint. It may be general or special interest, most often published daily or weekly. The first printed newspaper was published in 1605, and the form has thrived even in the face of competition from technologies such as radio and television. Recent—developments on the Internet are posing major threats to its business model. However paid circulation is declining in most countries, and advertising revenue, which makes up the bulk of a newspaper's income, is shifting from print to online; some commentators, nevertheless, point out that historically new media such as radio and television did not entirely supplant existing media.

Software Publishing

A software publisher is a publishing company in the software industry between the developer and the distributor. In some companies, two or all three of these roles may be combined (and indeed, may reside in a single person, especially in the case of shareware). Software publishers often license software from developers with specific limitations, such as a time limit or geographical region. The terms of licensing vary enormously, and are typically secret. Developers may use publishers to reach larger or foreign markets, or to avoid focussing on marketing. Or publishers may use developers to create software to meet a market need that the publisher has identified.

Video and Computer Games

Computer game is a computer-controlled game. A video game is a computer game where a video display such as a monitor or television is the primary feedback device. The term "computer game" also includes games which display only text (and which can therefore theoretically be played on a teletypewriter) or which use other methods, such as sound or vibration, as their primary feedback device, but there are very few new games in these categories. There always must also be some sort of input device, usually in the form of button/joystick combinations (on arcade games), a keyboard and mouse/trackball combination (computer games), or a controller (console games), or a combination of any of the above. Also, more esoteric devices have been used for input. Usually there are rules and goals, but in more open-ended games the player may be free to do whatever they like within the confines of the virtual universe. The phrase interactive entertainment is the formal reference to computer and video games. To avoid ambiguity, this game software is referred to as *computer and video games* throughout this article, which explores properties common to both types of game. In common usage, a "computer game" or a "PC game" refers to a game that is played on a personal computer. "Console game" refers to one that is played on a device specifically designed for the use of such, while interfacing with a standard television set. "Video game" (or "videogame") has evolved into a catchall phrase that encompasses the aforementioned along with any game made for any other device, including, but not limited to, mobile phones, PDAs, advanced calculators, etc.

Contrast with Non-Mass Media

Non-mass or "personal" media (point-to-point and person-to-person communication) include:

- Speech
- Gestures
- Telephony
- Postal mail
- Some uses of the Internet

- Some Interactive media.

Arguably, blogs and other first-person, web-based communications are non-mass media.

MASS MEDIA IN INDIA

Media Penetration as of 2003

Media in India, especially news media, are undergoing significant changes in the current liberalized environment. To understand these changes, one needs to have some idea of the road traversed so far. It is useful to look at media in the two phases of India's history—pre-colonial and post-colonial. Each medium has taken its own evolutionary path.

	All India %	*Urban %*
Print	25	46
Terrestrial television	53	80
Cable and satellite television	20	46
Radio	22	25
Cinema	7	11
Internet	1	3

The National and the English press; Bofors and Tehelka; *The Hindu* and *Indian Express*; *Times of India* and *The Statesman*; *India Today* and *Outlook*; Pothan Joseph and G. Kasturi; N. Ram and Vinod Mehta; The Hoot and IndianOnlineJournalism.Org are not contrasts but a sampling of the range that needs to be covered here.

Introduction

William Bolts, an ex-employee of the British East India Company attempted to start the first newspaper in India way back in 1776. Bolts had to beat a retreat under the disapproving gaze of the Court of Directors of the Company. The *Bengal Gazette* by James Augustus Hicky was started in 1780. The *Gazette*, a two-sheet newspaper, "specialized" in writing on the private lives of the Sahibs of the Company. He dared even to mount "scurrillious attacks" on the Governor-General Warren Hastings' wife, which soon landed "the late printer to the Honourable Company" in trouble. Hicky landed himself a four months jail term and Rs. 500 fine, which did not deter him. After a bitter attack on the Governor-General and the Chief Justice, Hicky was sentenced to one year in prison and fined Rs. 5000, which finally drove him to penury. These are the first tentative steps of journalism in India. B. Messink and Peter Reed were plaint publishers of the *India Gazette,* unlike their infamous predecessor. The colonial establishment started the *Calcutta Gazette*. It was followed by another private initiative the *Bengal Journal*. The *Oriental Magazine of Calcutta Amusement,* a monthly magazine made it four weekly newspapers and one monthly magazine published from Calcutta, now Kolkata.

Madras, now Chennai: The *Madras Courier* was started in 1785 in the southern stronghold of Madras, which is called Chennai now. Richard Johnson, its founder, was a government printer. Madras got its second newspaper in 1791, Hugh Boyd, who was the editor of the *Courier* quit and founded the *Hurkaru*. Tragically for the paper, Boyd passed away within a year of its founding—it ceased publication too.

It was only in 1795 that competitors to the *Courier* emerged with the founding of the *Madras Gazette* followed by the *India Herald*. The latter was an "unauthorised" publication, which led to the deportation of its founder Humphreys. The *Madras Courier* was designated the purveyor of official information in the Presidency. Bombay, now Mumbai: Bombay, surprisingly was a late starter—the *Bombay Herald* came into existence in 1789. Significantly, a year later a paper called the *Courier* started carrying advertisements in Gujarati. The first media merger of sorts: The *Bombay Gazette,* which was started in 1791, merged with the *Bombay Herald* the following year. Like the *Madras Courier,* this new entity was recognized as the publication to carry "official notifications and advertisements."

'A Chronicle of Media and the State', by Jeebesh Bagchi in the *Sarai Reader 2001* is a handy timeline on the role of the state in the development of media in India for more than a century.

Bagchi divides the timeline into three 'ages'. The Age of Formulation, which starts with the Indian Telegraph Act in 1885 and ends with the Report of the Sub-Committee on Communication, National Planning Committee in 1948. The Age of Consolidation that follows stretches from 1951, with the extension of the Indian Telegraph Act to the whole of India and ends with the promulgation of the Indecent Representation of Women (Prohibition) Act in 1985. The current age is the Age of Uncertainty, which began in 1989 with the introduction of the Prasar Bharati (Broadcasting Corporation of India) Bill. The story gets better from now.

News Agencies

PTI (Press Trust of India) and UNI (United News of India) are the two primary Indian news agencies. The former was formed after it took over the operations of the Associated Press of India and the Indian operations of Reuters soon after independence on August 27, 1947. PTI is a non-profit cooperative of the Indian newspapers. UNI began its operations on March 21, 1961, though it was registered as a company in 1959 itself.

List of popular publications in urban India in 2003:

1. *Dainik Bhaskar* (Hindi daily).
2. *Malayalam Manorama* (Malayalam daily).
3. *Dainik Jagran* (Hindi daily).
4. *The Times of India* (English daily).
5. *Amar Ujala* (Hindi daily).
6. *Anand Bazar Patrika* (Bengali daily).
7. *Grihshobha* (Hindi magazine).
8. *Eenadu* (Tamil daily).
9. *Lokmat* (Hindi daily).
10. *India Today* (weekly; Hindi edition most popular).
11. *Gujarat Samachar* (Gujarati daily).

List of popular english dailies in urban India in 2003:

1. The Times of India.
2. Hindustan Times.
3. The Hindu.
4. The Telegraph.
5. Deccan Chronicle.
6. The Economic Times.
7. The New Indian Express.
8. Mid-Day.

9. Deccan Herald.
10. Indian Express.
11. The Week.
12. The Digest.
13. News Sources India.

Colonial Indian Media

Refer for other authoritative sources for the topic (Summarised at Factbites.com).

Media Hype

Other Description of Media Hype

A *media circus* is an event that occurs when an aspect of a popular news event receives almost ludicrously high levels of media attention. The image of a circus is thus evoked by the vast troop of reporters who are sent to cover the story, as well as a seemingly endless parade of pundits, spin doctors, and spokespeople. A media circus will commonly appear when a story revolves around one central location. For example, when "Baby Jessica" (Jessica McClure) fell down a well, the well became the site of a huge convocation of reporters and cameramen. Elián González's home in Miami following his custody conflict was also home to a enormous media circus, complete with tents, food vans, and dressing rooms camped outside for the television networks' vast staffs.

In some cases, increased coverage may be because of an underlying social issue that the case represents. For example, the Scott Peterson case may have been amplified because it concretely represented the opposing vocabulary in the abortion debate, *i.e.*, whether someone could be tried for the 'murder' of an unborn child. As compared to the 'termination' of a fetus/pregnancy.

Media hype is another word used frequently in reference to a critique of media for their giving undue focus on an issue that is less important than the coverage would warrant. The general critique is often that there is a significant opportunity cost when other more important news issues that should be covered get less air time as a result of coverage of the hyped issue.

Events

Events sometimes described as a media circus include:

In Australia

- The Azaria Chamberlain disappearance of 2 month old baby in outback Australia (1980).

In the United States

- Baby Jessica rescued from a well (1987).
- The trial of Pamela Smart (1990).
- Menendez brothers trial (Early 1990's).
- John Wayne Bobbitt.
- The trials of O. J. Simpson, especially his criminal trial (1994 and 1995).
- The Blizzard of '96 (1996).
- Titanic movie of 1997.
- The sex scandal of President Bill Clinton and Monica Lewinsky (1998).
- The Columbine High School Massacre (1999).
- Marketing/merchandizing for many of the Star Wars movies released in the 2000s.
- The Elián González custody conflict (2000).
- The Florida Recount of Election 2000.
- Y2K crisis (1999-2000).
- Chandra Levy (2001)—missing Washington, D.C. intern.
- The sex scandal of Congressman Gary Condit (2001).
- Andrea Yates (2001)—the Texas woman who drowned her five children.
- Jessica Lynch (2003)—female POW in the Iraq war.
- Janet Jackson's wardrobe malfunction (2004) during the super bowl.
- The trial of Martha Stewart (2004).
- The Scott and Laci Peterson case (2004).
- Ronald Reagan's funeral (2004).
- The trial of Kobe Bryant (2004).
- Last episode of Friends (2004).
- Breakup of Brad Pitt and Jennifer Aniston (2005).
- The Terri Schiavo coverage (2005).
- Death of Pope John Paul II (2005).

- The trials of Michael Jackson (2005).
- Britney Spears' pregnancy (2005).
- The runaway bride incident with Jennifer Wilbanks (2005).

In Canada

- The marriage of Janet Jones to Wayne Gretzky.

In the United Kingdom

- The marriage of Lady Diana Spencer to Charles, Prince of Wales.
- The death and funeral of Diana, Princess of Wales, in August/September 1997.
- The detention of general Augusto Pinochet.

In Brazil

- The Candelaria Church Massacre.
- The Chico Mendes murder case.

In Portugal

- The Casa Pia child abuse scandal (1993 onwards)

Targetting other Medias

In television and radio news shows, news editors, some reporters, and even anchors have input on the news to be aired. In other types of shows, often the producer decides which stories to cover in future broadcasts. Segment producers will produce the individual stories for a broadcast, while assistant producers may perform specialized functions, such as finding interview subjects.

Television

The same considerations of "newsworthiness" discussed for newspapers apply to television broadcast news, with the added element of visuals. There are several types of TV programming you will want to consider. These include educational and informational programmes, local and community news programmes, and perhaps a business programme. Understand the types of shows being produced and aired in your regional area, and then pitch your story for an in-studio interview or a feature.

Ensuring that you are pitching the right story to the right TV programme staffer.

Radio

Radio time for news stories is very limited. Usually there is only enough time for headlines and summaries of the day's top stories, but radio still has great opportunities for your organization.

Some radio stations offer expanded news coverage and features (this is sometimes called "foreground programming"). Most Linux news has a better chance of getting coverage or an interview in news programming than in regular programming. The best chance of all lies in targetting an all-news station. Approximately 45 minutes of each hour are devoted to news, sports, weather, special reports and features. (The remaining 15 minutes are for commercials.) All news radio stations operate more like a magazine or newspaper, with specific departments and editors, more producers, more reporters, and therefore, more available resources. Stories that interest a significant portion of their listening community or that appeal to deep-pocketed sponsors will be given the most attention. You could pitch a "Linux for business" type of story. Even if your underlying goal is to promote your organization, the story or interview must avoid advertising or commercial overtones of any kind. Nothing kills the news media's credibility faster or turns off listeners more than inappropriate jingoism.

Talk Shows

Talk shows, whether on television or radio, are excellent vehicles for covering a wide variety of topics. Talk shows often invite industry experts to be commentators or participants in a panel discussion. In addition, these shows often have phone-in segments, inviting listeners to ask questions or make comments. These characteristics make the talk show an ideal forum for raising your organization's visibility.

For these programmes, there is usually an assistant producer responsible for lining up interesting guests, as well as a producer who coordinates the overall process. Both e-mail and telephone contact with the assistant producer can prove rewarding. The host, interviewer, or moderator of the show does not usually choose the guests or have final say in who appears. Unless instructed otherwise, contacting the assistant producer or producer is best.

"Selling" Your Story to the Media

Clearly, editors and producers have to know the interests of their audiences. Often this knowledge comes from the editors' strong identification with their readers, which can develop into an almost paternal attitude. Editors are constantly making decisions about what their readers will and won't see. Any editor would correctly say that is their job. Part of this judgement is based on what the editor feels the readers are currently interested in, and part is based on what the editor feels the readers *should* or *will* be interested in. An astute editor keeps their sights as much on the future as on the present. Keep in mind that the role of the news media has never been confined to just reporting the news, but also includes analysis and interpretation. Analysis and interpretation are considered the domain of "experts," which presents a perfect opportunity for specialists in your organization to share their knowledge and bring visibility to your organization.

Editors, being journalists, abide by the five Ws tradition of reporting: who, what, where, when, and why (with an unofficial "how" tagging along). Always include clear, engaging answers to the five Ws in all news releases. Also, you can use the five Ws as a guideline for how to most effectively catch the attention of editors.

The way in which you present this information is crucial to being accepted by an editor as newsworthy for their audience. You have to "tell a story," make the news interesting and relevant, and choose an appropriate time and place to present the story.

Who

"Who" usually consists of your organization, spokespersons, and authorities quoted in your news releases. Your organization and those speaking as representatives must be presented as professional, authoritative, influential, and with strong credentials for speaking on matters related to your industry. By positioning your organization in this way, you have a much better chance of generating visibility and prestige.

The goal is to make your organization a recognized authority in your field. With this distinction, any time you issue a statement, your news will draw the attention of editors whose readers are interested in the specific work you do. All things being equal, the more influential your spokesperson, the better the chance your news has of being selected.

What

The "what" is the subject of your release—a new application, a new appointment, or any interesting event you choose to announce. Naturally, unusual or exciting announcements have a better chance of being covered. Anything you can do to make your story stand out from the ordinary will be viewed as a refreshing change and will increase the chance of your story being published.

If the "what" in your story is a personnel appointment (either paid or volunteer), look for some human interest in either the person or the job at hand. If this person is a well-known Linux expert or a pillar of their local community, all the better. The more noteworthy the individual, the more newsworthy the story.

If the "what" is an event such as a Linux trade show, that is a plus. Editors regard events as more urgent and newsworthy than other announcements.

Where

The "where" of your release plays a key role. As you begin to understand public relations, you will appreciate the role of staging events to generate news. Since the media appreciates visuals, try to produce events with images as well as a pertinent story.

In planning a pitch or a release, ensure that you clearly indicate the address of every event you hope to have reporters attend. Reporters' time is wasted if they have to call for directions to every event. A special media contact person is a good idea to have at all events. This person can prevent reporters from missing important or visual parts of events. Be aware of upcoming events or activities that you might be able to capitalize on or borrow interest from. Again, the goal is promote the unusual, the unique, the unexpected that will pique the editor's curiosity or sense of humour—and get your story into print.

When

Remember that for most organizations, "when" can be just about any time. There is no need to wait for once-a-year events (like trade shows) to provide news. With creative thinking, you can come up with news stories that capitalize on current events. For example, news about the economy and what proprietary operating systems cost organizations to run can provide a background for Linux news. New computer applications running on Linux also present rich opportunities.

"When" is extremely important in terms of releasing the news. For instance, if you are publicizing special events or trade show appearances, you want to allow ample time for an editor to assign a reporter to cover the story (if the news is deemed of interest). If the editor doesn't have enough time to assign a reporter to cover your event, you can count on no reporters being available. Fortunately, though, while timing is critically important, avoiding bad timing is easy. The first rule is always to provide a reasonable amount of advance notice. For news-breaking media such as radio, television, and some newspapers, two days is an absolute minimum, and a week is more prudent. For magazines and trade journals, one to two weeks is the minimum in most cases, and three to four weeks is even better.

The second rule is to use your common sense and avoid scheduling pitches when you know the editor is on deadline or is involved with other events. Also avoid periods when the editor is working with little or no support staff (such as when reporters are away at an important trade show). Generally, business hours between 9:30 a.m. and 2:00 p.m. is best, since this gives reporters time to write and file their stories. Mondays and Fridays are always more difficult than mid-week, but don't be afraid to ask if the editor prefers specific days. If you are requesting reporters attend and cover an event, never ask the editor to confirm their attendance. The editor will not appreciate the pressure, and besides they cannot guarantee they will have the resources (reporters and camera operators) at the appointed time. News changes by the second. A reporter may be ready to go to your event and, at the last minute, be reassigned to something else. This happens all the time, so don't take the rejection personally. If you show respect for the editor's time, they will appreciate your consideration and may be more likely to cover at least some of your stories.

Why

So far, we have discussed *who* the news media is interested in, *what* news is most likely to be covered, and *where* and *when* you are going to make your pitch. Now, in looking at the "why" of your organization's story, we will address two questions. First, *why* did your news item come to pass, and second, *why* should an editor (and their readers, listeners, or viewers) find your event newsworthy? Unless there is something terribly interesting about the who, what, where, or when, "why" is the single most compelling factor available to an editor in determining newsworthiness. Why is the news important to the audience? Why do they need to know about this? Why is your particular event unusual or out of the ordinary?

Most organization's activities can be analyzed in terms of their cause and/or their effect. The more you can identify causes or effects in your story, the better chance your organization has of receiving coverage. As an example, if there is a trend of Linux being increasingly used in the enterprise, there must be a reason why. Giving the editor just a few of these reasons can make your story more newsworthy than just a simple, bland announcement. Even including some statistics to support your why will likely have a tremendous effect. The same principle holds true for something as seemingly mundane as a new personnel selection. Why was there a vacancy? Why was this person selected to fill the spot? Adding either or both pieces of information to the release greatly increases the news interest.

One of the cardinal rules of media and public relations is: "Never promote features, always promote benefits." A feature is any specific aspect that makes a product or service unique; features belong to products or services. A benefit is an advantage gained by the user in selecting a specific product or service; benefits belong to users. What a product or service does is nowhere near as meaningful as why there is some advantage or benefit to the user.

You don't need to completely ignore describing features, but you do need to present them in the context of their benefits to the end user. The reason for doing this is simple. Readers are potential users, and the better job you do of relating to the user, the more you will attract readers. Readers, as we already know, are the editor's Holy Grail. If your release is about an event, there are numerous "whys" you need to address. Why now? Why is your organization involved or being a sponsor? Why would anyone want to come to the event?

Be proactive and open in sharing the causes and anticipated effects of these accomplishments. Don't leave the editor wondering: "So what?" Failing to provide answers to why your activity is news is a sure-fire way of getting your release "filed" in the recycle bin.

How

Cause and effect, and explaining why your news is happening, will very naturally lead to the "how" of your story. How did this come to pass? How are you accomplishing this? How did your organization decide to embark on this new and exciting initiative? How will this change affect people and the marketplace? Describing the *hows* gives colour and interest to your story.

Media Studies

Media studies, a communication science, studies the nature and effects of mass media upon individuals and society. A cross-disciplinary field, media studies uses techniques from cultural studies, psychology, art theory, sociology, information theory, and economics. Media studies has greatly influenced the development of multimedia and of performance art.

Media studies pioneers include Marshall McLuhan, Denis McQuail, Harold Innis, Walter Ong, Neil Postman and Jean Baudrillard. The socialist and media critic Robert McChesney has become a major figure. Tom McPhail's theory of electronic colonialism has gained some international recognition.

Development

Media studies emerged in the 1960s from the academic study of English, and from literary criticism more broadly. It grew through schools, colleges and polytechnics, but not through established universities.

It can partially be understood as a response to the McCarthyist paranoia of the influences of the mass media. Mary Whitehouse's right-wing National Viewers' and Listeners' Association was concerned at the growing 'permissiveness' of broadcasting, and the more liberal Television and Radio Committee (led by Richard Hoggart) and Television Viewers' Council, which had a special interest in educational broadcasting.

In 1959, Joseph Trenaman left the BBC's Further Education Unit to become the first holder of the Granada Research Fellowship in Television at Leeds University. The Centre for Mass Communication Research was founded at Leicester University soon after (Crisell, 2002: 186). Hoggart founded the Centre for Contemporary Cultural Studies (CCCS) at the University of Birmingham in 1964.

The *critical paradigm* was formed in the early 1970s, raising questions about media and power. The CCCS was pivotal in developing the field, producing a number of key researchers. Under the directorship of Stuart Hall, who wrote the seminal *Encoding/Decoding* model, the centre produced key empirical research about the relationship between texts and audiences. Amongst these was *The Nationwide Project* by David Morley and Charlotte Brunsdon.

Derogatory Attitudes

Media studies is regularly the victim of derogatory jokes and attitudes. Ironically, then, it is the victim of the ideology and power relations it attempts to expose. Its relation to polytechnics, and subsequently the post-1992 New Universities, are also a target for ridicule. The now annual moral panic in the UK every August when GCSE and A'level results are released normally focusses upon media studies as an example of the supposed dumbing down of education (Barker, 2001). It is often labelled as a Mickey Mouse degree. The irony is that the discipline utilizes many theorists and philosophers which many detractors might associate with "proper" (traditional) degrees.

Strands

In addition to the interdisciplinary nature of the academic field, popular understandings of media studies encompass:

1. Media production (TV/Radio),
2. Mass communication, and
3. Journalism.

Although most production and journalism courses incorporate media studies for contextual purposes, the terms are not interchangeable. Separate strands are being identified within media studies, such as *Audience Studies, Television Studies* and *Radio Studies*. Film studies is a separate discipline, with a different history and focus. *Critical media theory* looks at how the corporate ownership of media production and distribution affects society, and provides a common ground to social conservatives (concerned by the effects of media on the traditional family) and liberals and socialists (concerned by the corporatization of social discourse). The study of the effects and techniques of advertising forms a cornerstone of media studies. New Media Studies is developing, concentrating upon the Internet, video games and other forms of mass media which developed from the 1990s.

New Media Studies

An emerging academic discipline, new media studies explores the intersections of computing, science, the humanities, and the visual and performing arts, what Dr. Janet Murray calls "a single new medium of representation, the digital medium, formed by the braided interplay of technical invention and cultural expression at the end of the 20th century..."

In a course on New Media Studies, students are exposed to ideas and insights on media from communication theorists, programmers, educators and technologists. Among others, the work of Marshall McLuhan is viewed as one of the cornerstones of the study of media theory. McLuhan's slogan, "the medium is the message" (elaborated on his 1964 book, *Understanding Media: The Extensions of Man*) calls attention to the intrinsic effect of communications media. A programme in New Media Studies may incorporate lessons, classes, and topics within Communication, Journalism, Computer Science, Programming, Graphic Design, Web design, Human-computer interaction, Media theory, English, and other related fields.

3

Profession and Education in Journalism and Electronic Journalism: An Overview

JOURNALISM

Journalism is the discipline of gathering, writing and reporting news, and broadly it includes the process of editing and presenting the news articles. Journalism applies to various media, but is not limited to newspapers, magazines, radio and television. Some high schools promote journalism as an elective class. While under pressure to be the first to publish its stories, each news media organization adheres to its own standards of accuracy, quality, and style—usually editing and proofreading its reports prior to publication. Many news organizations claim proud traditions of holding government officials and institutions accountable to the public, while media critics have raised questions on the accountability of the press. The word *journalism* is taken from the French *journal* which in turn comes from the Latin *diurnal* or daily; The *Acta Diurna,* a handwritten bulletin, was put up daily in the Forum, the main public square in ancient Rome, and was the world's first newspaper. News-oriented journalism was described by former Washington Post editor, Phil Graham, as "a first rough draft of history," because journalists often record important historical events as they are happening, but at the same time, they must produce their news articles on short deadlines.

Journalism's activities include stating What, When, Where, How, and Why, famously quoted by Rudyard Kipling (see the Five Ws), and stating the significance and effects of certain events or trends. Journalism exists in a number of media: newspapers, television, radio, magazines and, most recently, the World Wide Web through the Internet.

Journalists report and write on a wide variety of subjects: politics on the international, national, provincial and local levels, economics and business on the same four levels, health and medicine, education, sports, hobbies and recreation, lifestyles, clothing, food, pets, and relationships; journalists report on anything that news organizations think consumers will read. Journalists can report for general interest news outlets like newspapers, news magazines and broadcast sources; general circulation speciality publications like trade and hobby magazines, or for news publications and outlets with a select group of subscribers. Journalists are usually expected and required to go out to the scene of a story to gather information for their reports, and often may compose their reports in the field. They also use the telephone, the computer and the internet to gather information. However, more often those reports are written, and they are almost always edited in newsrooms, the offices where journalists and editors work together to prepare the content of news items.

Journalists, especially if they cover a specific subject or area (a 'beat') are expected to cultivate sources, people in the subject or area, that they can communicate with, either to explain the details of a story, or to provide leads to other subjects for stories yet to be reported. They are also expected to develop their investigative skills to research and report stories better. Print journalism can be split into several categories: newspapers, news magazines, general interest magazines, trade magazines, hobby magazines, newsletters, private publications, online news pages and others. Each genre can have its own requirements for researching and writing reports. For example, newspaper journalists in the United States have traditionally written reports using the inverted pyramid style, although this style is used more for straight or hard news reports rather than features. Written hard news reports are expected to be spare in the use of words, and to list the most important information first, so that if the story must be cut because there is not enough space for it, the least important facts will be automatically removed. Editors usually ensure that reports are written with as few words as possible. Feature stories are usually written in a looser style which usually depends on the subject-matter of the report, and are in general granted more space.

News magazine and general interest magazine articles are usually written in different styles, with less emphasis on the inverted pyramid. Trade publications can be more news-oriented, while hobby publications can be more feature-oriented.

Broadcast Journalism

Radio journalists must gather facts to present them fairly and accurately, but also must find and record relevant and interesting sounds to add to their reports, both interviews with people involved in the story and background sounds that help characterize the story. Radio reporters may also write the introduction to the story read by a radio news anchor, and may also answer questions live from the anchor.

Television journalists rely on visual information to illustrate and characterize their reporting, including on-camera interviews with people involved in the story, shots of the scene where the story took place, and graphics usually produced at the station to help frame the story. Like radio reporters, television reporters also may write the introductory script that a television news anchor would read to set up their story. Both radio and television journalists usually do not have as much "space" to present information in their reports as print journalists. Television Journalists have to be well presented and well prepared.

Online (Cyber) Journalism

The World Wide Web has spawned the newest medium for journalism, online (Cyber) journalism. The speed at which news can be disseminated on the web, and the profound penetration to anyone with a computer and web browser, have greatly increased the quantity and variety of news reports available to the average web user. The bulk of online journalism has been the extension of existing print and broadcast media into the web via web versions of their primary products. News reports that were set to be released at expected times can now be published as soon as they are written and edited, increasing the deadline pressure and fear of being scooped which many journalists must deal with.

The digitalization of news production and the diffusion capabilities of the internet are challenging the traditional journalistic professional culture. The concept of participatory or (citizen journalism) proposes that amateur reporters can actually produce their own stories either inside or outside professional media outlets.

Most news websites are free to their users—one notable exception being the *Wall Street Journal* website, for which a subscription is required to view its contents—but some outlets, such as the *New York Times* website, offer current news free, but archived reports and access to opinion columnists and other non-news sections for a periodic fee. Attempts to start unique web publications, such as *Slate* and *Salon*, have met with limited success, in part because they do or did charge subscription fees.

Many newspapers are branching into new mediums because of the Internet. Their websites may now include video, podcasts, blogs and slideshows. Story chat, where readers may post comments on an article, has changed the dialogue newspapers foster. Traditionally kept to the confines of the opinion section as letters to the editor, story chat has allowed readers to express opinions without the time delay of a letter or the approval of an editor. The growth of blogs as a source of news and especially opinion on the news has changed journalism for ever. Blogs now can create news as well as report it, and blur the dividing line between news and opinion. The debate about whether blogging is really journalism rages on.

Variations of Journalism

Newspapers and periodicals often contain features written by journalists, many of whom specialize in this form of in-depth journalism. Feature articles usually are longer than straight news articles, and are combined with photographs, drawings or other "art." They may also be highlighted by typographic effects or colours. Writing features can be more demanding than writing straight news stories, because while a journalist must apply the same amount of effort to accurately gather and report the facts of the story, the reporter must also find a creative and interesting way to write the article, especially the lead, or the first one or two paragraphs of the story. The lead must grab the reader's attention yet accurately embody the ideas of the article. Often the lead of a feature article is dictated by its subject matter. Journalists must work even harder to avoid clichéd images and words when writing the lead and the rest of the article.

In the last half of the 20th century the line between straight news reporting and feature writing blurred as more and more journalists and publications experimented with different approaches to writing an article. Tom Wolfe, Gay Talese, Hunter S. Thompson and other journalists used many different approaches to writing news articles. Urban and alternative weekly newspapers went even further in blurring the distinction, and many magazines include more features than straight news.

Some television news shows experimented with alternative formats, and many TV shows that claimed to be news shows were not considered as such by many critics, because their content and methods did not adhere to accepted journalistic standards. National Public Radio, on the other hand, is considered a good example of a good mixture of straight news reporting, features, and combinations of the two, usually meeting standards of high quality. Other U.S. public radio news organizations have achieved similar results. A majority of newspapers still maintain a clear distinction between news and features, as do most television and radio news organizations.

Sports Journalism

Sports journalism covers many aspects of human athletic competition, and is an integral part of most journalism products, including newspapers, magazines, and radio and television news broadcasts. While some critics don't consider sports journalism to be true journalism, the prominence of sports in Western culture has justified the attention of journalists to not just the competitive events in sports, but also to athletes and the business of sports.

Sports journalism in the United States has traditionally been written in a looser, more creative and more opinionated tone than traditional journalistic writing; the emphasis on accuracy and underlying fairness is still a part of sports journalism. An emphasis on the accurate description of the statistical performances of athletes is also an important part of sports journalism.

Science Journalism

Science journalism is a relatively new branch of journalism, in which journalists' reporting conveys information on science topics to the public. Science journalists must understand and interpret very detailed, technical and sometimes jargon-laden information and render it into interesting reports that are comprehensible to consumers of news media. Scientific journalists also must choose which developments in science merit news coverage, as well as cover disputes within the scientific community with a balance of fairness to both sides but also with a devotion to the facts.

Many, but not all, journalists covering science have training in the sciences they cover, including several medical journalists who cover medicine.

Investigative Journalism

Investigative journalism, in which journalists investigate and expose unethical, immoral and illegal behaviour by individuals, businesses and government agencies, can be complicated, time-consuming and expensive—requiring teams of journalists, months of research, interviews (sometimes repeated interviews) with numerous people, long-distance travel, computers to analyze public-record databases, or use of the company's legal staff to secure documents under freedom of information laws.

Because of its inherently confrontational nature, this kind of reporting is often the first to suffer from budget cutbacks or interference from outside the news department. Investigative reporting done poorly can also expose journalists and media organizations to negative reaction from the subjects of investigations and the public, and accusations of gotcha journalism. When conducted correctly it can bring the attention of the public and government to problems and conditions that the public deem need to be addressed, and can win awards and recognition to the journalists involved and the media outlet that did the reporting.

New Journalism

New Journalism was the name given to a style of 1960s and 1970s news writing and journalism which used literary techniques deemed unconventional at the time. The term was codified with its current meaning by Tom Wolfe in a 1973 collection of journalism articles.

It is typified by using certain devices of literary fiction, such as conversational speech, first-person point of view, recording everyday details and telling the story using scenes. Though it seems undisciplined at first, new journalism maintains elements of reporting including strict adherence to factual accuracy and the writer being the primary source. To get "inside the head" of a character, the journalist asks the subject what they were thinking or how they felt. Because of its unorthodox style, new journalism is typically employed in feature writing or book-length reporting projects. Many new journalists are also writers of fiction and prose. In addition to Wolfe, writers whose work has fallen under the title "new journalism" include Norman Mailer, Hunter S. Thompson, Joan Didion, Truman Capote, George Plimpton and Gay Talese.

Gonzo Journalism

Gonzo journalism is a type of journalism popularized by the American writer Hunter S. Thompson, author of *Fear and Loathing in Las Vegas, Fear and Loathing on the Campaign Trail* '72, among other stories and books. Gonzo journalism is characterized by its punchy style, rough language, and ostensible disregard for conventional journalistic writing forms and customs. Gonzo journalism attempts to present a multi-disciplinary perspective on a particular story, drawing from popular culture, sports, political, philosophical and literary sources. Gonzo journalism has been styled eclectic or untraditional. It remains a feature of popular magazines such as *Rolling Stone* magazine. It has a good deal in common with new journalism and online journalism.

'Celebrity' or 'People' Journalism

Another area of journalism that grew in stature in the 20th century is 'celebrity' or 'people' journalism, which focusses on the personal lives of people, primarily celebrities, including movie and stage actors, musical artists, models and photographers, other notable people in the entertainment industry, as well as people who seek attention, such as politicians, and people thrust into the attention of the public, such as people who do something newsworthy.

Once the province of newspaper gossip columnists and gossip magazines, celebrity journalism has become the focus of national tabloid newspapers like the *National Enquirer*, magazines like *People* and *Us Weekly*, syndicated television shows like *Entertainment*

Tonight, Inside Edition, The Insider, Access Hollywood and *Extra,* cable networks like E!, A&E Network and The Biography Channel, and numerous other television productions and thousands of websites. Most other news media provide some coverage of celebrities and people. Celebrity journalism differs from feature writing in that it focuses on people who are either already famous or are especially attractive, and in that it often covers celebrities obsessively, to the point of these journalists behaving unethically in order to provide coverage. Paparazzi, photographers who would follow celebrities incessantly to obtain potentially embarrassing photographs, have come to characterize celebrity journalism.

'Convergence Journalism'

An emerging form of journalism, which combines different forms of journalism, such as print, photographic and video, into one piece or group of pieces. Convergence Journalism can be found in the likes of CNN and many other news sites. *The Washington Post* has a notable amount of this.

Ambush Journalism

Ambush journalism refers to aggressive tactics practiced by journalists to suddenly confront with questions people who otherwise do not wish to speak to a journalist. The practice has particularly been applied by television journalists, such as those on the CBS-TV news show 60 minutes and by Geraldo Rivera, currently on the Fox News cable channel, and by hundreds of American local television reporters conducting investigations.

The practice has been sharply criticized by journalists and others as being highly unethical and sensational, while others defend it as the only way to attempt to provide those subject to it an opportunity to comment for a report. Ambush journalism has not been ruled illegal in the United States, although doing it on private property could open a journalist to being charged with trespassing.

Gotcha Journalism

Gotcha journalism refers to the deliberate manipulation of the presentation of facts in a report in order to portray a person or organization in a particular way that varies from an accurate portrayal based on a balanced review of the facts available. In particular, it is applied to broadcast journalism, where the story, images and interviews are tailored to create a particular impression of the subject-matter.

It is considered highly unethical to engage in gotcha journalism. Many subjects of reporting have claimed to have been subjected to it, and some media outlets are guilty of deliberately biased reporting.

Role of Journalism in a Democracy

In the 1920s, as modern journalism was just taking form, writer Walter Lippmann and American philosopher John Dewey debated over the role of journalism in a democracy. Their differing philosophies still characterize a debate about the role of journalism in society and the nation-state.

Lippmann understood that journalism's role at the time was to act as a mediator or translator between the public and policy-making elites. The journalist became the middleman. When elites spoke, journalists listened and recorded the information, distilled it, and passed it on to the public for their consumption. His reasoning behind this was that the public was not in a position to deconstruct the growing and complex flurry of information present in modern society, and so an intermediary was needed to filter news for the masses. Lippmann put it this way: The public is not smart enough to understand complicated, political issues. Furthermore, the public was too consumed with their daily lives to care about complex public policy. Therefore, the public needed someone to interpret the decisions or concerns of the elite to make the information plain and simple. That was the role of journalists. Lippmann believed that the public would affect the decision-making of the elite with their vote. In the meantime, the elite (*i.e.* politicians, policy-makers, bureaucrats, scientists, etc.) would keep the business of power running. In Lippmann's world, the journalist's role was to inform the public of what the elites were doing. It was also to act as a watchdog over the elites, as the public had the final say with their votes. Effectively that kept the public at the bottom of the power chain, catching the flow of information that is handed down from experts/elites.

Dewey, on the other hand, believed the public was not only capable of understanding the issues created or responded to by the elite, it was in the public forum that decisions should be made after discussion and debate. When issues were thoroughly vetted, then the best ideas would bubble to the surface. Dewey believed journalists not only had to inform the public, but should report on issues differently than simply passing on information. In Dewey's world, a journalist's role changed. Dewey believed that journalists should take in the information, then weigh the consequences of the policies being enacted by the elites on the public. Over time, his idea has been implemented in various degrees, and is more commonly known as "community journalism." This concept of *Community Journalism* is at the centre of new developments in journalism. In this new paradigm, journalists are able to engage citizens and the experts/elites in the proposition and generation of content. It is important to note that while there is an assumption of equality, Dewey still celebrates expertize. Dewey believes the shared knowledge of many is far superior to a single individual's knowledge. Experts and scholars are welcome in Dewey's framework, but there is not the hierarchical structure present in Lippmann's understanding of journalism and society. According to Dewey, conversation, debate, and dialogue lie at the heart of a democracy.

While Lippmann's journalistic philosophy might be more acceptable to government leaders, Dewey's approach is a better description of how many journalists see their role in society, and, in turn, how much of society expects journalists to function. Americans, for example, may criticize some of the excesses committed by journalists, but they tend to expect journalists to serve as watchdogs on government, businesses and other actors, enabling people to make informed decisions on the issues of the time.

The Elements of Journalism

According to *The Elements of Journalism* by Bill Kovach and Tom Rosensteil, there are nine elements of journalism. In order for a journalist to fulfill their duty of providing the people with the information they need to be free and self-governing. They must follow these guidelines:

1. Journalism's first obligation is to the truth.
2. Its first loyalty is to the citizens.
3. Its essence is discipline of verification.
4. Its practitioners must maintain an independence from those they cover.
5. It must serve as an independent monitor of power.
6. It must provide a forum for public criticism and compromise.
7. It must strive to make the significant interesting and relevant.
8. It must keep the news comprehensive and proportional.
9. Its practitioners must be allowed to exercise their personal conscience.

On the April, 2007 edition of the book, they have added one additional element, *the rights and responsibilities of citizens* to make it a total of ten elements of journalism.

Professional and Ethical Standards

Since the development of professional journalism at the beginning of the 20th century, journalists have been expected to follow a stringent code of journalistic conduct that requires them to, among other things:

- Use original sources of information, including interviews with people directly involved in a story, original documents and other direct sources of information, whenever possible, and cite the sources of this information in reports;
    - *For more information on using sources.*
- Fully attribute information gathered from other published sources, should original sources not be available (not to do so is considered plagiarism; some newspapers also note when an article uses information from previous reports);
- Use multiple original sources of information, especially if the subject of the report is controversial;
- Check every fact reported;
- Find and report every side of a story possible;

- Report without bias, illustrating many aspects of a conflict rather than siding with one;
- Approach researching and reporting a story with a balance between objectivity and skepticism.
- Use careful judgement when organizing and reporting information;
- Be careful about granting confidentiality to sources (news organizations usually have specific rules that journalists must follow concerning grants of confidentiality);
- Decline gifts or favours from any subject of a report, to avoid the appearance of being influenced;
- Abstain from reporting or otherwise participating in the research and writing about a subject in which the journalist has a personal stake or bias that cannot be set aside.

This was in stark contrast to the media climate prior to the 20th century, where the media market was dominated by smaller newspapers and pamphleteers who usually had an overt and often radical agenda, with no presumpton of balance or objectivity.

Recognition of Excellence in Journalism

There are several professional organizations, universities and foundations that recognize excellence in journalism in the USA. The Pulitzer Prize, administered by Columbia University in New York City, is awarded to newspapers, magazines and broadcast media for excellence in various kinds of journalism. The Columbia University Graduate School of Journalism gives the Alfred I. duPont-Columbia University Awards for excellence in radio and television journalism, and the Scripps Howard Foundation gives the National Journalism Awards in 17 categories. The Society of Professional Journalists gives the Sigma Delta Chi Award for journalism excellence. In the television industry, the National Academy of Television Arts and Sciences gives awards for excellence in television journalism.

Failing to Uphold Standards

Such a code of conduct can, in the real world, be difficult to uphold consistently. Journalists who believe they are being fair or objective may give biased accounts—by reporting selectively, trusting too much to anecdote, or giving a partial explanation of actions. Even in routine reporting, bias can creep into a story through a reporter's choice of facts to summarize, or through failure to check enough sources, hear and report dissenting voices, or seek fresh perspectives.

As much as reporters try to set aside their prejudices, they may simply be unaware of them. Young reporters may be blind to issues affecting the elderly. A 20-year veteran of the "police beat" may be deaf to rumours of departmental corruption. Publications marketed to affluent suburbanites may ignore urban problems. And, of course, naive or unwary reporters and editors alike may fall prey to public relations, propaganda or disinformation.

News organizations provide editors, producers or news directors whose job is to check reporters' work at various stages. But editors can get tired, lazy, complacent or biased. An editor may be blind to a favourite reporter's omissions, prejudices or fabrications. Provincial editors also may be ill-equipped to weigh the perspective (or check the facts of) a correspondent reporting from a distant city or foreign country.

A news organization's budget inevitably reflects decision-making about what news to cover, for what audience, and in what depth. Those decisions may reflect conscious or unconscious bias. When budgets are cut, editors may sacrifice reporters in distant news bureaus, reduce the number of staff assigned to low-income areas, or wipe entire communities from the publication's zone of interest. Publishers, owners and other corporate executives, especially advertising sales executives, can try to use their powers over journalists to influence how news is reported and published. Journalists usually rely on top management to create and maintain a "firewall" between the news and other departments in a news organization to prevent undue influence on the news department. One journalism magazine, Columbia Journalism Review, has made it a practice to reveal examples of executives who try to influence news coverage, of executives who do not abuse their powers over journalists, and of journalists who resist such pressures.

Self-censorship is a growing problem in journalism, particularly in covering countries that sharply restrict press freedom. As commercial pressure in the media marketplace grows, media organizations are loath to lose access to high-profile countries by producing unflattering stories. For example, CNN admitted that it had practiced self-censorship in covering the

Saddam Hussein regime in Iraq in order to ensure continued access after the regime had thrown out other media. CNN correspondent Christiane Amanpour also complained of self-censorship during the invasion of Iraq due to the fear of alienating key audiences in the US. There are claims that the media are also avoiding covering stories about repression and human rights violations by the Iranian regime in order to maintain a presence in the country.

Reporting Versus Editorializing

Generally, publishers and consumers of journalism draw a distinction between reporting—"just the facts"—and opinion writing, often by restricting opinion columns to the editorial page and its facing or "op-ed" (opposite the editorials) page. Unsigned editorials are traditionally the official opinions of the paper's editorial board, while op-ed pages may be a mixture of syndicated columns and other contributions, frequently with some attempt to balance the voices across some political or social spectrum.

The distinction between reporting and opinion can break down. Complex stories often require summarizing and interpretation of facts, especially if there is limited time or space for a story. Stories involving great amounts of interpretation are often labelled "news analysis," but still run in a paper's news columns. The limited time for each story in a broadcast report rarely allows for such distinctions.

Legal Status

Journalists around the world often write about the governments in their nations, and those governments have widely varying policies and practices towards journalists, which control what they can research and write, and what press organizations can publish. Many Western governments guarantee the freedom of the press, and do relatively little to restrict press rights and freedoms, while other nations severely restrict what journalists can research and/ or publish. Journalists in many nations have enjoyed some privileges not enjoyed by members of the general public, including better access to public events, crime scenes and press conferences, and to extended interviews with public officials, celebrities and others in the public eye. These privileges are available because of the perceived power of the press to turn public opinion for or against governments, their officials and policies, as well as the perception that the press often represents their consumers. These privileges extend from the legal rights of journalists but are not guaranteed by those rights. Sometimes government officials may attempt to punish individual journalists who irk them by denying them some of these privileges extended to other journalists.

Nations or jurisdictions that formally license journalists may confer special privileges and responsibilities along with those licenses, but in the United States the tradition of an independent press has avoided any imposition of government-controlled examinations or licensing. Some of the states have explicit shield laws that protect journalists from some forms of government inquiry, but those statutes' definitions of "journalist" were often based on access to printing presses and broadcast towers. A national shield law has been proposed.

In some nations, journalists are directly employed, controlled or censored by their governments. In other nations, governments who may claim to guarantee press rights actually intimidate journalists with threats of arrest, destruction or seizure of property (especially the means of production and dissemination of news content), torture or murder.

Journalists who elect to cover conflicts, whether wars between nations or insurgencies within nations, often give up any expectation of protection by government, if not giving up their rights to protection by government. Journalists who are captured or detained during a conflict are expected to be treated as civilians and to be released to their national government.

Rights of Journalists Versus those of Private Citizens and Organizations

Journalists enjoy similar powers and privileges as private citizens and organizations. The power of journalists over private citizens is limited by the citizen's rights to privacy. Many who seek favourable representation in the press (celebrities, for example) do grant journalists greater access than others enjoy. The right to privacy of a private citizen may be reduced or lost if the citizen is thrust into the public eye, either by their own actions or because they are involved in a public event or incident. Citizens and private organizations can refuse to deal with some or all journalists; the powers the press enjoy in many nations often make this tactic ineffective or counter-productive. Citizens in most nations also enjoy the right against being libelled or defamed by journalists, and citizens can bring suit against journalists who they claim have published damaging untruths about them with malicious disregard for the truth. Libel or defamation lawsuits can also become conflicts between the journalists' rights to publish versus the private citizen's right to privacy. Some journalists have claimed lawsuits brought against them and news organizations—or even the threat of such a lawsuit—were intended to stifle their voices with the threat of expensive legal proceedings, even if plaintiffs cannot prove their cases. This is referred to as the Chilling effect.

In the United Kingdom, it is up to the journalist and/or their employers to defend against claims of defamation, as opposed to other nations where the burden of proof is on the claimant.

In many nations, journalists and news organizations must function under a similar threat of retaliation from private individuals or organizations as from governments. Criminals and criminal organizations, political parties, some zealous religious organizations, and even mobs of people have been known to punish journalists who speak or write about them in ways they do not like. Punishments can include threats, physical damage to property, assault, torture and murder.

Right to Protect Confidentiality of Sources

Journalists' interaction with sources sometimes involves confidentiality, an extension of freedom of the press giving journalists a legal protection to keep the identity of a source private even when demanded by police or prosecutors; withholding sources can land journalists in contempt of court, or in jail.

The scope of rights granted to journalists varies from nation to nation; in the United Kingdom, for example, the government has had more legal rights to protect what it considers sensitive information, and to force journalists to reveal the sources of leaked information, than the United States. Other nations, particularly Zimbabwe and the People's Republic of China, have a reputation of persecuting journalists, both domestic and foreign. In the United States, there has never been a right to protect sources in a federal court. Some states provide varying degrees of such protection. However, federal courts will refuse to force journalists to reveal sources, unless the information the court seeks is highly relevant to the case, and there is no other way to get it. Journalists, like all citizens, who refuse to testify even when ordered to can be found in contempt of court and fined or jailed.

Right of Access to Government Information (USA)

Like sources, journalists depend on the rights granted by government to the public and, by extension, to the press, for access to information held by the government. These rights also vary from nation to nation and, in the United States, from state to state. Some states have more open policies for making information available, and some states have acted in the last decade to broaden those rights. New Jersey, for example, has updated and broadened its Sunshine Law to better define what kinds of government documents can be withheld from public inquiry. In the United States, the Freedom of Information Act (FOIA) guarantees journalists the right to obtain copies of government documents, although the government has the right to redact, or black out, information from documents in those copies that FOIA allows them to withhold. Other federal legislation also controls access to information.

REPORTING AND EDITORIALIZING

Journalism has as its main activity the reporting of events—stating who, what, when, where, why and how, and explaining the significance and effect of events or trends. Journalism exists in a number of media: newspapers, television, radio, magazines and, since the end of 20th century, the Internet.

Generally, publishers and consumers of journalism draw a distinction between reporting ("just the facts") and opinions (such as editorials, [(the official opinions of the paper) and op-ed columns ("opposite the editorial page" commentary)]. However, this distinction sometimes can break down. Journalists may unintentionally fall prey to propaganda or disinformation. Journalists may give a biased account of facts by reporting selectively, for instance, focussing on anecdote or giving partial explanation of actions. Foreign reporting may become more susceptible to bias, because the writers or editors of a newspaper in a given geographical area may find it more difficult to fact-check reports originating at a distance.

Feature-Writing

Newspapers and periodicals often will contain features written by journalists, many of whom specialize in this form of "in-depth" journalism.

Sources

Journalists' interaction with sources sometimes involves confidentiality. Many western governments guarantee the freedom of the press. By extension, these freedoms sometimes also add legal protection for journalists, allowing them to keep the identity of a source private even when demanded by police or prosecutors.

Blogging

Recently there has been some controversy as to whether blogging constitutes a form of journalism. There have been arguments on both sides of the debate further fueled by a March 2005 court ruling in a case involving Apple Computer and several Apple rumour blogs. In that ruling the judge declared that the blogs were not entitled to journalist protections with regards to preserving the anonymity of sources because they don't qualify as a form of journalism. This set a legal precedent.

Types of Journalism

1. Advocacy journalism.
2. Alternative journalism.
3. Broadcast journalism.
4. Business journalism.
5. Citizen journalism.
6. Computer-assisted reporting.
7. Gonzo journalism.
8. Electronic journalism—news aquisition by means of analogue and digital electronic recording devices.
9. Investigative journalism.
10. Literary journalism related to creative non-fiction.
11. Muckraking.
12. New journalism.

13. Online journalism.
14. Photo journalism.
15. Sports journalism.
16. Tabloid journalism.
17. Trade journalism—Trade publications covering news specific to industries and professions.
18. Yellow journalism.

A Statement of Shared Purpose

After extended examination by journalists themselves of the character of journalism at the end of the twentieth century, we offer this common understanding of what defines our work.

The central purpose of journalism is to provide citizens with accurate and reliable information they need to function in a free society.

This encompasses myriad roles—helping define community, creating common language and common knowledge, identifying a community's goals, heros and villains, and pushing people beyond complacency. This purpose also involves other requirements, such as being entertaining, serving as watchdog and offering voice to the voiceless. Over time journalists have developed nine core principles to meet the task. They comprise what might be described as the theory of journalism:

1. *Journalism's first obligation is to the truth*: Democracy depends on citizens having reliable, accurate facts put in a meaningful context. Journalism does not pursue truth in an absolute or philosophical sense, but it can—and must—pursue it in a practical sense. This "journalistic truth" is a process that begins with the professional discipline of assembling and verifying facts. Then journalists try to convey a fair and reliable account of their meaning, valid for now, subject to further investigation. Journalists should be as transparent as possible about sources and methods so audiences can make their own assessment of the information. Even in a world of expanding voices, accuracy is the foundation upon which everything else is built—context, interpretation, comment, criticism, analysis and debate. The truth, over time,

emerges from this forum. As citizens encounter an ever greater flow of data, they have more need—not less—for identifiable sources dedicated to verifying that information and putting it in context.

2. *Its first loyalty is to citizens*: While news organizations answer to many constituencies, including advertisers and shareholders, the journalists in those organizations must maintain allegiance to citizens and the larger public interest above any other if they are to provide the news without fear or favour. This commitment to citizens first is the basis of a news organization's credibility, the implied covenant that tells the audience the coverage is not slanted for friends or advertisers. Commitment to citizens also means journalism should present a representative picture of all constituent groups in society. Ignoring certain citizens has the effect of disenfranchising them. The theory underlying the modern news industry has been the belief that credibility builds a broad and loyal audience, and that economic success follows in turn. In that regard, the business people in a news organization also must nurture—not exploit—their allegiance to the audience ahead of other considerations.
3. *Its essence is a discipline of verification*: Journalists rely on a professional discipline for verifying information. When the concept of objectivity originally evolved, it did not imply that journalists are free of bias. It called, rather, for a consistent method of testing information—a transparent approach to evidence—precisely so that personal and cultural biases would not undermine the accuracy of their work. The method is objective, not the journalist. Seeking out multiple witnesses, disclosing as much as possible about sources, or asking various sides for comment, all signal such standards. This discipline of verification is what separates journalism from other modes of communication, such as propaganda, fiction or entertainment. But the need for professional method is not always fully recognized or refined. While journalism has developed various techniques for determining facts, for instance, it has done less to develop a system for testing the reliability of journalistic interpretation.

4. *Its practitioners must maintain an independence from those they cover*: Independence is an underlying requirement of journalism, a cornerstone of its reliability. Independence of spirit and mind, rather than neutrality, is the principle journalists must keep in focus. While editorialists and commentators are not neutral, the source of their credibility is still their accuracy, intellectual fairness and ability to inform—not their devotion to a certain group or outcome. In our independence, however, we must avoid any tendency to stray into arrogance, elitism, isolation or nihilism.
5. *It must serve as an independent monitor of power*: Journalism has an unusual capacity to serve as watchdog over those whose power and position most affect citizens. The founders recognized this to be a rampart against despotism when they ensured an independent press; courts have affirmed it; citizens rely on it. As journalists, we have an obligation to protect this watchdog freedom by not demeaning it in frivolous use or exploiting it for commercial gain.
6. *It must provide a forum for public criticism and compromise*: The news media are the common carriers of public discussion, and this responsibility forms a basis for our special privileges. This discussion serves society best when it is informed by facts rather than prejudice and supposition. It also should strive to fairly represent the varied viewpoints and interests in society, and to place them in context rather than highlight only the conflicting fringes of debate. Accuracy and truthfulness require that as framers of the public discussion we cannot neglect the points of common ground where problem-solving occurs.
7. *It must strive to make the significant interesting and relevant*: Journalism is story-telling with a purpose. It should do more than gather an audience or catalogue the important. For its own survival, it must balance what readers know they want with what they cannot anticipate but need. In short, it must strive to make the significant interesting and relevant. Quality is measured both by how much a work engages its audience and enlightens it. This means journalists must continually ask what information has

most value to citizens and in what form. While journalism should reach beyond such topics as government and public safety, a journalism overwhelmed by trivia and false significance ultimately engenders a trivial society.

8. *It must keep the news comprehensive and proportional*: Keeping news in proportion and not leaving important things out are also cornerstones of truthfulness. Journalism is a form of cartography: it creates a map for citizens to navigate society. Inflating events for sensation, neglecting others, stereotyping or being disproportionately negative all make a less reliable map. The map also should include news of all our communities, not just those with attractive demographics. This is best achieved by newsrooms with a diversity of backgrounds and perspectives. The map is only an analogy; proportion and comprehensiveness are subjective, yet their elusiveness does not lesson their significance.
9. *Its practitioners must be allowed to exercise their personal conscience*: Every journalist must have a personal sense of ethics and responsibility—a moral compass. Each of us must be willing, if fairness and accuracy require, to voice differences with our colleagues, whether in the newsroom or the executive suite. News organizations do well to nurture this independence by encouraging individuals to speak their minds. This stimulates the intellectual diversity necessary to understand and accurately cover an increasingly diverse society. It is this diversity of minds and voices, not just numbers, that matters.

ELECTRONIC JOURNALISM

Electronic journalism, known as "EJ" or "ENG" for electronic news gathering is most associated with broadcast news where producers, reporters and editors make use of electronic recording devices for gathering and presenting information in telecasts and radio transmissions reaching the public. The acquisition mediums of choice in 2005 are characterized by a variety of competing types or "formats" of video tape sound recording and editing offer a large number of analogue and digital systems. Still images, graphics and animation have their own sets of tools. The editorial systems available provide journalists with tools for fast and flexible assembly and delivery of electronically gathered and edited news reports.

Video Journalism

News via video is seen daily by millions of people around the world. Some of the typical uses include interviews, panel discussions, press conferences, speeches. Live and pre-recorded video is also used in news coverage of accidents, natural disasters and war coverage.

Technical Standards

The National Archives of the United States holds a collection of some of earliest examples historically significant motion picture films for the country and similar collections exist in other nation's archives. From the earliest days of the medium's existence, film cameras have been used for the acquisition of news elements and documentary footage. Film remained important in daily news operations until the late 1960s when news outlets turned to portable video cameras, portable recorders, wireless microphones and joined those with various microwave and satellite linked delivery systems. The 1962 arrival of the "Handy-Looky", a portable video tape camera from Ikegami announced a revolution in journalism. This Handy Looky provided a self-contained system of camera with lens and video recorder, the precursor of today's hand held cameras. As systems have improved, components have been made smaller and lighter and performance has greatly improved. Improvements in image quality, colourimetry, lens types, tape formulation.

1. Early formats of video tape—2 Inch Quad, 1 Inch Video, 3/4 Umatic
2. Betacam Tape—Broadcast standard format
3. 1080i/720p—High definition video format
4. CCD Camera Technology
5. DVC Pro format
6. Mini DV
7. High8
8. Editng Systems, Avid, Final Cut Pro, Video Vegas
9. Satellite, broadcast, cable, microwave.

Photographs, Graphics, Animation

Apart from moving images and sound recording, electronic journalism makes liberal use of still images, graphics and animation in reports.

- In television, still photographs, may be used when no video camera can reach a correspondent or interview subject. A still photograph may also be used to show historically notable person and event or in any place where it aids the report. Photos may be recorded with a standard video camera or the photos can be placed on a special motion control device which allows precise computer controlled positioning. Whether shot in the field or in the studio, the camera operator might zoom, pan or tilt while recording the images. The director may use portions of this video or may digitally store some selected frames for insertion into the final report.
- Graphics are used to report on financial markets, labour statistics, crop reports, municipal budgets and other instances where tabular data or charts are the best choice for explaining a story element. In electronic journalism, graphics are displayed while the reporter continues to read the script. The graphics, including fonts and titles, convey newsworthy information, names and titles. The use of graphics also support a station or network's image. Graphics, in some cases, may open up some revenue generating opportunities to the content delivery channel.
- Animation is an effective tool for communicating views of a natural disaster or a tragic accident like a plain crash. Producers might turn to animation to explain a complex scientific process, economic or political polling trends; to illustrate news about space flights and many other appropriate uses. Meteorologists make use of simple and complex animation to show the path of storms.

Technical Standards

- CCD Camera technology.

- Digital storage and transmission to news room via high-speed Internet connections. Advanced storage allows shooting hundreds of images without need to reload camera.

Audio Journalism

Radio has long been used to broadcast news as quickly as possible. Many important speeches and public events were covered on radio and still are today. With the growing availability of small, yet high-quality, cassette recorders, such as those from Marantz and Sony, radio reporters are able to make use of natural sounds and interviews which brings great detail to their reports. National Public Radio's All Things Considered has been a pioneer in the use of such sound elements woven into the fabric of its reports.

Technical Standards

A wide variety of audio recording formats is used in news rooms around the world. The standard report kit includes a battery operated cassette recorder with a dynamic microphone and optional telephone interface. With this set-up, the reporter can record interviews and natural sound and then play these over a telephone line for rerecording or live broadcast by the content provider (radio or TV station, cable outlet, web radio system). This offers a rugged and relatively simple system which can be placed into a single bag along with extra batteries, tape and supplies.

In addition to the standard compact cassette another popular choice is the digital minidisc. This has the advantage of superior sound, digital indexing and is re-recordable, reusable medium. The small cassette format known as DAT is popular with film makers and other studio professionals because of its superior sound quality and its SMPTE time code and other synchronization features. News gathering may also be accomplished with the use of recordable CD and DVD players and various fixed medium recording system.

JOURNALIST

A journalist (also called a newspaperman) is a person who practices journalism, the gathering and dissemination of information about current events, trends, issues, and people while striving for non-bias viewpoint.

Reporters are one type of journalist. They create reports as a profession for broadcast or publication in mass media such as newspapers, television, radio, magazines, , and the Internet. Reporters find sources for their work, their reports can be either spoken or written, and they are often expected to report in the most objective and unbiased way to serve the public good. A columnist is a journalist who writes pieces that appear regularly in newspapers or magazines. Depending on the context, the term *journalist* also includes various types of editors and visual journalists, such as photographers, graphic artists, and page designers. Journalists put the information in their own words, making it creative in their own way so it will catch the reader's or viewer's attention.

Modern Journalists

Modern media, including the creation of Internet-based news sources and the possibility that citizen journalism will greatly expand the field, has made it all but impossible to identify which journalists are notable, in the sense that they could be identified in the past. The global justice protests in Seattle (1999) gave rise to the independent media movement, exemplified by the Indymedia network, a collective of independent media organizations and hundreds of journalists offering grassroots, non-corporate coverage.

Kid Journalists

The Scholastic News Kid Press crop. is a group of kids age 8-14 who report for Scholastic News website and classroom magazines.

Ethics in Journalism

Some journalists in the United States adhere to the standards and norms expressed in the Society of Professional Journalists ethical code. Foremost in the minds of most practicing journalists is the issue of maintaining credibility, "Professional integrity is the cornerstone of a journalist's credibility."

Educating Journalists

Journalists often either receive training directly in the type of news field that they wish to enter, or through various institutions of higher education.

United States

From Columbia University and Point Park University's School of Communications and Journalism on the East Coast of America, to University of Southern California and Arizona State University's Walter Cronkite School of Journalism and Mass Communication on the West Coast, there is a broad range of options for beginning journalists to choose from when entering the field. Perhaps best known though is the University of Missouri School of Journalism.

Australia

In Australia, the most notable alumni of journalists come from Charles Stuart University, J-school, RMIT University and University of Technology, Sydney.

JOURNALISM SCHOOL

A journalism school is a school or department, usually part of an established university, where journalists are trained. "Journalism is the key to life," said one famous Nebraskan. An increasingly used short form for a journalism department, school or college is 'J-school'. Many of the most famous and respected journalists of the past and present had no formal training in journalism, but learned their craft on the job, often starting out as *copy boys/copy girls*. Today, in many parts of the world it is usual for journalists to first complete university-level training which incorporates both technical skills such as research skills, interviewing technique and shorthand and academic studies in media theory, cultural studies and ethics.

Historically, in the United Kingdom entrants used first to complete a non-media studies related degree course, giving maximum educational breadth, prior to taking a specialist postgraduate pre-entry course. However, this has changed over the last ten years with journalism training and education moving to higher educational institutions. There are now over 60 universities in the UK offering BA honours degrees in journalism. Postgraduate courses are more well-established, some of which are either recognised by the National Union of Journalists (NUJ) or the National Council for the Training of Journalists (NCTJ).

History

The first programme for journalism education was introduced by former Confederate General, Robert E. Lee, during his presidency at Washington and Lee University, in Lexington, Virginia, in the 1860s. The world's first journalism school was founded by Walter Williams as the Missouri School of Journalism at the University of Missouri in 1908. Since then the journalism school has become standard at most major universities.

Top Journalism Schools

There have been various attempts to rank journalism schools, and the question of which are the "best" or "top" journalism schools is frequently raised on the internet by students. Many institutions claim to be leading schools of journalism, and there is inevitably debate about which are the most appropriate criteria with which to evaluate and judge journalism schools. Awards are obvious indicators of a quality J-school, as are the quality of school graduates.

Australia and New Zealand

In Australia, a ranking of all journalism schools in the country has been assembled based on graduating students' assessments of the quality of their courses: Top journalism schools in Australia include J-school and the University of the Sunshine Coast. The New Zealand Training Organization has published a list of that country's journalism schools recognised by industry.

Europe

The Centre de Formation des Journalistes (CFJ) was founded in 1946 by two Resistance leaders. Located on the rue du Louvre in Paris, many of the leading journalists in France today graduated from this school and come back to help train today's students.

Europe's most long-established postgraduate centre of journalism education is the highly-regarded Department of Journalism at City University, London.

The UK's top-rated course by the National Council for the Training of Journalists is at Nottingham Trent University.

Cardiff University, Sheffield; University of Central Lancashire and Kingston University also have well-respected journalism departments. Issues from a European perspective in evaluating journalism schools are discussed by the president of the European Journalism Training Association:

In Russia, the MSU Faculty of Journalism is the leading journalism school. The majority of textbooks on journalism in Russian were written by MSU scientists.

Latin America

An evaluation of developments in journalism education in Latin America has been undertaken by Professor Rosental Calmon Alves.

Colombia

In this country the high court determined in 1998 that journalism was not a career or a profession, this high court said that is a human right, not a profession. Because of that there are in Colombia many schools of communications where people study for working, most of all, in enterprises, not in mass media.

There are only two schools of journalism:

1. University of Antioquia, a public institution in Medellín, offers Journalsim inside the Communcations faculty.
2. University of Rosario in Bogotá, a private institution offers Public Opinion Journalism.

North America

A listing (unranked) of Canadian journalism schools has been assembled by Canadian-Universities.net. Journalism schools are listed and classified on the "J-Schools & Programmes" page of The Canadian Journalism Project.

In the United States the Accrediting Council on Education in Journalism and Mass Communications (ACEJMC) applies nine standards in evaluating university programmes: mission, governance and administration; curriculum and instruction; diversity and inclusiveness; full-time and part-time faculty; scholarship: research, creative and professional activity; student services; resources, facilities and equipment; professional and public service; and assessment of learning outcomes. The ACEJMC has awarded accreditation to 109 university and college programmes of study in journalism and mass communications, but does not attempt to rank the courses or programmes. It accredits colleges, schools, Departments or Divisions. The listing of a unit as accredited indicates that the unit has been judged by ACEJMC to meet its standards. That judgement is rendered after a self-study prepared by the faculty and administration of the unit and an independent evaluation of the unit by educators and practitioners. The listing shows the bachelor's and professional master's degree programmes that were examined during the unit's most recent accreditation review. Some units offer degrees in addition to those listed here. ACEJMC does not accredit programmes leading to the Ph.D., which is considered a research (and not a professional) degree. The Council does not list sequences or specialities.

Editor and Publisher has presented an unranked list of leading journalism schools, while U.S. News and World Report produces annual lists of the top schools in advertising, print, and other categories based on responses to questionnaires sent to Deans and faculty members. A list based on a variety of resources claims to identify the "ten most popular journalism schools in the United States." One critic has pointed to the anecdotal nature of much J-school ranking in the absence of effective tracking of journalism graduates' career paths. Generally, America's most prominent journalism programmes are considered those at Columbia University, Northwestern University, and the University of Missouri. Other well-known programmes include those at Ohio University, Indiana University, Michigan State University, Quinnipiac University, University of Florida, University of North Carolina, Chapel Hill, and University of Illinois at Urbana-Champaign.

Debate about the Role of Journalism Schools

One of the most cited critiques of a journalism school was Michael Lewis's article in *The New Republic* (1993), "J-school ate my brain", which was strongly criticized by University of Maryland College of Journalism dean Reese Cleghorn in *American Journalism Review*: Discussion of the issues raised by Lewis was evident a decade later in the *Chronicle of Higher Education* colloquy on journalism education, *Columbia Journalism Review*'s "Searching for the perfect J-school" and "The J-school debate" in the Christian Science Monitor. Alternative approaches to journalism education were suggested in Jack Shafer's *Slate* article "Can J-school be saved? Professional advice for Columbia University." An article in *The Australian* discusses "What makes a good school of journalism."

On the internet, a range of weblogs have been set up by journalism students to chronicle or to criticize their journalism colleges. Examples are: An example of a weblog criticizing university journalism education in Australia is one journalism school in the UK, at the University of Westminster, has established a clearing house where all students are expected to contribute to the development and content of their own education and training using blogs.

Various commentaries on journalism education are related to criticisms of contemporary news media standards and values. One example is a paper by Jan Schaffer, executive director of J-Lab: the Institute for Interactive Journalism. A controversial paper to Australia's peak newspaper industry body PANPA (Pacific Area Newspaper Publishers Association) by Professor John Henningham ("Journalism sold short in media courses") blamed industry lack of interest and university cost-cutting for falling standards in journalism education. In Canada, Mark Anderson of the Ottawa Citizen has argued the case for teaching business journalism in college rather than on the job.

List of Journalism Schools and Programmes

United States and Canada

- The Department of Journalism (http://www.brooklyn.liu.edu/journalism) at Long Island University's Brooklyn Campus.

- Henry W. Grady College of Journalism and Mass Communication at the University of Georgia.
- The W. Page Pitt School of Journalism and Mass Communications at Marshall University.
- The Elon University School of Communications.
- The Department of Journalism, Roy H. Park School of Communications, Ithaca College.
- The College of Communications Department of Journalism at the Pennsylvania State University.
- College of Journalism and Mass Communications at University of Nebraska-Lincoln.
- The Department of Journalism at Ball State University.
- The College of Communication and Information Sciences at The University of Alabama.
- The Department of Journalism at New York University.
- Annenberg School for Communication at the University of Southern California, and the University of Pennsylvania.
- University of Oregon School of Journalism and Communication.
- School of Journalism and Mass Communications at University of South Carolina.
- The Edward R. Murrow School of Communication at Washington State University.
- Philip Merrill College of Journalism at the University of Maryland.
- Columbia University Graduate School of Journalism.
- Gaylord College of Journalism and Mass Communication at the University of Oklahoma.
- S. I. Newhouse School of Public Communications at Syracuse University.
- Ernie Pyle School of Journalism at Indiana University.
- E.W. Scripps School of Journalism at Ohio University.
- University of Texas School of Journalism.
- Michigan State University School of Journalism.
- Medill School of Journalism at Northwestern University.
- Missouri School of Journalism at University of Missouri.
- NBC News School of Digital Journalism in affiliation with New York Film Academy (http://www.nyfa.com/film_school/programs/filmmaking/nbc.php).

- School of Journalism at Loyola University Chicago.
- Point Park University in Pittsburgh, Pennsylvania.
- Ryerson School of Journalism at Ryerson University.
- University of Florida School of Journalism.
- UC Berkeley Graduate School of Journalism.
- UC Irvine offers an undergraduate degree in Literary Journalism.
- USC School of Journalism and Mass Communication—Columbia, South Carolina.
- University of Colorado School of Journalism and Mass Communication.
- Donald W. Reynolds School of Journalism at the University of Nevada, Reno.
- University of Wisconsin-Madison.
- University of Iowa Adler School of Journalism.
- Walter Cronkite School of Journalism and Mass Communication at Arizona State University.
- Boston University College of Communication.
- School of Communications and Theater at Temple University.
- School of Journalism and Communication at University of Oregon.
- School of Journalism and Mass Communication at Kent State University.
- School of Journalism and Mass Communication at University of Minnesota.
- School of Journalism and Mass Communication University of North Corolina, Chapel Hill.
- School of Communication at American University.
- College of Communication at DePaul University.
- The Department of Journalism at the University of Arizona.
- The Department of Journalism at the University at Albany.
- The Department of Journalism and Mass Communications at Washington and Lee University.
- College of Communications at University of Illinois Urbana-Champaign.
- The Washington Journalism Center in Washington, D.C.
- University of Western Ontario.

- School of Media and Public Affairs at The George Washington University.
- School of Media Arts and Design at James Madison University.
- The P. I. Reed School of Journalism at West Virginia University.
- School of Journalism Southern Illinois University.

Latin America (Colombia)

- University of Antioquia Journalsim career.
- Rosario University Public Opinion Journalism.

Asia

- Indian Institute of Mass Communication (IIMC), New Delhi.
- Asian College of Journalism, Chennai.
- A J K Mass Communication Research Centre, Jamia, New Delhi.
- Department of Journalism, Hong Kong Baptist University.
- Institute for Journalism and Society, Hong Kong Baptist University.
- Journalism and Media Studies Centre, University of Hong Kong.
- Department of Journalism at the College of Mass Communication, University of the Philippines Diliman.
- Department of Journalism, College of Communication, Polytechnic University of the Philippines.
- Asian Institute of Journalism and Communication.
- Department of Journalism, Shih Hsin University, Taiwan.
- Department of Journalism, National Chengchi University, Taiwan.
- Department of Journalism and Communication Studies, Fu Jen Catholic University, Taiwan.

Australia and New Zealand

- J-school: Journalism Education and Training.
- University of Technology, Sydney—Journalism Department.

Europe

- Nottingham Trent University Centre for Broadcasting and Journalism—Nottingham, England.
- CELSA Paris—Sorbonne University, France.
- CFJ Paris-based Journalism School and Training Centre, Paris, France.
- City University Journalism Department—London, England.
- JMG, University of Gothenburg—Gothenburg, Sweden.
- Leeds University—Institute of Communications Studies—Yorkshire, England.
- London College of Communication—University of the Arts, London—London, England.
- Moscow State University Faculty of Journalism—Moscow, Russia.
- Westminster University Journalism Department—London, England.
- Kingston University Journalism Department.

4

News, News Conference and News Writing: An Introductory Overview

NEWS

News is any *new information* or information on current events which is presented by print, broadcast, Internet, or word of mouth to a third party or mass audience, i.e. the reporting of current information on television and radio, and in newspapers and magazines.

Etymology

One theory is that "news" was developed as a special use of the plural form of "new" in the 14th century. In Middle English, the equivalent word was *newes,* based on the French *nouvelles.* A somewhat similar development is found in at least three Slavic languages (Czech, Slovak and Polish), where there exists a word *noviny* ("news"), developed from the word *nový* ("new"). Another theory is that the word, phonetically and its written style, is based upon the Germanic word "neues." A folk etymology suggests that it is an acronym of the cardinal directions: *north, east, west,* and *south,* it was because news is all around the world and *north, east, west* and *south* are obviously the cardinal directions.

History of News Reporting

In its infancy, news gathering was primitive by today's standards. Printed news had to be phoned in to a newsroom or brought there by a reporter, where it was typed and either transmitted over wire services or edited and manually set in type along with other news stories for a specific edition. Today, the term "Breaking News" has become trite as broadcast and cable news services use live satellite technology to bring current events into consumers' homes live as they happen. Events that used to take hours or days to become common knowledge in towns or in nations are fed instantaneously to consumers via radio, television, cell phones, and the Internet.

Newspapers

Most large cities had morning and afternoon newspapers. As the media evolved and news outlets increased to the point of near over-saturation, afternoon newspapers were shut down except for relatively few. Morning newspapers have been gradually losing circulation, according to reports advanced by the papers themselves. Commonly, news content should contain the "Five Ws" (who, what, when, where, why, and also how) of an event. There should be no questions remaining. Newspapers normally write hard news stories, such as those pertaining to murders, fires, wars, etc. in inverted pyramid style so the most important information is at the beginning. Busy readers can read as little or as much as they desire. Local stations and networks with a set format must take news stories and break them down into the most important aspects due to time constraints. Cable news channels such as Fox News Channel, MSNBC, and CNN, are able to take advantage of a story, sacrificing other, decidedly less important stories, and giving as much detail about breaking news as possible.

Objectivity in News

News organizations are often expected to aim for objectivity; reporters claim to try to cover all sides of an issue without bias, as compared to commentators or analysts, who provide opinion or personal point-of-view. However, several governments impose certain constraints or police news organizations for bias. In the United Kingdom, for example, limits are set by the government agency Ofcom, the Office of Communications. Both newspapers and broadcast news programmes in the United States are generally expected to remain neutral and avoid bias except for clearly indicated editorial articles or segments. Many single-party governments have operated state-run news organizations, which may present the government's views.

Even in those situations where objectivity is expected, it is difficult to achieve, and individual journalists may fall foul of their own personal bias, or succumb to commercial or political pressure. Similarly, the objectivity of news organizations owned by conglomerated corporations fairly may be questioned, in light of the natural incentive for such groups to report news in a manner intended to advance the conglomerate's financial interests. Individuals and organizations who are the subject of news reports may use news management techniques to try to make a favourable impression. Because no human being can remain entirely objective (each of us has a particular point-of-view), it is recognized that there can be no absolute objectivity in news reporting.

Newsworthiness

Newsworthiness is defined as a subject having sufficient relevance to the public or a special audience to warrant press attention or coverage. Normal people are not newsworthy unless they meet an unusual circumstance or tragedy. The news divides the population into two groups; those few whose lives are newsworthy, and the multitude who are born, live out their lives and die without the news media paying them any significant notice. The news has always covered subjects that catch people's attention and differ from their "ordinary lives." The news is often used for escapism and thus normal events are not newsworthy. Whether the subject is love, birth, weather, or crime, journalists' tastes inevitably run toward the unnatural, the extraordinary.

The subject and newsworthiness of a story depends on the audience, as they decide what they do and do not have an interest in. The denser the population, the more global the news becomes, as there is a broader range of interests involved in its selection.

NEWS CONFERENCE

A news conference or press conference is a media event staged by an individual or group wishing to attract media coverage for something claimed to have news value. Television stations and networks especially value news conferences: because today's TV news programmes air for hours at a time, or even continuously, assignment editors have a steady appetite for ever-larger quantities of "news" footage.

News conferences are often held by politicians (such as the President of the United States); by sports teams; by celebrities or film studios; by commercial organizations to promote products; by attorneys to promote lawsuits; and by almost anyone who finds benefit in the free publicity afforded by media coverage.

A news conference is announced by mailing or faxing an advisory or news release to assignment editors, preferably well in advance. Normally they are held in hotel conference rooms or other formal settings; they may also take place at disaster sites, courthouses or other places where news is breaking. In a news conference, one or more speakers may make a statement, which may be followed by questions from reporters. Sometimes only questioning occurs, sometimes there is a statement with no questions permitted. A media event at which no statements are made, and no questions allowed, is called a photo opportunity.

U.S. Presidential Press Conference

When the U.S. President holds a press conference, he takes questions from the press pool in a specific order: wire services (for decades, Helen Thomas of UPI had the first question), broadcast networks, national newspapers, newsmagazines, radio and, lastly, regional newspapers.

NEWS WRITING

News style (also journalistic style or news writing) is the particular prose style used for news reporting (*i.e.* in newspapers) as well as in news items that air on radio and television. News style encompasses not only vocabulary and sentence structure, but also the way in which stories present the information in terms of relative importance, tone, and intended audience.

News writing attempts to answer all the basic questions about any particular event in the first two or three paragraphs: *Who? What? When? Where? and Why? and occasionally How?* (*i.e.* "5 W's").

This form of structure is sometimes called the "inverted pyramid," to refer to decreased importance of information as it progresses.

News stories also contain at least one of the following important characteristics: proximity, prominence, timeliness, human interest, oddity, or consequence.

Overview

While newspapers, like encyclopedias, generally adhere to an expository writing mode and style, this has changed over time as journalism ethics and standards have (debatably) increased to become more objective and less sensationalistic. There are debated degrees of professionalism among particular news agencies, and their reputability or public value, according to professional standards of idealism and depending on what the reader wants from a news story, may be tied to their ability to be objective. In its most ideal form, news writing strives to be intelligible to the vast majority of potential readers, as well as to be engaging and succinct. Within the limits created by these goals, news stories also aim for a kind of comprehensiveness. However other factors are involved, some of which are practical and derived from the media form, and others stylistic.

Among the larger and more respected newspapers, fairness and balance is a major factor for the presentation of information. Commentary is usually confined to a separate section, though each paper may have a different overall slant. Editorial policy dictates the use of adjectives, euphemisms, and idioms. Papers with an international audience for example, usually use a more formal style of writing. The specific choices made by a news outlet's editor or editorial board are often collected in a style guide or stylebook; common commercial stylebooks are the "AP Style Manual" and the "US News Style Book." The main goals of news writing can be summarized by the ABCs of journalism: accuracy, brevity, and clarity.

Terms and Structure

Journalistic prose is explicit and precise, and tries not to rely on jargon. As a rule, journalists will not use a long word when a short one will do. They use subject-verb-object construction and vivid, active prose. They offer anecdotes, examples and metaphors, and they rarely depend on colourless generalizations or abstract ideas. News writers try to avoid using the same word more than once in a paragraph (sometimes called an "echo" or "word mirror").

Headline (or hed)

The head of a story, in newsman's jargon.

Subhead (or dek*)*

A phrase, sentence or several sentences near the title of an article or story.

Lede or Lead

The most important structural element of a story is the lede or lead—the story's first, or leading, sentence. Charnley (1966) stated that an effective lead is a "brief, sharp statement of the story's essential facts." The lede/lead is usually the first sentence, or in some cases the first two sentences, and is ideally 20-25 words in length. The top-leading principle applies especially to ledes, but the unreadability of long sentences constrains its size. This makes writing a lede an optimization problem, in which the goal is to articulate the most encompassing and interesting statement that a writer can make in one sentence, given the material with which he or she has to work. While a rule of thumb says the lede should answer most or all of the 5 Ws, few ledes can fit all of these. Article ledes are sometimes categorized into hard ledes and soft ledes. A hard lede aims to provide a comprehensive thesis which tells the reader what the article will cover. A soft lede introduces the topic in a more creative, attention-seeking fashion, and is usually followed by a nut graf (a brief summary of facts).

Media critics often note that the lede can be the most polarizing subject in the article. Often critics find bias based on an editor's choice in headline and lede.

Example Lede-and-Summary Design

Humans will be going to the moon again. The NASA announcement came as the agency requested ten gazillion dollars of appropriations for the project. ...

Example Soft-Lede Design

NASA is proposing another space project. The agency's budget request, announced today, included a plan to send another person to the moon. This time the agency hopes to establish a long-term facility as a jumping-off point for other space adventures. The budget requests approximately ten gazillion dollars for the project. ...

Two other terms common in editing are *hed* and *dek* or *deck*. Hed is used to denote an article's headline or heading. Dek refers to a quick blurb or article teaser.

Nut Graph

One or more paragraphs, particularly in a feature story, that explain the news value of the story.

Inverted Pyramid

Journalism instructors usually describe the organization or structure of a news story as an inverted pyramid. The journalist top-loads the essential and most interesting elements of his or her story, with supporting information following in order of diminishing importance. This structure enables readers to quit reading at any point and still come away with the essence of a story. It allows people to enter a topic to the depth that their curiosity takes them, and without the imposition of details or nuances that they would consider irrelevant. Newsroom practicalities represent another rationale. The inverted pyramid structure enables sub-editors and other news staff to quickly create space for ads and late-breaking news simply by cutting items ("*throw-aways*") from the bottom ("cutting", literally, at the papers that still use traditional paste up techniques). The structure frees sub-editors to truncate stories at almost any length that suits their needs for space.

Poor structure typically begins with a faulty lede. Steeped in the raw material of their interviews and research, apprentice news writers often fail to anticipate what readers will find most interesting or to sum up the information quickly. These elements of their story they present only after their lede and in an article's later paragraphs. This is the reason for the popular newsroom admonition: "*Don't bury the lede*!" Some writers start their stories with the "1-2-3 lede." This format invariably starts with a 5W's opening paragraph (as described above), followed by an indirect quote that serves to support a major element of the first paragraph, and then a direct quote to support the indirect quote.

Feature Style

News stories are not the only type of material that appear in newspapers and magazines. Longer articles, such as magazine cover articles and the pieces that lead the inside sections of a newspaper, are known as *features*. Feature stories differ from *straight* news in several ways. Foremost is the absence of a straight-news lead, most of the time. Instead of offering the essence of a story up front, feature writers may attempt to lure readers in.

While straight news stories always stay in third person point of view, it is not uncommon for a feature magazine article to slip into first person. The journalist will often detail his or her interactions with interview subjects, making the piece more personal. A feature's first paragraphs often relate an intriguing moment or event, as in an "anecdotal lede." From the particulars of a person or episode, its view quickly broadens to generalities about the story's subject. The section that signals what a feature is about is called the *nut graf* or *billboard*. Billboards appear as the third or fourth paragraph from the top, and may be up to two paragraphs long. Unlike a lede, a billboard rarely gives everything away. This reflects the fact that feature writers aim to hold their readers' attention to the end, which requires engendering curiosity and offering a "payoff." Feature paragraphs tend to be longer than those of news stories, with smoother transitions between them. Feature writers use the active-verb construction and concrete explanations of straight news, but often put more personality in their prose. Feature stories often close with a "kicker" rather than simply petering out.

5

News Editing and Copy Editing: Persons, Roles and Responsibilities

NEWS EDITING

Editing language, images, or sound through correction, condensation, organization, and other modifications in various media. A person who edits is called an *editor*. In a sense, the editing process originates with the idea for the work itself and continues in the relationship between the author and the editor. Editing is, therefore, also a practice that includes creative skills, human relations, and a precise set of methods.

Print Media

There are various levels of editorial positions in publishing industry. Typically, one finds junior editorial assistants reporting to the senior-level editorial managers and directors who report to senior executive editors. Senior executive editors are responsible for developing a product to its final release. The smaller the publication, the more these roles run together. In particular, the substantive editor and copy editor often overlap: fact-checking and rewriting can be the responsibility of either.

Newspaper and wire services copy editors correct spelling, grammar, and matters of house style, design pages and select of news stories for inclusion. At UK and Australian newspapers, the term is "sub-editor." As well, they choose the layout of the publication and communicating with the printer—a *production editor.* This and similar jobs are also called "layout editor," "design editor," "news designer," or—more so in the past—"make-up editor." Magazine editors include a top-level editor may be called an *editor-in-chief.* Frequent and esteemed contributors to a magazine may acquire a title of *editor at-large* or *contributing editor.*

In the book publishing industry, editors organize anthologies and other compilations, produce definitive editions of a classic author's works ("scholarly editor"); and organize and manage contributions to a multi-author book (symposium editor or volume editor). Finding marketable ideas and presenting them to appropriate authors: a *sponsoring editor*. Obtaining copy or recruiting authors such as: an *acquisitions editor* or a *commissioning editor* for a publishing house. Improving an author's writing so that they indeed say what they mean to say in an effective manner; a *substantive editor.* Depending on the writer's skill level, this editing can sometimes turn into ghost writing. Substantive editing is seldom a title. Many types of editors do this type of work, either in-house at a publisher or on an independent basis.

Newspapers

Editors at newspapers supervise journalists and improve their work. Newspaper editing encompasses a variety of titles and functions. These include:

- Copy editors
- Department editors
- Managing editors and assistant or deputy managing editors (the managing editor is often second in line after the top editor)
- News editors, who oversee the news desks
- Photo or picture editors
- Section editors and their assistants, such as for business, features, and sports
- Editorial page editor who oversees the coverage on the editorial page. This includes chairing the Editorial Board and assigning editorial writing responsibilities. The editorial page editor may also oversee the op-ed page or those duties are assigned to a separate op-ed editor
- Top editors, who may be called *editor-in-chief, executive editor* or sometimes just *editor*
- Readers' editors, sometimes known as the ombudsman, who arbitrate complaints

- Wire editors, who choose and edit articles from various international wire services, and are usually part of the copy desk, and
- Administrative editors (who actually don't edit but perform duties such as recruiting and directing training).

The term *city editor* is used differently in North America and South America, where it refers to the editor responsible for the news coverage of a newspaper's local circulation area (also sometimes called *metro editor*), than in the United Kingdom, where it refers to the editor responsible for coverage of business in the City of London and, by extension, coverage of business and finance in general.

Print editing is much different than online editing, that is why I am able to add this statement.

Scholarly Books and Journals

Editors of scholarly books and journals are of three types, each with particular responsibilities: the *acquisitions editor* (or *commissioning editor* in Britain), who contracts with the author to produce the copy, the *project editor* or *production editor,* who sees the copy through its stages from manuscript through bound book and usually assumes most of the budget and schedule responsibilities, and the *copy editor* or *manuscript editor,* who performs the tasks of readying the copy for conversion into printed form.

The primary difference between copy editing scholarly books and journals and other sorts of copy editing lies in applying the standards of the publisher to the copy. Most scholarly publishers have a preferred style guide, usually a combination of Merriam-Webster's Collegiate Dictionary and either the *Chicago Manual of Style,* the *MLA Style Manual,* or the *APA Publication Manual* in the US or New Hart's Rules [based on "Hart's Rules for Compositors and Readers at the University Press, Oxford" (1893)] in the UK. Since scholars often have strong preferences, very often a publisher will adopt different styles for different fields. For instance, psychologists prefer the APA style, while linguists might prefer the MLA style. These guidelines offer sound advice on making cited sources complete and correct and making the presentation scholarly.

EDITOR

Editor has four major senses:

1. *Print media*: There are various levels of editorial positions in publishing. Typically one finds junior editorial assistants reporting to senior level editorial managers and directors, who themselves report to senior executive editors responsible for project development to final releases.
2. *Visual media*: Editors in the visual mediums, film editor and video editors, perform a variety of tasks. Assistant editors and production assistants perform preliminary screening and logging of motion picture footage; senior editors are responsible for creative placement of scenes and shots, structural placement of major elements and organization of the entire presentation. Other editors will are involved with assembly of the final product and preparation for distribution.
3. *Sound media*: Motion pictures have many sound editors, this team works with various aspects of picture or programme's sound design. These editors construct tracks consisting of assembled pre-recorded dialogue, the audio mixing in of sound effects, foley and music to achieve the desired effect for the motion pictures and television programmes.
4. *Computer editor* is a programme used to make changes to files of a particular type. There are computer editing systems for visual and sound mediums as well as still images. Other types of editors are more technical and edit computer code in various ways needed by programmers and technicians.

Etymology

According to the *Oxford English Dictionary, editor* comes from the Latin phrase *e ditus* which means "to put forward." The *editor ludorum* in Ancient Rome was the person who put on the games. In French, *editeur* means "publisher." The word came into English from French. The verb *to edit* is a back formation from *editor*.

Print Media

Human editors in the print publishing industry include people who are responsible for:

- Newspapers and wire services.
- Organizing anthologies and other compilations.
- Organizing and publishing a magazine. The top editor may be called *editor-in-chief.*
- Producing a definitive edition of a classic author's works—a *scholarly editor.*
- Organizing and managing contributions to a multi-author book—*symposium editor* or *volume editor.*
- Finding marketable ideas and presenting them to appropriate authors—a *sponsoring editor.*
- Obtaining copy or recruiting authors—such as the *acquisitions editor* or *commissioning editor* for a publishing house.
- Improving an author's writing so that they indeed say what they want to say, in an effective manner—a *substantive editor.* Depending on the writer's skill, this editing can sometimes turn into ghost writing. Substantive editing is seldom a title. Many types of editors do this type of work, either in-house at a publisher or on an independent basis.
- Correcting spelling, grammar, and matters of house style—a *copy editor.* But copy editors at newspapers usually also have greater and higher responsibilities, which may include the design of pages and the selection of news stories for inclusion. At UK newspapers, the term is "sub-editor."
- Choosing the layout of the publication and communicating with the printer—a *production editor.* This and similar jobs are also called "layout editor," "design editor," "news designer," or—more so in the past—"makeup editor."

The smaller the publication, the more these roles run together. In particular, the substantive editor and copy editor often overlap:

- Fact-checking can be the responsibility of either.
- Copy editors who find an inappropriate term or phrase will often suggest or make an improvement.

Duties of an Editor

The eventual success of your organization's public and media relations efforts depends mainly on how often your news releases are issued and, more importantly, how often the news they contain is selected to run. The latter decision is in the hands of a person whose title is usually *editor*. Understanding an editor's job will help you do your job better.

Can you name the editor of your local computer magazine or local newspaper? The editor is a very importantally in public relations. The editor (whose title might also be *managing editor* or *editor-in-chief*) has overall responsibility for the publication's content. Below him or her, depending on the periodical's size, are subject editors who are assigned to specific beats (often called "departments"). These editors oversee the content for their departments. Sometimes each editor has additional staff, such as reporters, freelance writers, photographers, copy writers, copy editors, etc. The information contained in news releases is the primary source of information for most editors. Newsworthy releases are selected and edited or worked into an article. The selected releases are the lucky ones; most never see the light of day. When you consider that the editor at a daily publication receives upwards of 500 news releases on any given day, gauging the statistical possibility of an individual release being picked up for coverage is easy.

Newspaper Editors

Newspapers don't mean just the regular daily newspapers targetted at the general public. There are special-interest newspapers for business, computers, information technology, telecommunications, and other fields. The specialty papers may run weekly instead of daily, but, like their daily counterparts, they are primarily news-driven rather than feature-driven (which is more the case with magazines).

Newspaper editors reject many more releases than they use. The larger the paper's circulation or the more active the area being covered, the more releases the editor has to sort through.

Most newspapers have a space budget, which is not to be confused with a financial budget. The space budget consists of the total number of pages printed, divided between advertising and news articles. Advertisements are the lifeblood of a newspaper; advertisements consistently provide the largest portion of income. The advertisements must be accommodated first, after which the issue's remaining space is allocated to specific stories and departments by the key editors.

The selection of news releases to cover is based on the editor's personal and professional judgement. The main factor in that judgement can be summed up in a single word: "newsworthiness." Unfortunately, newsworthiness is defined by individual editor's opinions. Newsworthy stories are generally those that offer the most information with the most urgency to the most people.

If a news release issued on particular day is not covered in the following day's paper, this does not mean the news will not appear at all. Releases not considered newsworthy enough to appear in a weekday edition may be suitable for the weekend paper, where there is more room and less emphasis on breaking news. Even if a news item is selected for use, the article may still get pulled at the last minute. Perhaps an advertiser cancelled a large insert just prior to deadline, necessitating a layout change, or a big story emerged late in the day. When this happens, more expendable news is sacrificed.

What happens to releases that aren't selected for immediate coverage? Some are kept for future use, but more likely they are sent into the editor's trash can.

Magazine Editors

Magazines operate very much like newspapers, with departments, editors, space budgets, and advertising, but magazines differ in a few important ways. The potential lifespan of a news release is much longer for a magazine. A monthly publication might not use your news for several months. Depending on the printing and preparation schedule, your release could appear as soon as a week or two after you send the release or as late as six-months later. The nice thing is that whenever your news appears, the information remains in front of the reader for a full month instead of just one day.

The editorial focus and format of a magazine are usually more specialized than those of newspapers. "Focus" refers to the subjects a magazine covers; for instance, *Linux Journal* focusses on Linux in general while *ComputerWorld* might focus on Linux in the enterprise. "Format" refers to the way in which a magazine's news and information is presented, usually as a particular mix of regular columns, articles, features (main stories), shorter pieces, and editorials (opinion pieces). Magazine stories don't have to be as "newsy" as newspaper stories. To a greater degree, a magazine researches and creates news rather than relying on current events.

General-interest magazines try to appeal to a large segment of the population. (Examples are *Macleans, Readers' Digest,* and *People.*) Special-interest magazines target a limited, well-defined community of readers who share a particular interest along with associated activities and concerns. Special-interest magazines are good targets for the Linux community, especially those focussing on Linux, operating systems, storage, security, computers, and information technology.

Whether special interest or general interest, the closer your news release relates to the audience of a publication and the greater the impact on that audience, the more likely an editor will choose your news to publish. The key factors are editorial relevance and appeal to the publication's target audience.

Duties of Editor/Staff Writers

Putting together a base newspaper is a great responsibility. At times it can be frustrating when the editor feels as though he or she is being pulled in 10 different directions at the same time. It is this reason that editors must learn to delegate certain functions to their staff writers, when deemed necessary.

The following items are some of the functions that a newspaper editor is responsible for:

- Gathering base news and arranging photo coverage of wing events.
- Reviewing and localizing material received from Air Force and command news services.
- Editing and rewriting copy; writing headlines and cutlines, and cropping and marking photos for reproduction.
- Arranging and conducting interviews; researching, writing and coordinating articles.
- Designing newspaper layout using desktop publishing programmes and coordinating with the publisher on distribution, circulation and special issue production.

- Becoming very familiar with the provisions set forth in DOD Instruction 5120.4, *Department of Defense Newspapers, Magazines and Civilian Enterprise Publications, and* AFI 35-101, *Public Affairs Policies and Procedures,* concerning newspapers and abiding by them.
- Ensuring news coverage and content conform to policies of the Air Force and the commander, to include:
  - Being factual and objective.
- Ensuring accuracy is paramount.
- Avoiding morbid, sensational, or alarming details that are not essential to factual reporting.
- Distinguishing between facts and opinion, both of which may be part of a story.
  - When an opinion is expressed, identify the person or source.
- Ensuring locally originated editorials reflect the policies of the commander and are in the best interest of the Air Force. Ensure editorials meet these guidelines:
  - They should help readers understand Air Force policies and programmes.
- They must not imply criticism of other governmental agencies, nor advocate or dispute specific political, diplomatic, or legislative matters.
- Ensuring news content is based on local articles developed by the newspaper staff; news releases are by Air Force Print News, the MAJCOM news service, American Forces Press Service, or other agencies of the federal government.
- Ensuring sources of all material other than local, internal sources are properly credited. This includes, but is not limited to:
  - Air Force Print News.
- American Forces Press Service.
- MAJCOM news services.
- Ensuring that overseas newspapers obtain guidance concerning host country sensitivities from unified commands.

- Ensuring that commercial news and opinion materials are not used in the base paper.
  - Such material is outside the purpose of Air Force newspapers and would place them in direct competition with commercial newspapers.
- Use of such material may be authorized by AFNEWS/NS in a specific situation where other sources of national and international news are not available.
- Ensuring the newspaper does not contain any material which implies that Air Force units or people endorse or favour a specific commercial product, commodity or service.
- Ensuring the newspaper supports officially sanctioned fundraising campaigns consistent with AFI 36-3101.
- Ensuring that commercial sponsors are mentioned only routinely with other pertinent facts in news stories and announcements.
- Ensuring that news articles mentioning gifts from civilian sources tied to Air Force programmes honouring Airmen of the Month, top recruiter, and the like, are used only when:
  - Intent of the article is to report an Air Force individual honoured for professional achievement; the fact that a special gift has been donated to the Air Force will be of secondary consideration or mention in every case; special concessions or privileges have not been granted the donor, such as a requirement to accompany the article with a photograph of the recipient with the gift, or to publish a statement that implies endorsement of the product or organization by the Air Force or individual.
- Photographs of the recipient with the product are allowed, but must be used solely on their news value; the award is not made in exchange for any publicity requirement by the donor; or the commander determines the gift is acceptable and in good taste.
- Ensuring that book, radio, television, movie, and other entertainment reviews are written objectively, and there

is no implication of endorsement by the Department of the Air Force.

- Ensuring that political campaign news items or editorials dealing with candidates or issues are not used.
- Ensuring that unsolicited statements or articles on legislative matters by people or agencies outside the Department of Defense, including officials or candidates for public office, are not used.
- Ensuring the newspaper supports the Federal Voting Assistance Programme during election years by carrying factual information about registration and voting laws, especially about absentee voting requirements.

  ◆ Voting materials provided by the director of the Federal Voting Assistance Programme, DOD, and the Air Force are designed to encourage members to register as voters and exercise their right to vote.

- Ensuring that no poll, survey, or straw vote relating to a political campaign is conducted.
- Ratings of official inspections by the inspector general and inspectors may be used in Air Force newspapers. Check AFI 90-201, *Inspector General Activities* (Para. 2.14.3) to ensure the story complies with Air Force and DOD policy prior to publication.

  ◆ The fact an inspection has taken place may be reported when coordinated, in every case, with the commander to obtain his or her opinion on the inspection. The commander is in the best position to determine words that do not compromise the privileged status of an inspection report, yet publicly recognize the efforts of his or her people.

- Ensuring the Associated Press Stylebook and Libel Manual is used in preparing news, feature, and editorial material.
- Ensuring a newspaper readership survey is conducted at a frequency deemed necessary by the installation commander to meet his or her needs and those of readers.

  ◆ AFNEWS/NS has an approved standardized Base Newspaper Readership Survey.

- This standardized survey, with its control number, may be administered to active-duty military and their family members, retirees, and civilian employees of the Air Force without need for additional Air Force Personnel Center or AFNEWS/NS approval, provided questions are not altered significantly.
- Each MAJCOM public affairs office should have the survey and guidelines for administering it.
- Survey results should be reported to readers and used to develop new newspaper services or techniques.
- Ensuring that record copies of the base newspaper are maintained in annual blocks, with new files starting on January 1 or the anniversary of the first issue.
    - ◆ These may be permanently bound or microfilmed.
- Microfilmed source documents may be discarded after microfilmed copy is confirmed complete and accurate.
- Retain bound or microfilmed copies according to AFM 37-123, *Management of Records*.
- Developing close working relationship with the publisher and Services.
- Developing stringers and Unit Public Affairs Representatives to assist in ensuring the best possible coverage of all-base units and people.

Editorial

An editorial is a statement or article by a news organization (generally a newspaper) that expresses an opinion rather than attempting to simply report news. Editorials are not written by the regular reporters; rather, they are collectively authored by a group of individuals called the editorial board. They represent the newspaper's official positions on issues. Editorials are almost always printed on their own page of the newspaper, and are always labelled as editorials (to avoid confusion with news coverage). They are often about current events or public controversies.

For newspapers, the Op-Ed is the page opposite the editorial page. It may contain letters to the editor or other opinion pieces.

COPY EDITING

Copy editing is the process by which an editor makes formatting changes and other improvements to text. Copy, in this case a noun, refers to material (such as handwritten or typewritten pages) to be set (as in typesetting) for printing. A person who performs the task of copy editing is called a copy editor. Although copy editing is concerned with house style, there is no universal form for the term itself. In magazine and book publishing, it is often written as one word. The newspaper industry writes the expression as two words or hyphenates it, and the hyphenated form (*copy-editing*) is probably the one most commonly used in Britain. The term *copy editor* is similarly spelled as one word, two words, or hyphenated.

In British newspaper and magazine publishing (though not in book publishing), the job is generally called *sub-editing*.

Overview

Copy editing typically entails correcting spelling and punctuation; correcting grammatical and semantic errors; ensuring the typescript adheres to the publisher's house style; adding standardized headers, footers, headlines and so on. All these elements must be addressed before the typesetter can prepare a final proof copy.

The copy editor is expected to ensure the text flows well, that it makes sense and is fair and accurate, and that it will cause no legal problems for the publisher. Newspaper copy editors are sometimes responsible for choosing which wire copy the newspaper will use, and for re-writing it according to their house style. In many cases, a copy editor will be the only person other than the author to read an entire text before publication. Newspaper editors often regard their copy editors as their newspaper's last line of defense.

A copy editor may also abridge text, which is also called "cutting" or "trimming." This means reducing the length of a novel or article, either to fit broadcast or publishing limits, or to improve the material. This may involve simply cutting out parts of the text, but sometimes it is necessary to rewrite uncut parts to account for missing details or plot. Some abridged texts are only slightly shorter, whereas others may be reduced dramatically, particularly when a literary classic is abridged for the children's market.

Changes in the Profession

Traditionally, a copy editor would read a printed or written text, such as a manuscript, marking it with handwritten proofreader's marks for correction. Nowadays, the text is almost always read on a computer display and corrections are made directly to the text. Increasingly, a copy editor marks up the text using XML or a similar coding scheme, and is involved in preparing text for online publication, not just for printing.

The spread of desktop publishing means that many copy editors perform design and layout work that was once left to production crews for printed publications. As a result, the skills needed for the job are shifting, with technical knowledge sometimes considered as important as writing ability, particularly within journalism as compared with book publishing.

Traits, Skills and Training

Besides an excellent command of the language, copy editors should have broad general knowledge to be able to spot factual errors; good critical-thinking skills so they recognize inconsistencies; diplomatic skills to help them deal with writers; and a thick skin for when diplomacy fails. They also need to be able to set priorities so they can balance striving for perfection with working against deadlines. Many copy editors have a college degree, often in journalism or communications. Copy editing often is taught as a college journalism course, though the name of the course varies. News design and pagination often are taught in such classes.

In the United States, The Dow Jones Newspaper Fund sponsors internships that include two weeks of training. Also, midcareer training for newspaper copy editors and news editors (who supervise news copy desks) is offered at the American Press Institute, the Poynter Institute, the University of North Carolina at Chapel Hill, and conferences of the American Copy Editors Society. Most U.S. newspapers and many other publishers give candidates for copy-editing jobs a test or a try-out. These vary widely and often include general items such as acronyms, current events, simple mathematics and punctuation, and skills such as Associated Press style, headline writing, infographics editing, and journalism ethics.

Letters to the Editor

A letter to the editor (sometimes abbreviated LTTE) is a letter sent to the editors of a publication or periodical about materials that have appeared in the publication or issues of concern to the readership, usually intended for publication. Letters to the editor often appear in news media, though they also appear in non-news publications, such as many magazines. In many publications, letters to the editor may be sent either through conventional mail or electronic mail. Letters are usually short, as they must sometimes fit in a limited space. Many newspapers require that letters to the editor be under a certain number of words, and may attach other conditions, such as prohibiting anonymous letters, letters that contain misinformation or are meant to libel someone, are obscene or in poor taste, or are meant to resolve a personal conflict.

Letters to the editor are traditionally associated with newspapers and newsmagazines, though similar letters are sent to websites, radio stations, and television programmes, who may read them on air. Letters may support or oppose a publication's editorial stance, remark on materials that have appeared in the publication, or correct a perceived error or misrepresentation. They are also used in astroturfing campaigns to create the illusion of grassroots popular support in the community for a particular cause, candidate, or party.

Columnist

A columnist is a journalist who writes material on a regular basis for publication in a series. Columns appear in newspapers, magazines and other publications, including blogs on the Internet. Readers often open a publication with an expectation of reading a new essay by a specific writer who offers a personal point of view. Many columnists are strongly opinionated.

In defining a column, Dictionary.com provides a breakdown of a few popular subjects covered by columnists:

> A regular feature or series of articles in a newspaper, magazine, or the like, usually having a readily identifiable heading and the byline of the writer or editor, that reports or comments upon a particular field of interest, as politics, theater, or etiquette, or which may contain letters from readers, answers to readers' queries, etc.

In at least one situation, a column expanded to become an entire successful magazine. When Cyrus Curtis founded the *Tribune and Farmer* in 1879, it was a four-page weekly with an annual subscription rate of 50 cents. He introduced a women's column by his wife, Louise Knapp Curtis, and it proved so popular that in 1883, he decided to publish it as a separate monthly supplement, *Ladies Journal and Practical Housekeeper*, edited by Louise Curtis. With 25,000 subscribers by the end of its first year, it was such a success that Curtis sold *Tribune and Farmer* to put his energy into the new publication, which became the *Ladies Home Journal*.

Radio and Television

Newspaper columnists of the 1930s and 1940s, such as Franklin Pierce Adams (aka FPA), Nick Kenny, Jimmie Fidler, Walter Winchell. Louella Parsons, Drew Pearson, Ed Sullivan and Walter Winchell, achieved a celebrity status and used their columns as a springboard to move into radio and television. In some cases, such as Winchell and Parsons, their radio programmes were quite similar in format to their newspaper columns. Rona Barrett began as a Hollywood gossip columnist in 1957, duplicating her print tactics on television by the mid-1960s. One of the more famous syndicated columnists of the 1920s and 1930s, O. O. McIntyre, declined offers to do a radio series because he felt it would interfere and diminish the quality of writing in his column, "New York Day by Day."

Books

However, FPA and McIntyre both collected their columns into a series of books, as did other columnists. McIntyre's book, *The Big Town: New York Day by Day* (1935) was a bestseller. FPA's *The Melancholy Lute* (1936), collected selections from three decades of his columns. H. Allen Smith's first humor book, *Low Man on a*

Totem Pole (1941) and his two following books were so popular during World War II that they kept Smith on the *New York Herald Tribune*'s Best Seller List for 100 weeks and prompted a collection of all three in *3 Smiths in the Wind* (1946). While Smith's column, *The Totem Pole,* was syndicated by United Features, he told Time:

> Just between you and me it's tough. A typewriter can be a pretty formidable contraption when you sit down in front of it and say: 'All right, now I'm going to be funny.'

The Miami Herald promotes humor columnist Dave Barry with this description: "Dave Barry has been at *The Miami Herald* since 1983. A Pulitzer Prize winner for commentary, he writes about issues ranging from the international economy to exploding toilets." Barry has collected his columns into a series of successful books, and the newspaper offers a selection of memorable Barry columns on its website.

Types of Columnists

- Agony aunt, an advice columnist,
- Critic reviewer,
- Editorial opinion columnist,
- Gossip columnist,
- Humor columnist, and
- Food columnist.

Pundit (Expert)

A pundit is someone who offers to mass-media his/her opinion or commentary on a particular subject area (most typically political analysis, the social sciences or sport), on which he/she is presumed to be knowledgeable. The term has been increasingly applied to popular media personalities. In certain cases, it may be used in a derogatory manner as well.

Origins

The term originates from the Hindi term *pandit,* which in turn is derived from Sanskrit *pandita,* learned, and is first found in English in 1672. It refers to someone who is erudite in various subjects and who conducts religious ceremonies and offers counsel to the king or mayor.

Past English Use

The Oxford English Dictionary cites the first English Language use of the word "Pundit" as referring to an official of the Supreme Court in Colonial India who advised the English Judges on questions of Hindu law. In Anglo-Indian use, "pundit" also referred to a native of India who was trained and employed by the British to survey inaccessible regions beyond the British frontier. By extension, the word came to refer to, "A learned expert or teacher."

Speculation exists that the term's contemporary use may have its origins in a Yale University society known as "The Pundits" which, founded in 1884, developed a reputation for including among its members the school's most incisive and humorous critics of contemporary society. The group's late-nineteenth and early-twentieth century focus on lampooning the social and political world were well-documented in the university's yearbook and the Yale Daily News, the entries of which are considered among the first use of the term "Pundit" to refer to a critic of or expert on contemporary matters. Several members of the society have also gone on to become leading political pundits, including Pulitzer Prize-winning author and energy expert Daniel Yergin. Other notable Yale Pundits include A. Whitney Griswold, Lewis H. Lapham and Joe Lieberman.

Current Use

In the English-speaking West, *pundits* write signed articles in print media (blurbs included), and appear on radio, television, or the internet with opinions on current events. Television *pundits* may also be referred to as *talking heads*.

Punditry has become a more popular vehicle in nightly newscasts on American cable news networks. A rise of partisanship among popular *pundits* began with Bill O'Reilly of Fox News Channel. His opinion-oriented format led him to ratings success and has led others, including Lou Dobbs, Keith Olbermann, and Nancy Grace, to express their opinions on matters on their own respective programmes.

Internet authors trying to create a name for themselves by non-traditional means, may refer to themselves as *pundits*, and in fact can be considered experts of their particular life experiences or observations.

Comedian Stephen Colbert satirizes punditry in his show, *The Colbert Report*, most notably based on Bill O'Reilly but including others as well.

The term *pundit* is also used to refer to sports experts. Often, a 'pundit' will be partnered alongside a commentator, who will describe the action while asking the *pundit* for analysis. Alternatively, *pundits* may be asked for their opinions during breaks in the play.

List of Pundits

This is a list of some well-known contemporary *pundits*:

Australia

- Andrew Bolt
- Phil Cleary
- Germaine Greer
- John Laws
- Glenn Milne.

Brazil

- Olavo de Carvalho
- Reinaldo Azevedo.

Canada

- Michael Coren.

Chile

- Hermógenes Pérez de Arce
- Gonzalo Rojas Sánchez
- Patricio Navia
- Miljenko R. Marinkovic.

Hong Kong, China

- Ivan Choy.

India

- Cho Ramaswamy.

Spain

- Federico Jiménez Losantos
- Iñaki Gabilondo
- Luis del Olmo.

United Kingdom

- David Aaronovitch
- Gary Lineker
- Matthew Le Tissier
- Tim Henman
- Andy Gray
- John Motson
- Martin Tyler
- Vanessa Feltz
- Germaine Greer
- Christopher Hitchens
- Peter Hitchens
- John McCririck
- George Monbiot
- Melanie Phillips.

United States

- Glenn Beck
- Neal Boortz
- Tucker Carlson
- Stephen Colbert
- Alan Colmes
- Ann Coulter
- Lou Dobbs
- Roger Ebert
- Al Franken
- Nancy Grace
- Sean Hannity
- Christopher Hitchens
- Ezra Klein

- Rush Limbaugh
- Rachel Maddow
- Bill Maher
- Michelle Malkin
- Chris Matthews
- Keith Olbermann
- Bill O'Reilly
- Joe Scarborough
- Michael Savage
- Mark Steyn
- Jon Stewart.

Sports Pundits

- Skip Bayless
- Mike Francesa
- Peter Gammons
- Mike Golic
- Mike Greenberg
- Jay Mariotti
- Woody Paige
- Jim Rome
- Chris Russo
- Stephen A. Smith
- Dick Vitale
- Michael Wilbon
- Tony Kornheiser
- Lou Holtz.

Editorial Independence

Editorial independence is the freedom of editors to make decisions without interference from the owners of a publication. Editorial independence is tested, for instance, if a newspaper runs articles that may be unpopular with its advertising customers.

6

News Sourcing, News Release and Press Release: Elements and Dimensions

NEWS SOURCING

In journalism, a source is a person, publication or other record or document that gives information.

Overview

Examples of sources include: official records, publications or broadcasts, officials in government or business, organizations or corporations, witnesses of crime, accidents or other events, and people involved with or affected by a news event or issue. According to Shoemaker (1996) and McQuail (1994) there are a multitude of factors that tend to condition the acceptance of sources as bona fide by investigative journalists. Reporters are expected to develop and cultivate sources. This applies especially if they regularly cover a specific topic, known as a "beat." However, beat reporters must be cautious of becoming too close to their sources. Reporters often, but not always, give greater leeway to sources with little experience. For example, sometimes a person will say they don't want to talk, and then proceed to talk. If that person is not a public figure, reporters are less likely to use that information. Journalists are also encouraged to be skeptical without being cynical ("If your mother says she loves you, check it out."). As a rule of thumb, but especially when reporting on controversy, reporters are expected to use multiple sources. Outside journalism, sources are sometimes known as a "news source."

Embargo

In journalism and public relations, an embargo (sometimes called a press embargo) is an agreement or request that a news organization refrain from reporting certain information until a specified date and/or time, in exchange for advance access to the information. For example, if a government official is preparing to make a short speech announcing a policy initiative at 1:00 pm, the official's staff might transmit expanded details of the initiative to news organizations several hours ahead of the scheduled announcement, with a notice indicating that the contents are *embargoed* until 1:00. This gives the news organizations time to research and prepare complete stories that are ready to be disseminated when the embargo is lifted. In theory, press embargoes reduce inaccuracy in the reporting of breaking stories by reducing the incentive for journalists to cut corners in hopes of "scooping" the competition.

Embargoes are typically used by government or corporate representatives working in publicity or public relations, and are often arranged in advance as part of a formal or informal agreement. Sometimes publishers will release advance copies of a book to reviewers with the agreement that reviews of it will not appear before the official release date of the publication. Complex scientific news might also require advance notice with an embargo. Governments also have legitimate reasons for imposing embargoes, often so as to prevent news reports being an unfair or undue influence over votes in legislative bodies. Artists' names and locations of performances are sometimes embargoed pending the official announcement of the scheduled performance tour. Sometimes publicists will send embargoed press releases to newsrooms unsolicited in hopes that they will respect the embargo date without having first agreed to do so.

News organizations sometimes break embargoes and report information before the embargo expires, either accidentally (due to miscommunication in the newsroom) or intentionally (to get the jump on their competitors). Breaking an embargo is typically considered a serious breach of trust and can result in the source barring the offending news outlet from receiving advance information in the future.

Using Confidential Information

Off-the-record material is often valuable and reporters may be eager to use it, so sources wishing to ensure the confidentiality of certain information are generally advised to discuss the "terms of use" before actually disclosing the information, if possible. Some journalists and news organizations have policies against accepting information "off the record" because they believe it interferes with their ability to report truthfully, or because they suspect it may be intended to mislead them or the public.

Even if they cannot report certain information directly, journalists can use "off the record" information to uncover related facts, or to find other sources that are willing to speak on the record. This is especially useful in investigative reporting. Information about a surprise event or breaking news, whether on or off the record is known as a "tip-off." Information that leads to the uncovering of more interesting information is called a "lead."

Anonymous Sources

The identity of anonymous sources is sometimes revealed to senior editors or a news organization's lawyers, who would be considered bound by the same confidentiality. (Lawyers are generally protected from subpoena in these cases by attorney/client privilege.) Legal staff may need to give counsel about whether it is advisable to publish certain information, or about court proceedings that may attempt to learn confidential information. Senior editors are in the loop to prevent reporters from fabricating non-existent, anonymous sources, and to provide a second opinion about how to use the information obtained, how or how not to identify sources, and whether other options should be pursued.

The use of anonymous sources has been a controversial subject for many years. Some news outlets insist that anonymous sources are required to get certain information while others hold strict prohibitions against the use of unnamed sources at all times. News outlets are often embarrassed by a report from an anonymous source that turns out to be wrong. For instance, much of the O.J. Simpson reporting from unnamed sources was later deemed inaccurate. Newsweek retracted a story about a Qur'an being flushed down a toilet that led to riots in the Middle East. The Qur'an desecration controversy of 2005 was based upon one unnamed military source. The L.A. Times retracted an article that implicated Sean "Diddy" Combs in the beating of Tupac Shakur.

The original article was based on documents and a large assortment of unnamed sources. When reporting on the original story, the Associated Press noted that "[n]one of the sources was named."

After the embarrassment, a news organization will often "clamp down" on the guidelines for using unnamed sources, but those guidelines are often forgotten after the scandal dies down. One study found that large newspapers' use of anonymous sources dropped dramatically between 2003 and 2004. The Project for Excellence in Journalism, a research group found use of anonymous sources dropped from 29 per cent of all articles in 2003 to just 7 per cent in 2004.

Not on Tape

Whether in a formal, sit-down interview setting or an improptu meeting on the street, some sources request that all or part of the encounter not be captured in an audio or video recording ("tape"), but continue speaking to the reporter. As long as the interview is not confidential, the reporter may report the information given by the source, even repeating direct quotes (perhaps scribbled on a notepad or recalled from memory). This often shows up in broadcasts as "John Brown declined to be interviewed on camera, but said..." or simply "a spokesman said...".

Some interview subjects are simply uncomfortable being recorded. Some are afraid that they will be inarticulate and make fools of themselves when the interview is broadcast. Others might be uncooperative or distrust the motives or competence of the journalist, and wish to prevent them from being able to broadcast an unflattering soundbite or part of the interview out of context. Professional public relations officers know that having the reporter repeat their words, rather than being on the air themselves, will blunt the impact of their words. The audience need not see or hear them being uncomfortable (if they have unpleasant news), and not being on air also allows them to be anonymous or identified only by title.

Attribution

In journalism Attribution is the identification of the source of reported information. Journalists' ethical codes normally address the issue of attribution, which is sensitive because in the course of their work journalists may receive information from sources who wish to remain anonymous. In investigative journalism important news stories often depend on such information. For example, the Watergate scandal that lead to the downfall of U.S. President Richard Nixon was in part exposed by information revealed by an anonymous source ("Deep Throat") to investigative reporters Bob Woodward and Carl Bernstein.

Ethics

Divulging the identity of a confidential source is frowned upon by groups representing journalists in many democracies. In some jurisdictions journalists can be compelled by law to identify their sources, and journalists can and have been jailed for upholding this principle.

There are several reasons to protect confidential sources:

(*a*) In some cases serious harm might be fall the source if their identity is uncovered.
(*b*) The willingness of other potential sources to share information with reporters may be eroded if confidential sources are identified.
(*c*) The public perception of journalistic integrity is damaged when assurances about confidentiality are breached.
(*d*) The so-called "chilling effect," which serves to dissuade sources in the future from stepping forward with unknown information for fear of reprimand or retaliation.

"Speaking Terms"

There are several categories of "speaking terms" (agreements concerning attribution) that cover information conveyed in conversations with journalists. In the UK the following conventions are generally accepted:

(*a*) *"On-the-record"*: all that is said can be quoted and attributed.
(*b*) *"Unattributable"*: what is said can be reported but not attributed.
(*c*) *"Off-the-record"*: the information is provided to inform a decision or provide a confidential explanation, not for publication.

However, confusion over the precise meaning of "unattributable" and "off-the-record" has led to more detailed formulations:

(*a*) *"Chatham House Rule(s)"*: so called after Chatham House (the Royal Institute of International Affairs) which first introduced the rule in 1927, now in widespread use:

> *"When a meeting, or part thereof, is held under the Chatham House Rule, participants are free to use the information received, but neither the identity nor the affiliation of the speaker(s), nor that of any other participant, may be revealed."*

(*b*) *"Lobby Terms"*: in the UK accredited journalists are allowed in to the otherwise restricted Members' Lobby on the basis that information received there is never attributed and events there are not reported. "Lobby terms" are agreed to extend this arrangement to cover discussions that take place elsewhere.

(*c*) *"Not for attribution"* (as described by the Canadian Association of Journalists). The comments may be quoted directly, but the source may only be identified in general terms (e.g., "a government insider"). In practice such general descriptions may be agreed with the interviewee.

(*d*) *"On background"* (Canadian Association of Journalists). The thrust of the briefing may be reported (and the source characterized in general terms as above) but direct quotes may not be used.

(*e*) *"Deep background"*: This term is used in the U.S., though not consistently. Most journalists would understand "deep background" to mean that the information may not be included in the article but is used by the journalist to enhance his or her view of the subject matter, or to act as a guide to other leads or sources. Most deep background information is confirmed elsewhere before being reported.

Neologisms

Double Super Secret Background: It is a neologism, often used humorously, referring to the journalistic concept of keeping a background source secret. The phrase, coined by *Time Magazine* reporter Matthew Cooper, gained notoriety in July 2005 during the Plame affair. The phrase originally appeared in an e-mail of

July 11, 2003 from Cooper to his *Time* bureau chief, referring to a conversation with Karl Rove. In compliance with a court order, the magazine released Mr. Cooper's notes, thus breaking the anonymity of Mr. Rove. Cooper stated the phrase was "a play on a reference to the film Animal House, in which John Belushi's wild Delta House fraternity is placed on Double Secret Probation."

NEWS RELEASE

A news release, media release, press release or press statement is a written or recorded communication directed at members of the news media for the purpose of announcing something claimed as having news value. Typically, it is mailed, faxed, or e-mailed to assignment editors at newspapers, magazines, radio stations, television stations, and/or television networks. Commercial press-release distribution services are also used to distribute news releases. Sometimes news releases are sent for the purpose of announcing news conferences. A press release is different from a news article. A news article is a compilation of facts developed by journalists published in the news media, whereas a press release is designed to be sent to journalists in order to encourage them to develop articles on the subject. A press release is generally biased towards the objectives of the author. The use of news releases is common in the field of public relations, the aim of which is to attract favourable media attention to the PR firm's client, and publicity, the aim of which is to attract favourable media attention for products marketed by the clients.

Origins

One anecdote on an origin of modern press releases is about an incident in 1906 involving Ivy Lee, who is often referred to as the first real public relations practitioner. At that time, Lee's agency was working with the Pennsylvania Railroad, which had just fallen victim to a tragic accident. Ivy Lee convinced the company to issue the first press release to journalists, before other versions of the story, or suppositions, could be spread among them and reported. He used a press release, in addition to inviting journalists and photographers to the scene and providing their transportation there, as a means of fostering open communication with the media.

Elements

While there are several types of press releases (such as the general news release, event release, product press release and, more recently, the social media release). Press releases very often have several traits of their structure in common. This helps journalists separate press releases from other PR communication methods, such as pitch letters or media advisories. Some of these common structural elements include:

1. *Headline*—used to grab the attention of journalists and briefly summarize the news.
2. *Dateline*—contains the release date and usually the originating city of the press release.
3. *Introduction*—first paragraph in a press release, that generally gives basic answers to the questions of who, what, when, where and why.
4. *Body*—further explanation, statistics, background, or other details relevant to the news.
5. *Boilerplate*—generally a short "about" section, providing independent background on the issuing company, organization, or individual.
6. *Close*—in North America, traditionally the symbol "-30-" appears after the boilerplate or body and before the media contact information, indicating to media that the release is ending. A more modern equivalent has been the "###" symbol. In other countries, other means of indicating the end of the release may be used, such as the text "ends".
7. *Media Contact Information*—name, phone number, email address, mailing address, or other contact information for the PR or other media relations contact person.

Video News Releases

Some public relations firms send out video news releases (VNRs) which are pre-taped video programmes that can be aired intact by TV stations. Often, the VNRs are aired without the stations' identifying or attributing them as such.

TV news viewers can often detect the use of VNRs within television newscasts; for example, many movie-star "interviews" are actually VNRs, taped on a set which is located at the movie studio and decorated with the movie's logo. Another frequent example of VNRs masquerading as news footage is videotapes of particular medical "breakthroughs," that are really produced and distributed by pharmaceutical companies for the purpose of selling new medicines. Video News Releases can be in the form of full blown productions costing tens of thousands or even hundreds of thousands. They can also be in the TV news format, or even produced for the web. Recently, many broadcast news outlets have discouraged the use of VNRs. Many stations, citing an already poor public perception, want to increase their credibility. Public relations companies are having a tougher time getting their pre-edited video aired.

VNRs can be turned into podcasts then posted onto newswires. Further to this, a story can be kept running longer by engaging "community websites", which are monitored and commented on by many journalists and features writers.

Criticism

News releases have been a large source of criticism against various types of journalists, who sometimes rely on them heavily. Some people criticize writers for creating articles in this way, contending that it constitutes free advertising for the company on whose behalf the news release was issued, especially if it is not contrasted with criticism of that company or product in the same article. On the other hand, few dispute that news releases remain a valuable way for media to be made aware of new products and services, and recent and upcoming events of interest.

Embargoed News Release

Sometimes a news release is embargoed—that is, news organizations are requested not to report the story until a specified time. For example, news organizations usually receive a copy of presidential speeches several hours in advance. In such cases, the news organizations generally do not break the embargo. If they do, the agency that sent the release may blacklist them. A blacklisted news organization will not receive any more embargoed releases, or possibly any releases at all.

However, it is very hard to enforce embargoes on journalists, as there is constant pressure by editors to be first to a story. It is unlikely that a PR agency will blacklist a form of media, as other clients may want to be featured in this publication. This problem is sometimes overcome by controlling the timing of a release via email rather than relying on the journalist to do so.

A news release or press release is a written or recorded communication directed at members of the news media for the purpose of announcing something claimed as having news value. Typically, it is mailed or faxed to assignment editors at newspapers, magazines, radio stations, television stations, and/or television networks. Sometimes news releases are sent for the purpose of announcing news conferences. A news release is different from a news article. A news article is a compilation of facts developed by journalists published in the news media, whereas a news release is designed to be sent to journalists in order to encourage them to develop articles on the subject. A news release is generally biased towards the objectives of the author.

The use of news releases is common in the field of public relations, the aim of which is to attract favourable media attention to the PR firm's client, and publicity, the aim of which is to attract favourable media attention for products marketed by the client.

WRITING NEWS RELEASES

Who, what, where, when, why, and how—these are the six critical ingredients of all news releases. But don't forget, a little spice can make your news release stand out from the crowd. In this part, you will learn how to write a professional-looking news release, the most important tool in any public relations programme.

The Headline

The headline is the first thing—and sometimes the only thing—an editor will read. Releases are often rejected as a result of a weak headline. Create headlines with impact. The most effective words in a news release headline are eye-catching words like "announces" and "new." Comparative words like "better" or "more" can also draw attention to your article. The headline is the "hook" that lures editors and reporters into reading more. Headlines must be compelling.

Many public relations novices make the mistake of embellishing their headlines. Your organization has to earn the respect of editors. Nobody owes you a reading. Too much information, or confusing information, is a turnoff. Most importantly, you should never sacrifice accuracy for the sake of a flashy headline.

Here are some guidelines for writing headlines:

(*a*) Determine the most significant benefit your most important reader will derive from the news.
(*b*) Try and state those benefits in seven words or less.
(*c*) Ask yourself if your statement is meaningful to someone not closely involved with your business.

When actually writing the headline, try to achieve the greatest impact using the fewest words. Your headline doesn't need to be quite as dramatic as a newspaper headline. Editors are looking for information in the headline, so try to at least include who, what, and why. Whatever, the headline, you must accurately reflect the content that follows.

The First Paragraph

Many news releases are accepted or rejected on the basis of the headline and first paragraph or two. These introductory paragraphs are often all an editor will have time to read. Many releases are rejected due a simple downfall: failure to include any *news* in the first paragraph.

An important news-writing concept is *collapsible copy.* Collapsible copy reads well from the beginning to the end of any given paragraph. The information is "chunked" to stand on its own, if need be. Each sentence could be pulled from the news release and used as a quotation. This type of copy should be used as extensively as possible in all paragraphs.

Editors expect to see the five W's covered in the first few sentences. Here's an example:

NEW YORK—January 22, 2003—The Linux Professional Institute (LPI), the premier professional certification

> programme for the Linux community, and UnitedLinux LLC, an industry initiative to streamline Linux development and certification around a global, uniform distribution, have signed a cooperative agreement to market a UnitedLinux professional certification programme.
>
> Under the memorandum of understanding, LPI and UnitedLinux will work jointly to create new UnitedLinux specific exams which, when passed together with the current LPI Levels 1 and 2 exams, will lead to two new UnitedLinux certifications. The new exams are expected to be available during the first quarter of 2003.

Let's look more closely at this example. The *where* and *when* of this and most releases are specified in the *slug* ("New York, January 22, 2003"). The *who* is LPI and UnitedLinux. The *what* is signing a cooperative agreement. The *why* is marketing a UnitedLinux professional certification programme. And the *how* is LPI and UnitedLinux working jointly to create new UnitedLinux-specific exams. These two paragraphs alone communicate the essential points of this announcement. In print, there may not be enough space for more than this. Some special-interest journals devote a column or a page to announcements, which are printed verbatim from the news release. Unless the announcement is deemed more newsworthy, this may be all the coverage you get.

The Middle Paragraphs

Limited space in publications and time in broadcasting means the first paragraph may get covered. Paragraphs should always be ordered by importance for two important reasons. First, editors read through releases quickly and often will not finish entire releases. You must consider what things are most important, and place them next in the release. Often, a statement from your spokesperson explaining the expected impacts on the marketplace or something related can be catchy enough to be quoted. Follow this with the next most important thing, and so on to the end of the release. Second, sequence frequently indicates importance (unless the story is an in-depth feature that can establish pacing and shape). Stacking your news, in what some editors call the "inverted pyramid," can show editors the relative importance of your details. By following the inverted pyramid, you will make the editor's job easier and also accomplish your goal of getting the most critical information covered.

Final Details

You need to mark the end of your news release, so that editors know there is no further news. In journalism, this is traditionally done by putting "-30-" or "-end-" on a new, centered line, after the last line of copy, as follows:

–30–

After ending the release, it is important to include the *boilerplate*—standard, reusable background information about the organization issuing the news and contact information for editorial follow-up. The boilerplate includes the organization's web address where the editor can go for further details. Boilerplates can be reviewed and revised periodically, but they should maintain consistency. Wildly different boilerplates are unprofessional from one release to the next.

Below is an example of boilerplate and contact information.

About Linux Professional Institute

The Linux Professional Institute (LPI) develops professional certification for the Linux operating system independent of software vendors or training providers. Established as an international non-profit organization in 1999 by the Linux community, LPI develops accessible, internationally-recognized certification programmes which have earned the respect of vendors, employers and administrators. LPI's activities involve hundreds of volunteers and professionals throughout the world in many different capacities, and the group encourages active public involvement through mailing lists and its website at *http://www.lpi.org/*. LPI's multi-level programme of exams is administered globally through Virtual University Enterprises (VUE) and Prometric testing centres. LPI's major financial sponsors are Platinum Sponsors Caldera International (NASDAQ : CALD), IBM (NYSE : IBM), Linuxcare, Maxspeed, SGI (NYSE : SGI), SuSE Linux AG and TurboLinux as well as Gold Sponsors Hewlett-Packard (NYSE : HWP) and Wave Technologies.

What Makes a News Release Good (or Bad)

Print editors and journalists are notoriously overworked and underpaid. A well-written news release will often be used word for word, with may-be a few changes for "objectivity" or to accommodate the publication's format.

The editorial staff at the *Los Angeles Times* says this about news releases:

1. *Good news release* is a concise, complete description of an upcoming event; a timely report of an event has just occurred; notification of important personnel or procedural changes in an organization; or other news or feature tips.
2. *Bad releases*—the ones that don't get used—often have these common mistakes:
   (*i*) Lack of a local angle.
   (*ii*) Insufficient or inaccurate information (who, what, when, where, why, how).
   (*iii*) Failure to include contact information for the organization.
   (*iv*) Verbosity. (Try to keep the release to one or two pages, but balance brevity against failure to include necessary information.)
   (*v*) Lack of timeliness—the editor's deadline has passed or the news is released too long after the event.

Writing a news release does not have to be painful. What you need is a little time to gather all the facts: the who, what, when, where, why and how (and any additional information necessary to support). Sometimes your news won't be used right away or in the form you provided. A writer may need time to rewrite your outline into a news story. Or, if a feature is being developed on Linux, the writer may use many sources for depth and objectivity. They may use quotable quotes, first-person anecdotes, statistics, and causes and effects from your releases as well as those of your competitors.

Deadlines are hugely important because the news media cannot delay publication or broadcasting. Don't bother editors with untimely information. If you can't pitch your story in time, wait for another opportune moment to come around.

Top Ten Tips for Writing Releases

To summarize what we have said so far, here are ten tips for writing an excellent news release.

1. *Use an active headline to grab the editor's attention*: The headline makes your release stand out. Keep the headline short, active, and descriptive, with the most positive spin. Write "Jane Doe Named Person of the Year" instead of "Jane Doe Gets Award."
2. *Put the most important information at the beginning*: This is a tried and true rule of journalism. Remember that the first two paragraphs should contain the salient facts of who, what, when, where, why and how. Don't bury good information at the end.
3. *Avoid exaggeration and unsubstantiated claims*: A news editor can smell a sales pitch a mile away. Instead of making over-inflated statements, provide real, usable information. Find legitimate ways to set your organization apart, and stress those points.
4. *Write in an active, engaging, and concise style*: Use language that conveys your excitement about the news. If your release is boring or passively written, the editor may conclude the news itself is not very meaningful or you are not a good candidate for an interview. Interesting equals newsworthy.
5. *Keep your release to two pages or less*: Generally, if you can't state your message in two pages, you are not getting to the point fast enough. Editors are always looking for concise, easy-to-read releases that can be thrown onto a website or squeezed into a leftover space in a page layout. For highly important news with many details, you can include a third page, but this should be done sparingly.
6. *Include a contact*: *Every* news release should include a contact person who the media can reach for more information. This contact is your spokesperson and must be familiar with all the news in the release. They should be prepared to answer questions.
7. *Keep jargon to the minimum*: Avoid using highly technical terms and buzzwords familiar only to Linux insiders.

Jargon can date quickly, and complicated language irritates people who don't know what you mean. Your goal is to tell your story to as wide an audience as possible, not to unduly limit the audience. Even special-interest publications mostly write in plain language and only use jargon and acronyms generally familiar to their readers.

8. *Stress "benefits, benefits, benefits"*: This falls under the category of "show, don't tell." Avoid claiming something is "unique" or "the best" when you can't substantiate this. Instead, provide specific examples of benefits, supported by evidence and anecdotes.
9. *Be specific and detailed*: Marcia Yudkin, author of *Six Steps to Free Publicity,* talks about the "Yes, but what *is* it?" syndrome. Nothing is more irritating than seeing constant references to a product name or service name, but no information on what that product or service is. The reader needs to be able to visualize a new product or understand what a service offers. This is particularly critical for launches (announcements of new offerings). You should ask someone unfamiliar with your product or service to read your release and then describe the product or service in their own words.
10. *Proofread*: This is easily forgotten, but extremely important. Always proofread your work before issuing the final release. Better yet, give the document to someone else (perhaps a copy editor) who can readily spot spelling and grammatical errors. Nothing signals unprofessionalism more than a typo-filled communication.

Distributing the News Release

Your media contact database is your best source for editors, journalists, and freelancers who should receive your news, but if you want to include a broader range of news media targets, you may consider using one of the many news release distribution services available. Asking one or two of your news media contacts will likely reveal a creditable service. These services can be expensive, so base your decision on how broad an appeal your news has.

In North America, the more popular distribution services include:

(*a*) PR Newswire (*http://www.prnewswire.com/*)
(*b*) Canada Newswire (*http://www.newswire.ca/*)
(*c*) BusinessWire (*http://www.businesswire.com/*)

These firms will customize your distribution based on the subject-matter, and can target specific media such as technology editors, medical editors, daily news editors, and so on. A customer service representative will explain your options and the cost involved.

News releases are very important in a public relations campaign. News releases give editors and the public a glimpse into your company. When these documents are done professionally, your organization will receive the recognition you deserve. Remember, though, that news releases are not the only tool of public relations professionals.

7

News Reporting, Presentation and News Designing: Persons and Processes

NEWS REPORTING

News Reporting (*Reportage*) sometimes refers to the total body of media coverage of a particular topic or event, including news reporting and analysis: "*the extensive reportage of recent events in x.*" This is typically used in discussions of the media's general tone or angle or other collective characteristics.

Reportage is also a term for an eye-witness genre of journalism: an individual journalist's report of news, especially when witnessed firsthand, distributed through the media. This style of reporting is often characterized by travel and careful observation.

Literary reportage is the art of blending documentary, reportage-style observations, with personal experience, perception, and anecdotal evidence, in a non-fiction form of literature. This is perhaps more commonly called creative nonfiction and is closely related to New Journalism. The prose of such reporting tends to be more polished and longer than in newspaper articles.

Etymology

All forms have a common route, being adapted into English in the late 19th century from the French word of the same spelling.

Examples of Reportage in Photography

Reportage styles of photography can be applied outside of photojournalism. People who have worked in the journalistic profession sometimes move their skills acquired into other areas of photography such as weddings or portraits, pets and animals or event photography.

REPORTER

A reporter is a type of journalist who researches and presents information in certain types of mass media. Reporters gather their information in a variety of ways, including tips, press releases, sources (individuals with newsworthy information) and witnessing events. They perform research through interviews, public records and other sources. The information-gathering part of the job is sometimes called "reporting" as distinct from the production part of the job, such as writing articles. Reporters generally split their time between working in a newsroom and going out to witness events or interview people.

Most reporters working for major news media outlets are assigned an area to focus on, called a beat or patch. They are encouraged to cultivate sources to improve their information gathering.

Analyzing Reporting

It is important when reading or watching a news report to understand how to assess the information that is being provided. Ask the following questions: Is the reporter being paid for the story? Ask who posted the report? Who posted it? Who said it? What was the question? What is the answer? Why should I believe you? How can I believe you? Do Americans really believe this or say that? Are the words loaded? Do you really care?(VAW, 2008, CCPOSC111).

Career

Reporters working for major Western news media usually have a university or college degree. The degree is sometimes in journalism, but in most countries, that is generally not a requirement. When hiring reporters, editors tend to give much weight to the reporter's previous work (such as newspaper clippings), even when written for a student newspaper or as part of an internship.

Reporters in the UK and the United States

In the United Kingdom, editors often require that prospective trainee reporters have completed the NCTJ (National College for the Training of Journalists) preliminary exams. After 18 months to two years on the job, trainees will take a second set of exams, known collectively as the NCE. Upon completion of the NCE, the candidate is considered a fully-qualified senior reporter and usually receives a (very) small pay raise. In the United States, there is no set requirement for a particular degree (and licensing journalists would be unconstitutional under the First Amendment), although almost all newspapers, wire services, television news, and radio news operations hire only college graduates and expect prior experience in journalism, either at a student publication or through an internship.

Although their work can also often make them into minor celebrities, most reporters in the United States and the United Kingdom earn relatively low salaries. It is not uncommon for a reporter fresh out of college working at a small newspaper to make $20,000 annually or less. But according to the 2006 survey of journalism/mass communication graduates released in August 2007 by Dr. Lee B. Becker (University of Georgia), the average starting salary for a daily newspaper reporter in 2006 was $26,000, and the average salary at a weekly newspaper was $22,880. The average salary in radio was $23,400, while the average salary in broadcast television was $21,840, and in cable television $25,012. Despite many college students' perceptions that newspapers pay the most poorly, both dailies and weeklies are paying more than broadcast television, which actually pays the poorest of any mass communication industry or profession (advertising graduates got $26,988 and public relations graduates got $28,964 in 2006). Around £12,000 is a typical starting wage in the UK. In order to move to larger papers, it is common for reporters to start with newspapers in small towns and move their way up the ladder, though *The New York Times* has been known to hire reporters with only a few years experience, based on talent and expertize in particular areas. Many reporters also start as summer interns at large papers and then move to reporting jobs at medium sized papers. ... The same job prospects fall into the television reporting business, with reporters starting in small markets and moving up the larger markets and to national news programmes.

NEWS PRESENTER

A news presenter is, broadly speaking, a person that presents a news show on radio or the Internet. The term is not commonly used by people in the industry as they tend to use more descriptive—and sometimes country-specific—terms. Examples include "newsreader", "newscaster" and "news anchor."

Different Roles

Newscaster

A newscaster is a presenter of a news bulletin who is himself or herself a working journalist and news gatherer as well as a participant in compiling the script to be delivered in a news bulletin. Prior to the television era, radio-news broadcasts often mixed news with opinion and each presenter strove for a distinctive style. These presenters were referred to as commentators. The last remaining news presenter of this type is Paul Harvey. The term newscaster came into common use to distinguish presenters of straight news broadcasts from commentators. However in the UK, ITN's presenters are referred to as newscasters (and have been since the 1950s), whilst those working at the BBC are called newsreaders.

News Anchor

In the United States and Canada, presenters of news broadcasts are referred to as news anchors (sometimes anchorperson, anchorman, or anchorwoman) instead of "newscasters." An anchor traditionally is a television personality who presents material prepared for a news programme and, at times, must improvise commentary for live presentation. Many news anchors are also involved in writing and/or editing the news for their programmes.

The term "anchor" was coined by producer Don Hewitt. PBS cites its first usage as being on July 7, 1952, to describe Walter Cronkite's role at the Democratic and Republican National Conventions. According to Hewitt, the term was in reference to the "anchor leg" of a relay race.

NEWS DESIGN

News design is the process of arranging material on a newspaper page, according to editorial and graphical guidelines and goals. Main editorial goals include the ordering of news stories by order of importance, while graphical considerations include readability and balanced, unobtrusive incorporation of advertising.

News design incorporates principles of graphic design and is taught as part of journalism training in schools and colleges. Overlapping and related terms include layout, makeup (formerly paste up) and pagination. The era of modern newspapers begins in the mid-nineteenth century, with the Industrial Revolution, and increased capacities for printing and distribution. Over time, improvements in printing technology, graphical design, and editorial standards have led to changes and improvements in the look and readability of newspapers. Nineteenth-century newspapers were often densely packed with type, often arranged vertically, with multiple headlines for each article. A number of the same technological limitations persisted until the advent of digital typesetting and pagination in late 20th century.

"USA Today" was a leader in design changes, and was largely responsible for adding tools such as colour and infographics to newspapers' design vocabulary. These changes are partly intended to help readers "navigate", to scan and see priorities.

Some of these changes included:

- Fewer articles per page.
- Modules, or squaring off of articles and packages of related materials. Modules avoid what is known as "doglegs" or inverted- "L" shapes.
- More standardized column widths.
- More standardized fonts.
- More "art"—nontext elements, usually photos, but often including advertising or outline (or shaded) boxes for featured stories.
- More white space, known as "air." An area with too little white space is called "tight", and too much white space is called "loose."
- Colour.

Process

Designers typically use desktop publishing software to arrange the elements on the pages directly. In the past, before digital pre-press pagination, designers used precise "lay out dummies" to direct the exact layout of elements for each page. A complete layout dummy was required for designating proper column widths by which a typesetter would set type, and arrange columns of text. Layout also required the calculation of lengths of copy (text in "column inches"), for any chosen width.

Much of the variance and incoherence of early newspapers was due to the fact that last minute corrections were exclusively handled by typesetters. With photographic printing process, typesetting gave way to paste-up, whereby columns of type were printed by machines (phototypesetters) on high-resolution film for paste-up on photographed final prints. These prints in turn were "shot to negative" with a large format production camera—directly to steel-emulsion photographic plates.

Though paste-up put an end to cumbersome typesetting, this still required planned layouts and set column widths. Photographic plates are (still) wrapped on printing drums to directly apply ink to newsprint (paper). In the mid-1990s, the paste-up process gave way to the direct to plate process, where computer-paginated files were optically transmitted directly to the photographic plate. Replacing several in-between steps in newspaper production, direct to plate pagination allowed for much more flexibility and precision than before.

Design Options

Designers choose photo sizes and headline sizes (both the size of the letters and how much space the headline will take). They may decide what articles will go on which pages, and where on the page, alone or in consultation with editors. They may choose typefaces for special pages, but newspapers usually have a design style that determines most routine uses.

Notable News Designers

Notable in the field include Roger Black, Phil Autelitano, Bill Ostendorf, Richard Curtis, Mario Garcia, Tim Harrower, Lucie

Lacava, Tony Majeri, Monica Moses, Deborah Withey, Alan Jacobson and Ron Reason. Some other newspapers influential to the expanded role of design in the newsroom include the Detroit Free Press, the San Jose Mercury News, The Guardian, and the Virginian-Pilot.

Edmund Arnold, who recently died, is widely credited as the father of modern newspaper design.

8

News Printing and Publishing: An Overview of Ways and Means

PRINTING

Printing is news printing an industrial process for reproducing copies of texts and images, typically with ink on paper using a printing press. It is an essential part of publishing. Books and newspapers are usually printed today using the technique of offset printing. Other common printing techniques include relief print, (which is principally used for catalogues), screen printing, rotogravure, and digital-based inkjet and laser printing. The largest commercial and industrial printer in the world is Montréal, Quebec-based Quebecor World.

The Folder of Newspaper Web Offset Printing Press

History of Printing

Printing was first discovered and developed in China. Primitive *Woodblock printing* was already in use by the 6th century BC. The oldest surviving book printed using the more sophisticated block printing dates from 868 AD (The *Diamond Sutra* of AD 868, a Buddhist scripture). The movable type printer was invented by Pi Sheng in 1040. The movable type metal printing press was invented in Korea between 1234 and 1241. By the 12th and 13th centuries many Arabic and Chinese libraries contained tens of thousands of printed books.

There is little direct evidence, but it is highly probable that Chinese printing technology diffused into Europe through trade links that went through India and on through the Arabic world. Johann Gutenberg, of the German city of Mainz, developed European printing technology in 1440. Basing the design of his machine on a wine press, Gutenberg developed the use of raised and movable type, and from the start used oil-based inks.

This development of the printing press revolutionized the spread of knowledge: a printing press was built in Venice in 1469, and the city had 417 printers by 1500. In 1476, a printing press was developed in England by William Caxton; in 1539, the Italian Juan Pablos set up an imported press in Mexico City, Mexico. Stephen Day built the first printing press in North America at Massachusetts Bay in 1628, and helped establish the Cambridge Press.

In *Prints and Visual Communication*, William Ivins offers the following concise history of a series of rapid innovations in image and type printing at the end of the eighteenth century:

> At the end of the eighteenth century there were several remarkable innovations in the graphic techniques and those that were utilized to make their materials. Bewick developed the method of using engraving tools on the end of the wood. Senefelder discovered lithography. Blake made relief etchings. Early in the nineteenth century Stanhope, George E. Clymer, Koenig and others introduced new kinds of type presses, which for strength surpassed anything that had previously been known.

Computer Printing

A document can also be printed by a laser printer, inkjet, or other computer printer. In recent years, computer printing and industrial printing processes have converged, leading to the development of digital printing and on-demand printing. The artistic process of printmaking is also known as printing, as is photographic printing.

Printing is a process for production of texts and images, typically with ink on paper using a printing press. It is often carried out as a large-scale industrial process, and is an essential part of publishing and transaction printing.

Block Printing in China

Woodblock printing on paper, whereby individual sheets were pressed against wooden blocks with the text and illustrations carved into them, was first recorded in China in the Tang Dynasty, although as a method for printing patterns on cloth the earliest surviving examples from China date to before 220, and from Egypt to the 6th or 7th century.

In the Tang Dynasty, a Chinese writer named Fenzhi first mentioned in his book "Yuan Xian San Ji" that the woodblock was used to print Buddhist scripture during the Zhenguan years (627~649 A.D.). The oldest known Chinese surviving printed work is a woodblock-printed Buddhist scripture of Wu Zetian period (684~705 A.D.); discovered in Tubofan, Xinjiang province, China in 1906, it is now stored in a calligraphy museum in Tokyo and Japan. The oldest surviving documented printed book, a copy of the Buddhist Diamond Sutra, is dated 848 AD, but a recent excavation at a Korean pagoda may have unearthed an even earlier Buddhist text dating to AD 750-751. In the modern Chinese historiography, printing is considered one of the Four Great Inventions of ancient China. In a memorial to the throne in 1023, Northern Song Dynasty China, it recorded that the central government at that time used copperplate to print the paper money also the copper-block to print the numbers and characters on the money, nowadays we can find these shadows from the Song paper money. Later in the Jin Dynasty, people used the same but more developed technique to print paper money and formal official documents, the typical example of this kind of movable copper-block printing is a printed "check" of Jin Dynasty in the year of 1215.

Block Printing in Europe

Block printing came to Christian Europe as a method for printing on cloth, where it was common by 1300. Images printed on cloth for religious purposes could be quite large and elaborate, and when paper became relatively easily available, around 1400, the medium transferred very quickly to small woodcut religious images and playing cards printed on paper. These prints were produced in very large numbers from about 1425 onwards.

Around the mid-century, block-books, woodcut books with both text and images, usually carved in the same block, emerged as a cheaper alternative to manuscripts and books printed with movable type. These were all short heavily illustrated works, the bestsellers of the day, repeated in many different block-book versions: the Ars moriendi and the Biblia pauperum were the most common. There is still some controversy among scholars as to whether their introduction preceded or, the majority view, followed the introduction of movable type, with the range of estimated dates being between about 1440-1460.

The volume of Joseph Needham's *Science and Civilization in China* dealing with paper and printing has a chapter that suggests that "European block printers must not only have seen Chinese samples, but perhaps had been taught by missionaries or others who had learned these un-European methods from Chinese printers during their residence in China." But he also admitted that the "only evidence of European printing transmitted from China is a lack of counterevidence."

Movable Type Printing

Movable type allowed for a much more flexible processes than hand copying or block printing.

In East Asia

For a description of

- the oldest surviving metal type,
- early books printed with such metal type,
- the oldest surviving movable metal print book printed in Korea in 1377,
- the Korean font casting process as recorded by Song Hyon in the 15th c., and
- problems due to the nature of the Chinese language.

Movable type printing was first invented in 1041 by Bi Sheng in China. Sheng used clay type, which broke easily, but Wang Zhen later carved a more durable type from wood.

The transition from wood type to metal type occurred during the Goryeo Dynasty of Korea and is credited to Chwe Yun-Ui.

Movable type, though known in China, was not extensively used there until the European-style printing press was introduced in relatively recent times.

East Asian printing technology may possibly have diffused into Europe through the trade routes from China through India or the Arabic world, although there is no evidence. The lack of known intermediaries and profound technical differences in detail indicate that Gutenberg's invention of movable type was done independently.

In Europe

Johann Gutenberg, of the German city of Mainz, developed European printing technology in 1440, with which the classical age of printing began. Also, Johann Fust and Peter Schöffer experimented with him in Mainz. Genealogically, all modern movable type printing can be traced back to a single source, Gutenberg's printing press which he derived from the design of long known agricultural presses. East Asian style movable type printing, which was based on laborious manual rubbing and which had been scarcely used, practically died out after the introduction of European style printing in the 19th century.

Gutenberg is also credited with the introduction of an oil-based ink which was more durable than previously used water-based inks. Having worked as a professional goldsmith, Gutenberg made skillful use of the knowledge of metals he had learned as a craftsman. Gutenberg was also the first to make his type from an alloy of lead, tin, and antimony, which was critical for producing durable type that produced high-quality printed books, and proved to be more suitable for printing than the clay, wooden or bronze types used in East Asia. To create these lead types, Gutenberg used what some considered his most ingenious invention, a special matrix wherewith the moulding of new movable types with an unprecedented precision at short notice became feasible. Within a year after his B42, Gutenberg also published the first coloured prints.

Gutenberg's invention of the printing press revolutionized communication and book production leading to the spread of knowledge. Rapidly, printing spread from Germany by emigrating German printers, but also by foreign apprentices returning home. A printing press was built in Venice in 1469, and by 1500 the city had 417 printers. In 1470 Johann Heynlin set up a printing press in Paris. In 1473 Kasper Straube published the Almanach Cracoviense ad annum 1474 in Kraków. In 1476 a printing press was developed in England by William Caxton. The Italian Juan Pablos set up an imported press in Mexico City in 1539. Stephen Day was the first to build a printing press in North America at Massachusetts Bay in 1628, and helped establish the Cambridge Press.

Printing Houses

Early printing houses (near the time of Gutenberg) were run by "master printers." These printers owned shops, selected and edited manuscripts, determined the sizes of print runs, sold the works they produced, raised capital and organized distribution. Some master printing houses became the cultural centre for literati such as Erasmus.

(*a*) *Print shop apprentices*: Apprentices, usually between the ages of 15 and 20, worked for master printers. Apprentices were not required to be literate, and literacy rates at the time were very low, in comparison to today. Apprentices prepared ink, dampened sheets of paper, and assisted at the press. An apprentice who wished to learn to become a compositor had to learn Latin and spend time under the supervision of a journeyman.

(*b*) *Journeyman printers*: After completing their apprenticeships, *journeyman* (so-called from the French "journée" for day) printers were free to move employers. This facilitated the spread of printing to areas that were less print-centred.

(*c*) *Compositors*: Those who set the type for printing.

(*d*) *Pressmen*: The person who worked the press. This was physically labour intensive.

The earliest-known image of a European, Gutenberg-style print shop is the *Dance of Death* by Matthias Huss, at Lyon, 1499.

This image depicts a compositor standing at a compositor's case being grabbed by a skeleton. The case is raised to facilitate his work. The image also shows a pressman being grabbed by a skeleton. At the right of the printing house a bookshop is shown.

Financial Aspects

Court records from the city of Mainz document that Johannes Fust was, for sometime, Gutenberg's financial backer. By the sixteenth century jobs associated with printing were becoming increasingly specialized. Structures supporting publishers were more and more complex, leading to this division of labour. In Europe between 1500 and 1700 the role of the Master Printer was dying out and giving way to the bookseller-publisher. Printing during this period had a stronger commercial imperative than previously. Risks associated with the industry however were substantial, although dependent on the nature of the publication. Bookseller publishers negotiated at trade fairs and at print shops. Jobbing work appeared in which printers did menial tasks in the beginning of their careers to support themselves.

1500–1700: Publishers developed several new methods of funding projects:

1. *Cooperative associations/publication syndicates*: A number of individuals shared the risks associated with printing and shared in the profit. This was pioneered by the French.
2. *Subscription publishing*: Pioneered by the English in the early 17th century. A prospectus for a publication was drawn up by a publisher to raise funding. The prospectus was given to potential buyers who signed up for a copy. If there were not enough subscriptions the publication did not go ahead. Lists of subscribers were included in the books as endorsements. If enough people subscribed a reprint might occur. Some authors used subscription publication to bypass the publisher entirely.
3. *Installment publishing*: Books were issued in parts until a complete book had been issued. This was not necessarily done with a fixed time period. It was an effective method of spreading cost over a period of time. It also allowed earlier returns on investment to help cover production costs of subsequent installments.

The *Mechanick Exercises*, by Joseph Moxon, in London, 1683, was said to be the first publication done in installments. Publishing trade organizations allowed publishers to organize business concerns collectively. Systems of self-regulation occurred in these arrangements. For example, if one publisher did something to irritate other publishers he would be controlled by peer pressure. Such systems are known as cartels, and are in most countries now considered to be in restraint of trade. These arrangements helped deal with labour unrest among journeymen, who faced difficult working conditions. Brotherhoods predated unions, without the formal regulations now associated with unions.

In most cases, publishers bought the copyright in a work from the author, and made some arrangement about the possible profits. This required a substantial amount of capital in addition to the capital for the physical equipment and staff. Alternatively, an author who had sufficient money would sometimes keep the copyright himself, and simply pay the printer for the production of the book. For further developments, as described in *Prints and Visual Communication*, by William Ivins.

Eighteenth Century Innovations

At the end of the eighteenth century there were several remarkable innovations in the graphic techniques and those that were utilized to make their materials. Bewick developed the method of using engraving tools on the end of the wood. Senefelder discovered lithography. Blake made relief etchings.

Nineteenth Century Innovations

Early in the nineteenth century Stanhope, George E. Clymer, Koenig and others introduced new kinds of type presses, which for strength surpassed anything that had previously been known.

Modern Printing Technology

In 2006, there are approximately 30,700 printing companies in the United States, accounting for $112 billion, according to the *2006 U.S. Industry and Market Outlook* by Barnes Reports. Print jobs that move through the Internet made up 12.5 per cent of the total U.S.

Printing market last year, according to research firm InfoTrend/CAP Ventures.

Books and newspapers are printed today using the technique of offset lithography. Other common techniques include:

(*a*) flexography used for packaging, labels, newspapers;
(*b*) relief print (mainly used for catalogues);
(*c*) screen printing from T-shirts to floor tiles;
(*d*) rotogravure mainly used for magazines and packaging;
(*e*) inkjet used typically to print a small number of books or packaging, and also to print a variety of materials from high quality papers simulate offset printing, to floor tiles; inkjet is also used to apply mailing addresses to direct mail pieces;
(*f*) hot wax dye transfer; and
(*g*) laser printing mainly used in offices and for transactional printing (bills, bank documents). Laser printing is commonly used by direct mail companies to create variable data letters or coupons, for example.

Gravure

For this process, the image to be printed is made up of small holes sunk into the surface of the printing plate. The cells are filled with ink and the excess is scraped off the surface, then a rubber-covered roller presses paper onto the surface of the plate and into contact with the ink in the cells. The printing plates are usually made from copper and may be produced by engraving or etching.

Gravure printing is used for long, high-quality print runs such as magazines, mail-order catalogues, packaging, and printing onto fabric and wallpaper. It is also used for printing postage stamps and decorative plastic laminates, such as kitchen worktops.

Digital Printing

Printing at home or in an office or engineering environment is subdivided into

(*a*) *small format* (up to ledger size paper sheets), as used in business offices and libraries, and (*b*) *wide format* (up to 3′ or 914 mm wide rolls of paper), as used in drafting and design establishments.

Some of the more common printing technologies are:

(*a*) line printing—where pre-formed characters are applied to the paper by lines,

(*a*) daisy wheel—where pre-formed characters are applied individually,

(*a*) dot-matrix—which produces arbitrary patterns of dots with an array of printing studs,

(*a*) heat transfer—like early fax machines or modern receipt printers that apply heat to special paper, which turns black to form the printed image,

(*a*) blueprint—and related chemical technologies,

(*a*) inkjet—including bubble-jet—where ink is sprayed onto the paper to create the desired image, and

(*a*) laser—where toner consisting primarily of polymer with pigment of the desired colours is melted and applied directly to the paper to create the desired image.

Vendors typically stress the total cost to operate the equipment, involving complex calculations that include all cost factors involved in the operation as well as the capital equipment costs, amortization, etc. For the most part, toner systems beat inkjet in the long run, whereas inkjets are less expensive in the initial purchase price. Professional digital printing (using toner) primarily uses an electrical charge to transfer toner or liquid ink to the substrate it is printed on. Digital print quality has steadily improved from early colour and black and white copiers to sophisticated colour digital presses like the Xerox iGen3, the Kodak Nexpress and the HP Indigo Digital Press series. The iGen3 and Nexpress use toner particles and the Indigo uses liquid ink. All three are made for small runs and variable data, and rival offset in quality. Digital offset presses are called direct imaging presses; although these receive computer files and automatically turn them into print-ready plates, they cannot insert variable data.

Small press and fanzines generally use digital printing or more rarely xerography. Prior to the introduction of cheap photocopying the use of machines such as the spirit duplicator, hectograph, and mimeograph was common.

PRINTING PRESS

The printing press is a mechanical printing device for making copies of identical text on multiple sheets of paper. It was invented in Germany by the goldsmith and printer Johannes Gutenberg in 1445. Printing methods based on Gutenberg's printing press spread rapidly throughout first Europe and then the rest of the world, replacing most block printing and making it the sole progenitor of modern movable type printing. Printing's effect on civilization has often been discussed in terms of the effect of the "printing press" on civilization—a rhetorical device, which alludes to the pivotal role of the printing press in the global spread of printing.

Movable type printing, which allowed individual characters to be arranged to form words, is a separate invention from the printing press. In what is regarded as an independent invention, movable type printing as we know it today was invented in Germany by Gutenberg in the 1440s, although the first known invention was in China by Bi Sheng between 1041 and 1048.

Invention of the Printing Press

Johannes Gutenberg is credited with inventing the first printing press, although there are several local claims for the invention of the printing press in other parts of Europe, including Laurens Janszoon Coster in the Netherlands and Panfilo Castaldi in Italy. Screw presses for olives and wine were known in Europe since Roman times; presses for the binding of manuscript books were also in use. Gutenberg was the first to convert the concept for printing uses. Gutenberg's use of mechanical presses, along with other innovations of his, made printing from the start a proto-industrial process with a far greater printing output than with manual work.

Having previously worked as a professional goldsmith, Gutenberg also made skillful use of the knowledge of metals he had learned as a craftsman. He was the first to make his type from an alloy of lead, tin, and antimony, which was critical for producing durable type that produced high-quality printed books, and proved to be more suitable for printing than the clay, wooden or bronze types used in East Asia. To create these lead types, Gutenberg used what some considered his most ingenious invention, a special matrix enabling the moulding of new movable types at short notice and with unprecedented precision.

In the Gutenberg Bible, Gutenberg made a trial of coloured printing for a few of the page headings, present only in some copies. (Albert Kapr, "Johannes Gutenberg", Scolar 1996, p. 172).

A later work, the Mainz Psalter of 1453, presumably designed by Gutenberg but published under the imprint of his successors Johann Fust and Peter Schoeffer, had elaborate red and blue printed initials. (Kapr, p.203). Gutenberg is also credited with the introduction of an oil-based ink which was more durable than the previously used water-based inks. As printing material he used both vellum and paper, the latter having been introduced in Europe somewhat earlier from China by way of the Arabs, who had a paper mill in operation in Baghdad as early as 794.

Method of Using the Gutenberg-Style Printing Press

Adapted from Philip Gaskell, *A New Introduction to Bibliography* (Oxford: OUP, 1995)

The parts of the printing press:

(*a*) The frame—immovably braces and supports the two moving parts.

(*b*) The carriage assembly—carries the type and paper in and out of the impression assembly.

(*c*) The impression assembly—pushes (or presses) the paper onto the inked type.

The printing process:

1. *Buy the paper*: Paper from the same lot will give the resulting book a uniform look.
2. *Arrange the paper into stacks of 250 sheets*: These are called tokens and are the units for calculating a pressman's work. Most book editions are in multiples of 250 copies.
3. The night before printing, wet the stack of paper and let it stand under a heavy weight. This helps the paper to absorb ink.
4. Make register by loading the forme into the carriage assembly on the press stone so that when the paper was

printed on one side and then flipped over and printed on the other side, the pages printed squarely on top of each other. Press points on the tympan were adjusted to hold the paper in position.

5. Paste one sheet of paper to the tympan to serve as a guide to positioning the sheets of paper to be printed.
6. Paste another sheet of paper to the frisket, print the first forme on it and cut out the areas where text appears. This will protect the white areas of the sheet from dirt and ink.
7. The beater inks the type in the forme (called beating the forme) using two ink balls—leather-covered pads of horsehair or wool with handles. Ink rollers were not invented until after the hand-press era.
8. The puller lays the sheet of clean paper to be printed onto the tympan and then lowers the frisket onto it.
9. The beater folds the tympan, paper, and frisket down onto the forme.
10. The puller runs the front end of the carriage assembly under the impression assembly by turning the rounce.
11. The puller pulls on the bar to force the platen down onto the tympan, thereby pressing the paper onto the inked forme. When he releases the bar, the platen will spring back.
12. The rounce is turned again to pull the second half of the forme under the platen and the platen is lowered again.
13. Release the bar to lift the platen and turn the rounce to pull the carriage assembly out from under the impression assembly.
14. Unfold the carriage assembly to remove the printed sheet.
15. Repeat this procedure from step 8 for each sheet in the stack.

The same procedure was followed for printing the second side of the sheet, positioning the sheet on the already-adjusted points. Printing the second side is called perfecting. In the sixteenth century, the first side of the sheet was printed in the morning and the second side was printed in the afternoon. In the eighteenth century, one side was done on one press and the other side was done on another press.

Two pressmen could print 250 sheets an hour, going from step 8 to step 15 in about fifteen seconds but according to McKenzie, they seldom did. A full press-crew was two men—a puller and a beater, and often a boy to put on fresh ink.

Impact of Printing

Effects of Printing on Culture

The impact of printing is comparable to the development of writing and the invention of the alphabet or the internet, as far as its effects on the society. Printing did not achieve a position of total dominance, and handwritten manuscripts continued to be produced, and the continuing influences of the printed word and oral communication on each other meant that no one form of communication could dominate.

Printing also was a factor in the establishment of a community of scientists who could easily communicate their discoveries, which had previously been communicated by personal letters, helping to bring on the scientific revolution. Also, although early texts were printed in Latin, books were soon produced in common European vernaculars, leading over several centuries to the decline of the Latin language as the medium of scholarly communication.

Because of the printing press, authorship became more meaningful and profitable. It was suddenly important who had said or written what, and what the precise formulation and time of composition was. This allowed the exact citing of references, producing the rule, "One Author, one work (title), one piece of information" (Giesecke, 1989; 325). Before, the author was less important, since a copy of Aristotle made in Paris would not be exactly identical to one made in Bologna. For many works prior to the printing press, the name of the author was entirely lost.

Because the printing process ensured that the same information fell on the same pages, page numbering, tables of contents, and indices became common, though they previously had not been unknown. The process of reading was also changed, gradually changing over several centuries from oral readings to silent, private reading. And obviously, the availability of printed materials led to a continuing rise in the literacy level, revolutionizing education.

It can also be argued that printing changed the way Europeans thought. With the older illuminated manuscripts, the immediate visual emphasis was on the images and the beauty of the page. Early printed works emphasized principally the text and the line of argument. In the sciences, the introduction of the printing press marked a move from the medieval language of metaphors to the adoption of the scientific method.

In general, knowledge came closer to the hands of the people, since printed books could be sold for a fraction of the cost of illuminated manuscripts. There were also more copies of each book available, so that more people could discuss them. Within 50-60 years, the entire library of "classical" knowledge had been printed on the new presses (Eisenstein, 1969; 52). The spread of works also led to the creation of copies by other parties than the original author, leading to the formulation of copyright laws. Furthermore, as the books spread into the hands of the people, Latin was gradually replaced by the national languages. This development was one of the keys to the creation of modern nations.

Some theorists, such as McLuhan, Eisenstein, Kittler, and Giesecke, see an "alphabetic monopoly" as having developed from printing, removing the role of the image from society. Other authors stress that printed works themselves are a visual medium. Certainly, modern developments in printing have revitalized the role of illustrations.

The Art of Book Printing

For years, book printing was considered a true art form. Typesetting, or the placement of the characters on the page, including the use of ligatures, was passed down from master to apprentice. In Germany, the art of typesetting was termed the "black art" in allusion to the ink-covered printers. It has largely been replaced by computer typesetting programmes, which make it possible to get similar results with less human involvement. Some practitioners continue to print books the way Gutenberg did. For example, there is a yearly convention of traditional book printers in Mainz, Germany.

Printing in the Industrial Age

The Gutenberg press was much more efficient than manual copying, and as testament to its effectiveness, it was essentially unchanged from the time of its invention until the Industrial Revolution, some three hundred years later. The "old style" press (as it was termed in the nineteenth century) was constructed of wood and could produce 240 impressions per hour of simple work using a well experienced two-man crew. The invention of the steam powered press, credited to the German inventors Friedrich Koenig and Andreas Friedrich Bauer in 1812, made it possible to print over a thousand copies of a page per hour.

Koenig and Bauer sold two of their first models to *The Times* in London in 1814, capable of 1,100 impressions per hour. The first edition so printed was on November 28, 1814. They went on to perfect the early model so that it could print on both sides of a sheet at once. This began the long process of making newspapers available to a mass audience (which in turn helped spread literacy), and from the 1820s changed the nature of book production, forcing a greater standardization in titles and other metadata. Their company Koenig and Bauer AG is still one of the world's largest manufacturers of printing presses today.

Their press was improved by Applegath and Cooper. The diagram indicates the principle of operation of a Cooper and Applegath's Single Machine. The press is built up from a large flat inking table (*a*) which moves regularly back and forth, the form; (*b*) on the table holds the type. The paper travels clockwise round a large cloth covered cylinder, the impression roller (*c*), and is pressed against the table. The ductor roller (*d*) rotates and so draws ink from the attached reservoir. The ink passes from the ductor roller to the vibrating roller (*e*), this moves, on its arms, in a regular motion between the ductor roller and the table. The ink is spread thinly and evenly by the distributing rollers (*f*) and then, as the table moves, passes onto the inking rollers (*g*). The axles of the inking rollers rest in grooves, allowing them to rise and fall, they are also position at a slight angle to the table to improve ink distribution. As the table continues to move the form passes alternately under the inking rollers, twice, and then under the impression roller. Later on in the middle of the 19th century the rotary printing press (invented in 1833 in the United States by Richard M. Hoe) allowed millions of copies of a page in a single day. Mass production of printed works flourished after the transition to rolled paper, as continuous feed allowed the presses to run at a much faster pace.

Also, in the middle of the 19th century, there was a separate development of jobbing presses, small presses capable of printing small-format pieces such as billheads, letterheads, business cards, and envelopes. Jobbing presses were capable of quick set-up (average makeready time for a small job was under 15 minutes) and quick production (even on treadle-powered jobbing presses it was considered normal to get 1,000 impressions per hour [iph] with one pressman, with speeds of 1,500 iph often attained on simple envelope work). Job printing emerged as a reasonably cost-effective duplicating solution for commerce at this time.

Later inventions in this field include the following:

- Lithography
- Offset printing
- Desktop publishing
- Electronic publishing (on CD-ROM or online)
- Computer printer
- Composing stick.

NEWSPAPERS

A newspaper is a lightweight and disposable publication (more specifically, a periodical), usually printed on low-cost paper called newsprint. It may be general or special-interest, and may be published daily, weekly, biweekly, monthly, bimonthly, or quarterly. General-interest newspapers are usually journals of current news on a variety of topics. Those can include political events, crime, business, sports, and opinions (either editorials, columns, or political cartoons). Many also include weather news and forecasts. Newspapers increasingly use photographs to illustrate stories; they also often include comic strips and other entertainment, such as crosswords.

Overview

The general variety is issued every day (a daily newspaper), often with the exception of Sundays and some national holidays. Weekly newspapers, printed once a week, are also common; they tend to be smaller and less prestigious than daily papers. Most nations have at least one newspaper that circulates throughout the whole country: a national newspaper, as contrasted with a local newspaper serving a city or region. In the United States and Canada, there are few truly national newspapers, with the notable exceptions of *USA Today* in the United States and *The Globe and*

Mail and *The National Post* in Canada. Large metropolitan newspapers with expanded distribution networks such as *The New York Times, The Washington Post,* and *The Toronto Star* can fill the role of *de facto* national newspapers. Newspapers have been developed around very narrow topic areas, such as news for merchants in a specific industry, fans of particular sports, fans of the arts or of specific artists, and participants in the same sorts of activities or lifestyles.

History

According to the World Association of Newspapers:

> Regular publications have been created and distributed by governments for millennia, including *Acta Diurna,* a listing of events ordered by Julius Caesar in Ancient Rome in 59 B.C.
>
> In A.D. 713, the first newspaper, *Mixed News* in Kaiyuan, was published as hand-written newsheet in Beijing, China. Kaiyuan is the name given to the year in which the paper is published.

1605 : Johann Carolus publishes the first printed newspaper, Relation, in Strasbourg, now in France but at the time a part of the Deutsches Reich.
The first English-language private newspaper, *The Corante,* was first published in London in 1621.
The first English daily newspaper, the *Daily Courant,* was founded by Samuel Buckley on 11 March, 1702 (Publication ceased in 1735).

1631 : *The Gazette,* the first French newspaper, was founded.

1645 : the oldest newspaper still in circulation, *Post-och Inrikes Tidningar* of Sweden, began publishing.

1690 : *Publick Occurrences* in Boston became the first newspaper published in America. It was suppressed after one issue.

1701 : September 6, Estimated first issue of the *Norwich* Post, which was probably the first provincial newspaper.

1709 : *Worcester Post-Man* founded, which became Berrow's Worcester Journal in 1753, The Worcester Post-Man/ Berrow's Worcester Journal is Britain's oldest surviving un-official newspaper.

1785 : *The Daily Universal Register* was founded by John Walters. It became *The Times* on January 1st, 1788.

1803 : Just 15 years after the first British penal colony was established, Australia's military government published the *Sydney Gazette* and the *New South Wales Advertiser*, Australia's first newspapers.

1821 : *The Guardian* was founded.

1884 : Otto Merganthaler invented the linotype machine which casts type in full lines, using hot lead, a quantum leap in newspaper publishing, and issuing in the era of "hot lead." The systems remained in general production in the industry well into the 1980s, when computerized pagination became prominent.

1962 : *The Los Angeles Times* drives linotype hot metal typesetters with perforated tape created from RCA computers speeding up the typesetting. The key was development of a dictionary and method to automate the hyphenation and justification of text in columns (tasks that had taken 40 per cent of a manual operator's time).

1973 : Harris introduced editing terminals, which were quickly followed by terminals from Raytheon, Atex, Digital Equipment Corporation and others. The output was strips of type on film from phototypesetters ("cold type" replacing the "hot type" of Linotype machines. Atex worked with the *Minneapolis Star* to develop the first pagination system that allowed the creation and output of full editorial pages, eliminating the need for manual paste-up of strips of film. The Atex system featured "Atex Messaging" which is widely believed to be the forerunner of both e-mail and instant messenger applications.

Format

Most modern newspapers are in one of three sizes:

- broadsheets (29½ × 23½ inches), generally associated with more intellectual newspapers.

- tabloids: half the size of broadsheets, and often seen as sensationalist in contrast to them.
- "Berliner" or "midi" (470 × 315 mm), used by European papers such as *Le Monde*.

They are usually printed on a thin, somewhat rough paper known as *newsprint*. Since the 1980s, many newpapers have been printed with three-colour process photography and graphics. This highlights the fact that the layout of the newspaper is of major importance in getting attention so readers will see and enjoy large sections of the newspaper.

Circulation and Readership

The number of copies sold on an average day is called the newspaper's circulation, and is used to set advertising rates. According to United Nations data from 1995 Japan has three daily papers with a circulation well above 4 million. Germany's *Bild*, with a circulation of 4.5 million, was the only other paper in that category. In the United Kingdom *The Sun* is the top seller, with around 3,200,000 copies distributed daily (late-2004). In the United States and the United Kingdom at least, circulation has been declining for many years. *USA Today* has daily circulation of approximately 2 million, making it the most widely distributed paper in the country. However, the validity of USA Today's circulation figures are disputed by some in the newspaper community. This is because of the paper's contracts with hotels. Many of its papers are delivered to hotel guests who don't realize they are being charged for it. In 2004, several large US newspapers were found to have overstated their circulation.

Business Side

Almost all newspapers make nearly all their money from advertising. The income from the customer's payment at the newsstand is a pittance in comparison. That is why all newspapers cost little and some are free. The portion of the newspaper that is not advertising is called *editorial content* or *editorial matter*.

Publishers of commercial newspapers strive for higher circulation so that advertising in their newspaper becomes more effective, allowing the newspaper to attract more advertisers and charge more for the service. But some advertising sales also market demographics: Some newspapers might sacrifice higher circulation numbers in favour of an audience with a higher income.

Many paid-for newspapers offer a variety of subscription plans. For example, someone might only want a Sunday paper, or perhaps only Sunday and Saturday, or maybe only a workweek subscription, or perhaps a daily subscription.

Some newspapers provide some or all of their content on the Internet, either at no cost or for a fee. In some cases free access is only available for a matter of days or weeks, or readers must register and provide personal data. In other cases, extensive free archives are provided.

Newspaper Journalism

Since newspapers began as a *journal,* or record of current events, the profession involved in the making of newpapers began to be called *journalism*. Much emphasis has been placed upon the value of the journalist to be accurate and fair in the historical record. In the yellow journalism era of the 19th century, many newspapers in the United States relied on sensational stories that were meant to anger or excite, rather than to inform. The more restrained style of reporting that relies on fact checking and accuracy regained popularity around World War II.

Criticism of journalism is varied and sometimes vehement. Charges of sensationalism have diminished to a degree. But credibility is questioned because of anonymous sources; errors in facts, spelling, and grammar; real or perceived bias; and scandals involving plagiarism and fabrication. Newspapers have often been owned by so-called press barons, either as a rich man's toy, or used as a political tool. Even though the opinions of the owners are often relegated to the *editorial* section, and the opinions of the readers are in the *op-ed* ("opposite the editorial page") and *letters to the editors* sections of the paper, newspapers have been used for political purposes by insinuating some kind of bias outside of the editorial section and into straight *news*. For example, *The New York Times* is often criticized for a leftist slant to its stories, or, by others, for supporting the American political establishment in nearly all cases, whereas *The Wall Street Journal* has a history of emphasizing the position of the right. Some ways newspapers have tried to improve their credibility are: appointing ombudsmen, developing ethics policies and training, using more stringent corrections policies, communicating their processes and rationale with readers, and asking sources to review articles after publication.

The Future of Newspapers

The future of newspapers is cloudy, with overall readership slowly declining in most developed countries due to increasing competition from television and the Internet. The 57th annual World Newspaper Congress, held in Istanbul in June 2004, reported circulation increases in only 35 of 208 countries studied. Most of the increase came in developing countries, notably China.

A report at the gathering said China tops total newspaper circulation, with more than 85 million copies of papers sold every day, followed by India with 72 million—China and India are the two most populous countries in the world followed by Japan with 70 million and the United States with 55 million. The report said circulation declined by an average of 2.2 per cent across 13 of the 15 countries that made up the European Union before May 1. The biggest declines were in Ireland, down 7.8 per cent; Britain, down 4.7 per cent; and Portugal, where numbers fell by 4.0 per cent. One growth area is the distribution of free newspapers, which are not reflected in the above circulation data. They grew 16 per cent in 2003. Another growth area is high-quality tabloids, particularly in the UK, where several of the major broadsheets are experimenting with the format. Smaller and easier to hold than broadsheets, but presenting real journalism rather than traditional tabloid fodder, they appear to have drawn some younger readers who are otherwise abandoning newspapers.

Newspapers also face increased competition from the Internet for classified ads, especially for jobs, which have long been a key source of revenue.

Newspapers in Different Countries

Argentina

In Argentina, the broadsheet format is almost non-existent. The only remaining national newspaper published in that format is *La Nación*.

Germany

In Germany, the distinction between *serious* and tabloid papers is usually made according to whether they are available on subscription. The more sensational tabloids such as *Bild* are commonly called *Boulevardzeitungen* (boulevard papers), because they are normally available at the newsstand only; by contrast, the more serious *Abonnementzeitungen* (subscription papers) sell a large amount of their circulation to subscribers. National newspapers such as *Die Welt* are available, but local ones draw a much wider readership. Some local newspapers assume the role of national papers, such as the *Frankfurter Allgemeine* of Frankfurt/M. and the *Süddeutsche Zeitung* of Munich.

Hong Kong

Hong Kong has a vibrant newspaper publishing industry. Most papers use the broadsheet size. Almost all newspapers focus on the local Hong Kong market, but some may also target at the markets in Macao and Pearl River Delta. Although they are broadsheets, the three papers with the largest circulation are all considered tabloid-style, with large and colourful photos and sensational coverage to attract readers. Most papers adopt a daily magazine approach, with all sort of coverages range from local and international news, entertainment, culture, lifestyle, economic and finance, sport and horse-racing. Hong Kong Economic Journal, Hong Kong Economic Times and South China Morning Post have are stronger focus on economic and finance. Ta Kung Pao, Wen Wei Po and Oriental Daily are the mouthpieces of the communist government in Peking. There are also papers specifically published for horse-racing tips.

Mexico

In Mexico, there are many publications, and none that can be considered a national newspaper. The most important ones, like La Jornada, Excelsior, and Reforma are in Mexico City, and because of a heavy national centralization, a lot of redistribution happens (newspapers from Mexico City are sold in almost every city in the country, some with a day or two lag.)

The only attempts to create a national national newspaper originate in Monterrey:

- One of them is Milenio, a midi format newspaper, which is distributed in Mexico City, Monterrey, Nuevo León, Veracruz, Veracruz, Guadalajara, Jalisco, Tampico, Tamaulipas, and the state of Tabasco.
- The other attempt to make a national newspaper has been done by *Reforma* news group, which also originated in Monterrey but that now is run from Mexico City. Reforma publishes different newspapers with the same main content, but with specific local content in the major cities of the country: *El Norte* in Monterrey, *Reforma* in Mexico City, *Mural* in Guadalajara and *Palabra* in Saltillo. All of the newspapers by Reforma are published in the broadsheet format.
- Reforma is one of the most prestigious, and often considered among the most reliable, news sources in Mexico, in spite of its youth (it appeared in Mexico City in 1993). It has gained its prestige with its attractive editorial design, wide-spectrum editorialists and denouncements of government corruption.
- Until very recently, newsprint in Mexico was a product made only by the government-owned monopoly. Importing the product from other countries (such as the United States) was illegal. This allowed the Mexican government, for many years, to put out of circulation any dissident newspaper. Reforma survived the boycott and fought heavily until the government allowed for importing the product in the 1990s.

Since then, the Mexican Press has been undergoing a process towards more freedom of speech, especially after the election of President Vicente Fox in the year 2000.

United Kingdom

In the United Kingdom, newspapers can be classified by distribution as *local* or *national* and by page size as *tabloids* and *broadsheets*. The principal newspapers of England and Wales are all nationals edited in London. Scotland is a separate market with its own newspapers.

There is often an implication that *tabloids* cater for more vulgar tastes than *broadsheets*. Within the *tabloid* category the most down market titles are classed as *red-tops* because of the design of their front pages. This term is often used deprecatingly by newspapers that consider themselves more serious. There are also "middle-market" tabloids such as *The Daily Mail.*

This distinction began to be blurred in October 2003 as two *broadsheet* newspapers—*The Independent* and *The Times*—began to trial *tabloid* editions in some parts of the U.K. *The Independent* switched entirely to producing what it prefers to call a *compact* edition from May 2004 and *The Times* changed to this format at the beginning of November 2004, despite initial opposition to from its more traditional and conservative readership. *The Guardian* is expected to switch to the unusual (for the U.K.) "Berliner" format, slightly larger than a traditional tabloid, sometime in 2006.

There are daily paid papers in most of the larger cities, and weekly paid papers in some other areas. These focus on local news and do not attempt to be a direct substitute for the London based national newspapers. Most areas also typically have one or more free local papers, with extensive classified advertising.

United States

The vast majority of American newspapers are traditionally printed as broadsheets. A small number of daily papers are printed in the tabloid format.

US dailies commonly separate the physical newspaper into *sections* on particular topics. Most major American cities' papers will have sections covering at least a few of the following topics:

- *National and international news,* usually the first section. In the most prestigious newspapers like the *New York Times,* the majority of articles in this section are dispatched by the paper's own journalists from bureaus around the world. Smaller papers usually fill almost all of this section with stories taken from newswires like the Associated Press or Reuters.
- *Local and regional news,* usually the second section. This is often called the *metro* (from *metropolitan*) section. Many large newspapers use "zoning," with different zones, receiving somewhat different articles, or the same articles arranged differently. Zoning is most predominant in the local section, but also plays a role in the front page.

- *Sports*
- *Business*
- *Classified ads*
- *Features*: This may include *Arts, Home furnishing, Fashion, Style,* or some combination. This section usually also includes general advice columns and amusements, such as comic strips, horoscopes and puzzles.
- A weekly general-interest magazine-type feature, usually appearing on Sunday, such as *Parade,* USA Weekend, or their own magazine (for larger papers) such as *The New York Times Magazine* or the *Washington Post Magazine.*
- *Weekend* or *Entertainment*. This section includes many ads for upcoming entertainment events which usually occur on the weekend; this section usually appears on a Friday, or the last newspaper printed before the weekend.
- *Comics*. Typically only a separate section on Sundays; daily papers will include a page or more of comics in another section. Although new colour printing technology has seen the spread of the use of colour in comics (and other editorial content) to daily editions, for many years the expense of colour printing meant that only the Sunday editions of many newspapers carried most comics in full colour.
- *Opinion* or *Editorial*. Includes both editorials by the newspaper's editorial staff and letters to the editor from readers. Typically only a separate section on Sundays; daily papers will include these materials in the back of the national, regional, metro, or local news sections. Sometimes may include commentaries or "op-ed pieces" from nationally renowned writers.

MAGAZINE

A magazine is a periodical publication containing a variety of articles on various subjects. Magazines are typically published weekly, biweekly, monthly, or quarterly, with a date on the cover that is in advance of the date it is actually published. They are often printed in colour on coated paper.

Magazines usually have articles on popular topics of interest to the general public and are written at the reading level of most of the population. An academic periodical featuring scholarly articles written in a more specialist register is usually called a "journal." "Periodical" is the word usually used to describe magazines, journals, newspapers, newsletters, and anything else that is published in regular intervals for an indefinite period of time, but "serial" is sometimes used, especially in librarianship.

Many weekend newspapers incorporate magazine supplements, such as *Parade*; the *Times Literary Supplement*, and *LIFE* in its most recent incarnation. *The Gentleman's Magazine*, first published in 1731, is considered to be the first general-interest magazine. The oldest magazine still in print is *The Scots Magazine*, which was first published in 1739, though multiple changes in ownership and gaps in publication totaling over 90 years weaken that claim.

The most widely distributed magazine in the world is *Reader's Digest* (founded in 1922). Its worldwide circulation including all editions comprises 21 million copies and over 100 million readers. *The Watchtower* is the most widely distributed religious magazine in the world, with an average circulation of 26.4 million copies semimonthly in more than 150 languages.

9

Photojournalism: Elements, Advances and Jobs

PHOTOJOURNALISM IN MODERN TIMES

Photojournalism is a particular form of journalism (the collecting, editing, and presenting of news material for publication or broadcast) that creates images in order to tell a news story. It is now usually understood to refer only to still images, and in some cases to video used in broadcast journalism. Photojournalism is distinguished from other close branches of photography (such as documentary photography, street photography or celebrity photography) by the qualities of:

- *Timeliness*—the images have meaning in the context of a recently published record of events.
- *Objectivity*—the situation implied by the images is a fair and accurate representation of the events they depict in both content and tone.
- *Narrative*—the images combine with other news elements, to make facts relatable to the viewer or reader on a cultural level.

Like a writer, a photojournalist is a reporter but he or she must often make decisions instantly and carry photographic equipment, often while exposed to significant obstacles (physical danger, weather and crowds).

History

Foundations

The practice of illustrating news stories with photographs was made possible by printing and photography innovations that occurred between 1880 and 1897. While newsworthy events were photographed as early as the 1850s, printing presses could only publish from engravings until the 1880s. Early news photographs required that photos be re-interpreted by an engraver before they could be published.

The pioneering battlefield photographs from the Crimean War (1853 to 1856) by British press reporters such as William Simpson of the *Illustrated London News* and Roger Fenton were published as engravings. Similarly, the American Civil War photographs of Mathew Brady were engraved before publication in *Harper's Weekly.* Because the public craved more realistic representations of news stories, it was common for newsworthy photographs to be exhibited in galleries or to be copied photographically in limited numbers. On March 4, 1880, *The Daily Graphic* (New York) published the first halftone (rather than engraved) reproduction of a news photograph. Further innovations followed. In 1887, flash powder was invented, enabling journalists such as Jacob Riis to photograph informal subjects indoors, which led to the landmark work *How the Other Half Lives.* By 1897, it became possible to reproduce halftone photographs on printing presses running at full speed. Despite these innovations, limitations remained, and many of the sensational newspaper and magazine stories in the period from 1897 to 1927 (*see* Yellow Journalism) were illustrated with engravings. In 1921, the wirephoto made it possible to transmit pictures almost as quickly as news itself could travel. However, it was not until development of the commercial 35 mm Leica camera in 1925, and the first flash bulbs between 1927 and 1930 that all the elements were in place for a "golden age" of photojournalism.

Golden Age

In the "golden age" of photojournalism (1930-1950s), some magazines (*Picture Post* (London), *Paris Match* (Paris), Arbeiter-Illustrierte-Zeitung (Berlin), Berliner Illustrirte Zeitung (Berlin), *Life* (USA), *Sports Illustrated* (USA)) and newspapers (*The Daily Mirror* (London), *The New York Daily News* (New York)) built their huge readerships and reputations largely on their use of photography, and photographers such as Robert Capa, Alfred

Eisenstaedt, Margaret Bourke-White and W. Eugene Smith became well-known names. In particular Henri Cartier-Bresson is generally held as the the father of photojournalism. His candid shots of frozen moments, frozen in time are seen as ground breaking. His photo of a man jumping over a puddle has been called the greatest photograph of the 20th century. His Leica camera (introduced in 1925) is considered an enabler that allowed him to capture decisive moments in time. It was also the favoured tool of Robert Capa.

Soldier Tony Vaccaro is also recognized as one of the pre-eminent photographers of World War II. His images taken with the modest Argus C3 captured horrific moments in war, similar to Capa's soldier being shot. Capa himself was on Omaha beach on D-Day and captured pivotal images of the conflict on that occasion. Vaccaro is also known for having developed his own images in soldier's helmets, and using chemicals found in the ruins of a camera store in 1944.

Until the 1980s, most large newspapers were printed with turn-of-the-century "letterpress" technology using easily smudged oil-based ink, off-white, low-quality "newsprint" paper, and coarse engraving screens. While letterpresses produced legible text, the photoengraving dots that formed pictures often bled or smeared and became fuzzy and indistinct. In this way, even when newspapers used photographs well—a good crop, a respectable size—murky reproduction often left readers re-reading the caption to see what the photo was all about. The *Wall Street Journal* adopted stippled hedcuts in 1979 to publish portraits and avoid the limitations of letterpress printing. Not until the 1980s had a majority of newspapers switched to "offset" presses that reproduce photos with fidelity on better, whiter paper.

By contrast *Life*, one of America's most popular weekly magazines from 1936 through the early 1970s, was filled with photographs reproduced beautifully on oversize 11×14-inch pages, using fine engraving screens, high-quality inks, and glossy paper. *Life* often published a United Press International (UPI) or Associated Press (AP) photo that had been first reproduced in newspapers, but the quality magazine version appeared to be a different photo altogether. In large part because their pictures were clear enough to be appreciated, and because their name always appeared with their work, magazine photographers achieved near-celebrity status. *Life* became a standard by which the public judged photography, and many of today's photo books celebrate "photojournalism" as if it had been the exclusive province of near-celebrity magazine photographers.

The Best of Life (1973), for example, opens with a two-page (1960) group shot of 39 justly famous *Life* photographers. But 300 pages later, photo credits reveal that scores of the photos among *Life's* "best" were taken by anonymous UPI and AP photographers.

Thus even during the golden age, because of printing limitations and the UPI and AP syndication systems, many newspaper photographers laboured in relative obscurity.

Farm Security Administration

From 1935 to 1942, the Farm Security Administration and its predecessor the Resettlement Administration were part of Franklin Roosevelt's New Deal, and were designed to address agricultural problems and rural poverty associated with the Great Depression. A special photographic section of the agency, headed by Roy Stryker, was intended merely to provide public relations for its programmes, but instead produced what some consider one of the greatest collections of documentary photographs ever created in the U.S. Whether this effort can be called "photojournalism" is debatable, since the FSA photographers had more time and resources to create their work than most photojournalists usually have.

Acceptance by the Art World

Since the late 1970s, photojournalism and documentary photography have increasingly been accorded a place in art galleries alongside fine art photography. Luc Delahaye, VII Photo Agency and Chien-Chi Chang are among many who regularly exhibit in galleries.

Professional Organizations

The Danish Union of Press Photographers (Pressefotografforbundet) was the first national organization for newspaper photographers in the world. It was founded in 1912 in Denmark by six press photographers in Copenhagen. Today it has over 800 members. The National Press Photographers Association (NPPA) was founded in 1946 in the U.S., and has about 10,000 members.

Others around the world include the British Press Photographers Association (BPPA) founded in 1984, then relaunched in 2003, and now has around 450 members. Hong Kong Press Photographers Association (1989), Northern Ireland Press Photographers Association (2000), Pressfotografernas Klubb (Sweden, 1930), and PK—Pressefotografenes Klubb (Norway).

News organizations and journalism schools run many different awards for photojournalists. Since 1968, Pulitzer Prizes have been awarded for the following categories of photojournalism: 'Feature Photography', 'Spot News Photography.' Other awards are World Press Photo, Best of Photojournalism, and Pictures of the Year as well as the UK based The Press Photographer's Year.

Ethical and Legal Considerations

Photojournalism works within the same ethical approaches to objectivity that are applied by other journalists. What to shoot, how to frame and how to edit are constant considerations. Often, ethical conflicts can be mitigated or enhanced by the actions of a sub-editor or picture editor, who takes control of the images once they have been delivered to the news organization. The photojournalist often has no control as to how images are ultimately used. The emergence of digital photography offers whole new realms of opportunity for the manipulation, reproduction, and transmission of images. It has inevitably complicated many of the ethical issues involved.

The U.S. National Press Photographers Association, and other professional organizations, maintain codes of ethics to specify approaches to these issues. Major ethical issues are often inscribed with more or less success into law. Laws regarding photography can vary significantly from nation to nation. The legal situation is further complicated when one considers that photojournalism made in one country will often be published in many other countries.

The Impact of New Technologies

Smaller, lighter cameras greatly enhanced the role of the photojournalist. Since the 1960s, motor drives, electronic flash, auto-focus, better lenses and other camera enhancements have made picture taking easier. New digital cameras free photojournalists from the limitation of film roll length, as thousands of images can be stored on a single microdrive or memory card.

Content remains the most important element of photojournalism, but the ability to extend deadlines with rapid gathering and editing of images has brought significant changes. As recently as 15 years ago, nearly 30 minutes were needed to scan and transmit a single colour photograph from a remote location to a news office for printing. Now, equipped with a digital camera, a mobile phone and a laptop computer, a photojournalist can send a high-quality image in minutes, even seconds after an event occurs. Video phones and portable satellite links increasingly allow for the mobile transmission of images from almost any point on the earth. There is some concern by news photographers that the profession of photojournalism as it is known today could change to such a degree that it is unrecognizable as image-capturing technology naturally progresses. There is also concern that fewer print publications are commissioning serious photojournalism on timely issues.

Photojournalism in the Age of Scrutiny

A leading organization of visual journalists, the Society for News Design, has adopted a new ethics code, just as two new controversies emerged that questioned the integrity of photographic images.

Consider the landscape:

> Reporters who do their journalism with cameras now have at their disposal tools and techniques that provide them with more choices than ever in the ways they document and edit their images. Photographers who once had to abandon the scene of a story in order to process and print are now able to remain in the field as they file digitally direct from cameras or select, edit and transmit from their laptops. The resulting images are often distributed to audiences almost immediately via Website portals.

On the receiving end are news consumers far better equipped to evaluate the integrity of the photographs—both for accuracy and aesthetics—and to make themselves heard when they believe photojournalists and their news organizations have fallen short.

All of this has created an intense need for ethical standards and guidelines to help photographers measure up—and to provide a common understanding among journalists and viewers, readers and users about what constitutes fair and accurate visual reporting. We have had some great news on that front in recent weeks, along with some good news and some news that was not so good.

Let's start with the great news—the approval by SND of a set of standards that will help photojournalists address the issues raised by several recent controversies. As one of the drafters of the SND document, I'm especially anxious to see them put to use.

The first ethics code in SND's 27-year history aligns the organization with The National Press Photographers' Association in both groups' quest to raise the standards of ethical decision-making in the practice of visual journalism. Bill Gaspard, who coordinated the two-year development of the code, presented it to a luncheon crowd of more than 500 people during SND's recent national convention in Orlando. "I could not be more pleased with the efforts of this group," said Christine McNeal, deputy managing editor of *The Milwaukee Journal-Sentinel* and immediate past president of SND. "Our core group brought the discussion about these very critical topics to the journalism world. Now we must continue the discussion and help make this a reality. It is crucial."

Gaspard, who is deputy managing editor of *The Las Vegas Sun* and a former SND president, said he believes that "if you look into the language of the code you can find words that will guide you through any ethical situation that you face," and is joined in this effort by John Long, a veteran photojournalist who serves as picture editor for the *The Hartford Courant* and as ethics chair for NPPA. In an e-mail to Poynter Online, Long said: "We have to protect our integrity at all costs. The NPPA Code of Ethics and the new SND Code of Ethics show there is a thirst for integrity among visual journalists. We see our credibility, our integrity, our very existence as a profession threatened by today's ethical transgressions. These codes also show that we are in an age of transition and evolution in ethics.

"Our members want a 'Ten Commandments' set of rules, but that is not possible right now. As technology evolves, so do the ethics. Both codes try to address this. Both codes encourage their members to be as honest as they can be while being open to evolving conditions."

That progress on standards was accompanied by the two controversies—one involving *The New York Times*, the other, CBS News. The *Times* case centers on a photograph by accomplished staff photographer and former picture editor Jim Wilson. The photo shows soldiers in Iraq gazing upward at a member of the Purrfect Angelz dance group in Iraq. Suspicious critics of the photo, published on Page One of the Sunday, August 27 edition of the *Times*, questioned what happened to a microphone cord that appeared to disappear into thin air in the middle of the photo. Michele McNally, the *Times'* assistant managing editor for photography, characterized the controversy as more a reflection of the general questioning of photojournalism than as specific criticism aimed at the *Times*. "Ever since the most recent Reuters discovery (of altered photos of the Israeli-Hezbollah fighting) many people have taken it upon themselves to question the veracity of all images" she said in an e-mail to Poynter Online. "One should note, during this particular war, each side is continually trying to prove an 'agenda' in all media outlets. They call into question everything, every usage, balance. You cannot persuade either side that you have (no agenda) because to them, there is no other truth but their own." The *Times* has very clear guidelines in place that prohibit image manipulation without clear cause and disclosure.

Photography and Images

Images in our pages that purport to depict reality must be genuine in every way. No people or objects may be added, rearranged, reversed, distorted or removed from a scene (except for the recognized practice of cropping to omit extraneous outer portions). Adjustments of colour or gray scale should be limited to those minimally necessary for clear and accurate reproduction, analogous to the "burning" and "dodging" that formerly took place in darkroom processing of images. Pictures of news situations must not be posed. In the cases of collages, montages, portraits, fashion or home design illustrations, fanciful contrived situations and demonstrations of how a device is used, our intervention should be unmistakable to the reader, and unmistakably free of intent to deceive. Captions and credits should further acknowledge our intervention if the slightest doubt is possible. The design director, a masthead editor or the news desk should be consulted on doubtful cases or proposals for exceptions.

In an e-mail interview about the Iraq photo, Jim Wilson said that he could not believe that so many people believed there was some sort of conspiracy involved. He said he wanted to set the record straight: "The important thing to note is that this is a straight picture—there are no Photoshop tricks, manipulation or any other thing going on in this picture."

He said nothing was "removed from the image nor was anything enhanced." When asked to describe the circumstance of the coverage, here's how he responded:

> It was a terrible place to shoot and as you might well imagine, the Marines certainly did not want me standing anywhere that I might block their view of the action on stage. At one point, one of the Marines gave me a pretty hard time about standing on a chair at the edge of the stage. After the show was over, he lightened up and we had a decent conversation. He apologized and both of us departed with smiles on our faces. But at the time, it was a little tense. The dancer was standing still but moving the hand she held the microphone in as she spoke to the Marines. That's why that part of the cord is blurred. Some of the Marines were moving as well (you can see some blurred hands in the photo).

I shot the picture at ISO 800 at 1/6 sec f2.8. The cord was moving as the dancer held the microphone in her hand, moving it as she talked to the Marines. The blurred cord is in the photo (the sort of dark wavy line against the background). I used the one camera-mounted strobe (portable flash) I had with me in a cavernous room (it had 40-foot ceilings and was the size of a gym) lit only by a couple of flourescent lights—no stage lighting or anything like that existed. The stage was lit by the ambient light in the room. I shot five frames of that particular segment of the show.

McNally said she stands behind Wilson and the photograph, adding that "the Times relies on an art production team that prepares images for printing (and) scrutinizes pictures. If they see random pockets of odd pixilation, or other discrepancies as they enlarge the image, they will contact the desk."

The not-so-good news is brought to us by CBS's *Watch!* magazine—the miracle Katie Couric digital diet that reduced her neck and waistline digitally to make her look about 20 pounds lighter. In an interview with *USA Today*, Gil Schwartz who is the editor in chief of *Watch!* and a CBS news spokesperson confirmed, that an "overzealous" photo editor had improperly manipulated the photo and that "this is not something that is going to happen again." CBS said different standards govern the network's entertainment and news publicity operations and that Ms. Couric and CBS News management had no knowledge of the retouching.

Generally, news photography reflects high standards of accuracy and clarity to ensure integrity and trust with viewers and readers. When it comes to TV publicity photographs, on the other hand, digital corrections and alterations are commonplace. *Watch!* magazine has a reported circulation of 400,000, according to *USA Today*, and is distributed on American Airlines flights and at other national locations. Asked about such manipulation in an e-mail interview with Poynter Online, Mick Cochran, director of photography at *USA Today*, said: "Photojournalism has always been an art and a craft. The art is in a photographer's mental processes being translated into a visual image that is true and that can be understood by others. The craftsmanship is in the making of the image all the way through the final print.

"But now the final product is millions of pixels on a small screen. The print is gone once the image leaves the screen. So the craftsmanship will also disappear unless we leave time for the image to settle on the screen, be scrutinized for imperfections, and be made as accurate as it can be (not being reality). In the charged world of news photography, the time to do that is slipping away, both in the field and in the bureau." Photography always has—and should always continue to have—its creative dimension. In the end, the best way to maintain integrity is to provide skilled and thoughtful picture editors and other newsroom staff with the time they need to do their jobs. The good news here is the number of people in our communities and audiences who are really looking closely at pictures. With greater visibility—and respect for—the standards of photojournalism reflected in the new SND code, more of that audience will see how photographic techniques can be used to inform rather than deceive.

ETHICS AND TECHNIQUES OF PHOTOJOURNALISM

What is Photojournalism?

Photojournalism is a unique kind of journalism, wherein images tell a news story. Normally, photojournalism includes the use of frozen images, and commonly used for print in newspapers and magazines. In contrast, this type of journalism may take the form of video for broadcast news. The key goal of photojournalism is for the photojournalist to portray a story through snapshots. A shared problem amongst many writers is penning the right words to describe an incident or reaction. For example, a news writer reporting on a serious auto accident can use words like, "grave," or "mangle" to illustrate the wreck. Yet, words bring to mind limited emotions, and readers must rely on their imagination. On the other hand, photographs are compelling and convincing. What's more, images allow readers to grasp the printed or spoken word.

Distinguishing Photojournalism from other areas of Photography?

The use of images makes photojournalism distinct from other types of photography and journalism. News writers must rely on the written word to bring a story to life. This is a difficult craft, which generally entails the writer expanding their thinking and digging deep into their own emotions. Great journalism it capable of conveying a range of emotions—happiness, sadness, anger, and so forth. Unless a news writer connects with the story, he or she is unable to compose on an emotional level. Sometimes, this involves including a photo with the story. Other types of photography may use images as a simple means of capturing a moment or beautiful scenery. However, this type of photography lacks elements crucial to photojournalism. Three important aspects of photojournalism include:

1. *Timeliness or Relevance*: Images or photos are significant to a written story.
2. *Impartiality*: Depicted images are a non-discriminatory portrayal of actual events.
3. *Narrative Story*: Collective photographs and relevant news elements can effectively update and inform readers.

JOBS AND CAREERS IN PHOTOJOURNALISM

If you are planning to pursue a career in photojournalism, you should have keen interest in journalism. Photojournalists may work side by side with a reporter to decide which photograph will accompany with the news item.

There are many different structures of photo department management in a publication. A large newspaper or magazine may have a managing editor of photography and graphics that supervises a team of photo editors who work with the photographers, page designers and lab technicians.

The primary duty of the photojournalist is to take pictures. They are responsible for providing clear, easy-to-read, high quality, truthful images, that communicate a meaningful message to the readers of the publication they work for. Most newspapers also give the photographer other duties such as developing their film, editing film, scanning their pictures in the computer, adjusting the tone and colour of the pictures.

Salaries for photojournalists vary depending on the location, size and type of the publication, experience of the photographer.

Eligibility Criteria

In India there is no institution or university specifically offering degree or diploma course in photojournalism. The course is offered through different programmes of journalism and mass communication, art and craft, film and television and advanced information technologies. This education is recognized as professional education, usually referred to by different nomenclatures, viz., photo editing, layout and design, fundamentals of photography, electronic editing, advanced photography, digital imaging, fundamentals of digital technology, basic and advanced photojournalism, film editing, fundamental principles and practices on videography, moving and still photography, etc. depending on the emphasis on different aspects of photojournalism.

Graduates from any stream can join the above courses offered by various universities and media institutes. Almost all institutions and universities prefer to take the candidates through written and personality-test (interview) examinations due to limited seats.

- Institutions Offering Courses on Journalism and Photography.
- Amity School of Journalism and Communication, Saket, New Delhi.
- Amrit College, Railway Colony, Poojappura, Trivandrum.
- Asian College of Journalism, Kasturi Centre, 2-Anna Salai, Chennai.
- Bharatiya Vidhya Bhavan units at Trivandrum, Kottayam, Thrissur, Kochi, Kozhikode and other cities of India.
- Bhavan's Institute of Communication and Management, Andheri West, Mumbai.
- Bhavan's PDN College of Communication and Management, Somani College, Chowpatty, Mumbai.
- Biju Patnaik Film and Television Institute, Bhubaneswar.
- Centre for Convergence Media Studies (Kerala University), Senate House Campus, Trivandrum.
- Centre for Development of Imaging Technology, Chitranjali Studio Complex, Thiruvallom, Trivandrum.
- DCSMAT Media School, Kinfra Film and Video Park, Kazhakkoottam, Trivandrum.
- Film and Television Institute of India, Pune.
- Garware Institute of Career Education and Development, Vidyanagri, Kalina Campus, Santa Cruz (East) Mumbai.
- IILM Film and Media School, 3 Institutional Area, Lodhi Road, New Delhi.
- Indian Centre for Media and Communication, Agrasen Campus, S. No. 239/2, Yera-wada, Pune.
- Indian Institute of Mass Communication, Aruna Asaf Ali Marg, JNU Campus, New Delhi.
- Indian Television Training Institute, C-41, Gulmohar Park, New Delhi.
- Institute for Integrated Learning in Management, Lodhi Institutional Area, Lodhi Road, New Delhi.
- Jaipuria Institute, Lucknow and Noida.
- Manipal Institute of Communication, Old Tile Factory Road, Press Corner, Manipal.
- Mother Teresa Institute of Communication and E-journalism, TC 16/138 EVRA-29, Cotton Hill, Trivandrum.

- Pioneer Media School, 6, Toder Mal Lane, Bengali-Market, New Delhi.
- Ranade Institute, Fergusson College Road, Pune.
- School of Convergence, 208 A, Savitri Nagar, New Delhi.
- Satyajit Ray Film and Television Institute, EM Bypass Road, Kolkata.
- The Manorama School of Communication, P. B. No. 229, Kottayam.
- Rai Media Lab, B-II/58, MCIE, Mathura Road, New Delhi.
- School of Broadcasting and Communication, 108, Building 4, Kamdhenu Centre, Lokhandwala Complex, Andheri (West), Mumbai.
- School of Communication and Management Studies, Management House, South Kalamassery, Kochi.
- Sri Aurobindo Institute of Mass Communication, Sri Aurobindo Marg, Near IIT, New Delhi.
- St. Xavier's Institute of Communication, St. Xavier's College, Mumbai.
- Times Centre for Media Studies, 10-Daryaganj, New Delhi.
- National Institute of Social Communications, Research and Training, A-2, Sector-1, Vaishali, Ghaziabad, Uttar Pradesh.
- Symbiosis Institute of Communication, Pune.
- YMCA, Jai Singh Road, New Delhi.

DIGITAL PHOTOJOURNALISM

This workshop is for the practicing photojournalist who has been shooting professionally for sometime, currently using a digital camera. You must have the required knowledge of computers and should have worked with Adobe Photoshop to some extent. The course is designed to help the professional photographer make optimum use of digital technology to capture 'decisive moments.'

Teaching Methodology

The workshop will be conducted at the Light and Life Academy, Digital Studio. The faculty will have slide shows and demos and take participants through a step-by-step process in various areas. You will have to work on specific assignments and critique sessions will be conducted on a daily basis.

What to Bring

Digital SLR camera and lenses, portable flash like the Vivitar 285, Compact Flash cards. A laptop with photoshop loaded, will be useful (but optional). Cold weather clothing.

Enrollment

You should be a practising photojournalist and must be working with a Digital SLR Camera. To enroll for this workshop, please download the application form, fill in the relevant details and send it to the Academy with the fees by way of a Demand Draft favouring Light and Life Academy, payable in Ooty.

MERGER OF PHOTOJOURNALISM AND ETHICS: ISSUES AND OPTIONS

Civilization is a stream with banks. The stream is sometimes filled, with blood from people killing, stealing, shouting and doing things historians usually record, while on the banks, unnoticed, people build homes, make love, raise children, sing songs, write poetry. The story of civilization is the story of what happened on the banks....

—*Will Durant*

In a fitting tribute to the power and prevalence of photojournalism images, *Time* magazine recently produced the first issue in its history on a single topic with a single advertiser. Measured from the dual technological achievements announced in 1839 of Louis Daguerre's daguerreotype and Henry Talbot's calotype, the 150th year of photography has been celebrated throughout the world with gallery exhibitions and feature articles in all manner of media

Life magazine, a publication responsible for photojournalism's rise in respect, published an anniversary issue titled, "150 Years of Photography: Pictures that Made a Difference." *American Photographer*, a magazine that regularly features works by newspaper and magazine photojournalists, devoted its cover and over 30 pages to the subject of photojournalism. Marianne Fulton, associate curator of photographic collections at the International Museum of Photography at the George Eastman House in Rochester, New York, was the editor of a well-researched and richly illustrated book on photojournalism, *Eyes of Time: Photojournalism in America.*

Jim Dooley, photography editor and chief for the Long Island newspaper, *Newsday*, remarked that "newspaper photojournalism is in its heyday. It's going through a tremendous renewal." Professor of Photojournalism at the University of Missouri, Bill Kuykendall, also feels that there is now a photojournalism renaissance. "I think there has been a rebirth," said Kuykendall, "of interest in candid ... photojournalism." Just as discussions of photojournalism have received an abundance of media treatment, professional ethics has also received widespread attention in magazines, books and from experts in the field.

Ethical issues are hot topics in today's media-conscious society. Questions currently debated in formats that vary from newspaper articles to public forums broadcast on public television stations include: Is insider trading a result of greedy individuals or does it foretell a problem with the entire system of business? Are the temptations from profit motives too great for government employees to manage without outside monitoring? Should the organs from aborted fetusses be used for medical purposes? Does the media concentrate too much on scandals or other sensational events and miss the underlying issues that may be ultimately more important?

Icons with Ethical Problems

When photojournalism and ethics are combined as a topic for discussion, *Time* magazine's, "150 Years of Photojournalism" issue should be analyzed in a more critical manner. After consulting with experts in the field, the editors of the photojournalism issue reproduced in the introduction, "The Ten Greatest Images of Photojournalism." "There are hundreds of unforgettable news pictures," the subhead explains. "Some record great events, others the small but resonant ones. In our view these ten-images of war and peace, love and hate, poverty and triumph—are the ones indelibly pressed upon the mind and heart."

Ironically, 8 of the 10 photographs have ethical problems associated with them or the photographer. Another "unforgettable news picture" is made more unforgettable through computer digital manipulation. Civil War photographer

Alexander Gardner moved a corpse to illustrate, in separate images, a Union and a Confederate soldier. Robert Capa and Joe Rosenthal were accused of stage managing their famous photographs. Dorothea Lange and Alfred Eisenstaedt were criticized by their subjects for not paying them for their famous poses. The pictures of Bob Jackson and Eddie Adams were considered too gruesome by many members of the general public. Gene Smith regularly posed his subjects and manipulated his prints with a variety of techniques that included double printing. And finally, in a demonstration of the manipulative potential of computer technology, a photograph of the solitary moonscape portrait of Edwin Aldrin by fellow astronaut Neil Armstrong is transformed at the end of the issue to an invasion of the moon by a platoon of moon-walkers.

There is no doubt that for older Americans, the 10 images are among the strongest and most visually memorable icons of the 20th century. A committee from Britain or France might not have seven American related images. A group of younger students of photography might include photographs more recent than 1971. Another panel might not have five pictures that are war-related, a portrait of a destitute family, an international disaster, a political assassination and a mercury deformed child.

Ethical arguments are usually not satisfying. There is no clear winner or loser when perspective guides a determination. But there must be some way to defend your action to a reader who does not share your personal perspective. Writers and photographers for newspapers follow the same ethical principle of truthfulness outlined in ethics codes. Journalists would view as unethical a reporter who fabricated quotations. Likewise, a photographer who uses darkroom tricks to make a false image would probably be fired. The principle of truthfulness is easily defended by both writers and photographers.

It is Hard to Hide a Camera

Ethical worlds often collide, however, because of the fundamental techniques the two reporters use to gather information. During a controversial news event, when a father grieves visibly over the loss of a drowned child, a writer can stay behind the scenes with pen and paper hidden. Facts are gathered quietly and anonymously. A photographer is tied to a machine that must be out in the open and obvious to all who are present. A videographer during the 1967 riots in Newark, New Jersey said, 11 a newspaper guy can huddle in a doorway or get it over the phone. But we've got to be in it to get it."

Long lenses or hidden camera techniques can be used, but the results are usually unsatisfactory. Focus, exposure, and composition problems are increased with the use of telephoto lenses or hiding a camera. Besides being on ethically shaky ground, the use of hidden cameras is illegal in Delaware, Georgia, Hawaii, Maine, Michigan, New Hampshire, South Dakota, and Utah. The photographer, unlike the hidden writer, can be the target of policemen, family members, and onlookers who vent their anger and grief on the one with the camera. No call to journalistic principles of truthfulness will convince a mob not to attack a photographer in such an emotionally charged situation.

Because photographers must be out in the open to take pictures, the photographer's ethical orientation must be more clearly defined than with writers who can report over the telephone. A photographer must have a clear reason why an image of a grieving parent is necessary.

Photojournalism as a Profession

Although photojournalism is filled with many dark moments, the history of the field is also rich with pride and professionalism. Cliff Edom, one of the most well respected photojournalism educators in the country, credited Frank Mott, dean of the Journalism School at the University of Missouri, with inventing the term, photojournalism. In 1942, Mott helped establish a separate academic sequence for photojournalism instruction. For the first time, photojournalism was considered "as important to the field of communication" as its word equivalent.

In 1946, Joseph Costa, staff photographer for the *New York Daily News*, was elected president of the first national organization for newspaper photographers, the National Press Photographers Association (NPPA). *Editor and Publisher* magazine at the time wrote that the aim of the new organization was "to combine all elements of the working photographic press in America to raise and maintain the high levels of photography necessary to the advancement of pictorial journalism." Shortly thereafter, the first issue of *News Photographer*, the official publication of the NPPA, was printed. Academic standing, professional membership, and literature unique to the organization are fundamental criteria for the definition of a professional group. Since the early days of the NPPA, members of the photojournalism profession have seen academic sequences begun at universities across the country. NPPA membership has grown from a handful at their first meeting in Atlantic City to more than 9,000. *News Photographer* magazine has grown in coverage and stature to become one of the leading trade publications in the business.

Another standard of professionalism is the amount of self-criticism that occurs within the organization for the betterment of its members. From the first issue of *News Photographer*, articles have been written, not simply to introduce technical advances, but to critically examine the ethical behaviour of press photographers. From relations with the police to the coverage of tragic events, ethical issues get a fair hearing within the pages of *News Photographer*.

Reactions to controversial issues are a result of the underlying principles that guide a person. Many times photographers and the general public are on opposite sides of a philosophical wall. As part of the journalism community, photographers see their role as providing readers with a record of each day's events. The community at large is benefitted. That mission often leads to the taking and printing of disturbing, graphically violent images. Such an underlying philosophy at work for journalists could be interpreted as a form of utilitarianism. Many members of the general public, however, are disturbed by such images. Readers often complain that they either do not wish to see such gruesome photographs in their morning newspaper or are concerned that the pictures will contribute to the grief of the victim's family and friends. The underlying philosophy for those letter writers is most probably the Golden Rule. It is important to understand that the two conflicting philosophies have long been debated by philosophers without a satisfactory resolution. Emotional issues find little room for compromise. Again, a person's perspective guides a response to a controversial photograph.

The main concern of this textbook, the workbook, and the computer programme is to help you learn your own ethical perspective. Such an insight will help you understand the various perspectives in use by photojournalists, their editors, their subjects, and their readers. As photojournalism heads into the next sesquicentennial, the ethical principles photographers rely on, as never before, will be challenged. It is vitally important, as you start your career, that you consider being an ethical photojournalist. The photojournalism profession demands nothing less.

Photojournalism Ethics Timeless Issues

Photojournalism—the profession in which journalists make news-editorial images for print and screen (television and computer) media—is under attack.

Media critics and viewers question the use of gruesome images, dozens of photographers hounding celebrities, picture manipulations that present misleading views, visual messages that perpetuate negative stereotypes of individuals from various multicultural groups, and images that blur the distinction between advertising and journalism. What is happening? Nothing that hasn't been a part of photography since its invention in 1839. What is new, however, is the spread of computer technology that allows practically anyone to produce and disseminate visual messages in massive numbers for a world-wide audience.

Because images evoke almost immediate emotional responses among viewers, pictures have tremendous impact. With well-chosen words, visual messages combine to educate, entertain and persuade. But the flip side to such visual power is that images can also offend, shock, mislead, stereotype and confuse.

Consider some recent examples: Violent reports from a Miami television station, reporters camped out in front of O.J. Simpson's mansion, Olympic skaters and rivals Tonya Harding and Nancy Kerrigan digitally altered to look like best friends, an African-American cast as a Los Angeles rioter and a victim of AIDS used in an advertisement to sell sweaters. The stories featured above can be classified into five ethical concerns of most interest to photojournalism professionals: Victims of violence, right to privacy, picture manipulations, stereotyping and advertising/editorial blurring.

Victims of Violence

After a gruesome image of dead or grieving victims of a tragic event is presented to the public in either the print or screen media, many viewers are often repulsed and offended by the picture. Nevertheless, violence and tragedy are staples of American journalism. "If it bleeds, it leads" is a popular, unspoken sentiment in many newsrooms. The reason for this obvious incongruity is that a majority of viewers are attracted and intrigued by such stories. Photojournalists who win Pulitzer Prizes and other international competitions are almost always witness to excruciatingly painful human tragedies that nevertheless get published or broadcast. It is as if viewers want to see violent pictures, but through gaps in the fingers in front of their face.

When television station WSVN, Channel 7, in Miami lost its affiliation with NBC, it joined the FOX network and had to quickly generate high ratings in order to survive. In order to appeal to a younger audience, the station started specializing in gory crime news. The programming change was described as "a continuous barrage of the body bags on the street and the blood coming out of them." The content of the nightly news cast was so upsetting that nine area hotels banned the station from its television sets, lest out-of-town guests get the wrong impression about Miami (which backwards reads "I maim.") Complaints about hotel censorship from station executives were framed within a utilitarian context. As one television spokesperson said, "To mask crime stories would not be fair to the viewers." But to be honest, both sides presented hedonistic arguments based on a fear of lost revenue due to a decline in tourism or a decline in viewers.

Editors need to be sure that images of murder or automobile victims are really necessary to tell the story. Journalists often cite the reason for using such visual messages as a way to warn others of the dangers of modern living or to urge drivers to watch the speed limit. Another, perhaps more honest reason, is to avoid being scooped by a rival media organization. Despite well-rehearsed explanations, sensational images of victims of violence are shown as much for economic as utilitarian reasons. The media concentration on criminal activity creates an exaggerated perception of crime in the minds of viewers. Rather than focusing on bloody body bags, journalists need to explain the underlying social forces that cause such tragic events to occur.

Right to Privacy

Privacy concerns are almost always voiced by ordinary citizens or celebrities who are suddenly thrust in front of the unblinking lens of a camera because of connection to some sensational news story. Seldom do you hear viewers complain about violating someone else's right to privacy. Courts in America have consistently maintained that privacy rights differ between private and public persons. Private citizens have much more strictly enforced rights to their own privacy than celebrities who often ask for media attention. Not surprisingly, celebrities bitterly complain when they are the subject of relentless media attention because of some controversial allegation.

O. J. Simpson ran from defensive football players for teams in California and New York and over airport obstacles in Hertz car rental commercials. But when his mostly hidden violent personality was tragically revealed, he couldn't run from the media. With video cameras set in front of Simpson's mansion and in helicopters following his bizarre travels throughout Southern California freeways, news personnel were able to broadcast live his every move to a world-wide audience.

Critics were divided on the media's obsession with the sensational double murder case. But the attention is easily explained. The story involved one of the most hard-fought and fragile entities of any society—the celebrity. O. J. Simpson was beloved and respected by countless fans around the world. His fall from grace is at once shocking and extremely interesting. Such a story simply has to be covered. And part of that coverage involves the key and secondary characters that are caught in the media's story-telling web. When a news story is so compelling as to draw world-wide attention, a person—whether celebrity or neighbour—has a legal right to privacy that is defined by the height of the fence outside their house. For private or public citizens, perhaps the most stressful news story is the funeral of a loved one. A guiding principle for journalists in deciding to cover such a story is whether the event is newsworthy. Newsworthiness is not determined by the number of cameras pointed through the gate at the cemetery, but a concept with roots to unemotional, objective and reasoned journalism principles. In 1946, the Hutchins Commission came out with a definition of news that still applies today: A truthful, comprehensive, and intelligent account of the day's events in a context which gives them meaning. Unfortunately, media officials under pressure from circulation or rating figures make decisions that sensationalize rather than explain complex stories of interest to the public. Live pictures for the nightly newscast of a speculating reporter in front of a brightly lit brick mansion increase the charge of sensational coverage by critics. In an ideal world, journalists tell stories in words and pictures that explain rather than cause a viewer to ask more questions.

Picture Manipulations

Picture and subject manipulations have been a part of photography since it was first invented. But because of computer technology, digital manipulations are relatively easy to accomplish, hard to detect and perhaps more alarming, alter the original image so that checking the authenticity of the picture is impossible. Some critics have predicted that in a few years, images—whether still or moving—will not be allowed in trials as physical evidence because of the threat to their veracity created by digital alterations.

Tonya and Nancy. Who can (or would love to) forget the Harding v. Kerrigan soap opera that nearly froze the 1994 Winter Olympic games? In the dead of winter, editors at New York Newsday published a slick cover picture of the two cold-faced skaters under a large headline, "Fire on Ice" and above a confusing subhead, "Tonya, Nancy To Meet At Practice." But the colour photograph showed the two skating next to each other. Didn't they meet when the picture was taken? The obvious answer (at least in this context) is that the picture was a lie—it was a composite of two different images manipulated with a computer.

Newspaper editors across the country published a condemnation of the computer technique. How dare Newsday use an altered photo for a news event? But lost in the criticism is the fact that the editors for the publication did everything they were suppose to do when turning a news picture into an illustration. For also on the cover in bold, black, sans serif type is the cutline for the image:

- Tonya Harding, left, and Nancy Kerrigan appear to skate together in this New York Newsday composite illustration. Tomorrow, they'll take to the ice together.

- In addition, a byline beside the picture identified the photographers of the separate images.
- So what's the problem? Why was there so much criticism from fellow journalists? The answer is that admitting to a lie doesn't make the lie acceptable.
- Cameras and the images they produce are naively thought by many to never lie. But because humans operate the machine, technical, composition and content manipulations are unavoidable. Computer technology did not start the decline in the credibility of pictures, but it has hastened it. Photographic darkrooms are quickly being replaced by computer workstation lightrooms. But as long as photojournalists do not subtract or add parts of a picture's internal elements, almost any other manipulation once accomplished in a photographic darkroom is considered ethical for news-editorial purposes.

Two factors may guard against a further erosion of credibility in visual messages: Reputation of the media organization that publishes or broadcasts images and the words that accompany the manipulated picture.

Credibility is not an inherent quality of a particular picture, but a concept based on tradition, story choices, design considerations and reader perception of the company or individual that produces the image. Reputation is what separates the difference in picture credibility between The New York Times, *the* National Enquirer, *"CBS Evening News," or "Hard Copy."*

Words are also vital in assuring the credibility of a news organization and a picture. If a photojournalist or art director is tempted to combine parts from two separate pictures to create a third picture, the reader needs to know that such an action has taken place. The cutline for the image should include the details of the manipulation while the image itself should be labeled an illustration—not a news-editorial picture. Such an addition would at least solve one aspect of the ethical problem—letting the reader know of the illustrative technique.

However, a larger question remains: In this age of digital manipulation and desktop publishing, why do computer operators feel the need to turn news-editorial photographs into illustrations? Journalism professionals need to face the issue of photojournalism images being replaced by illustrations and not concern themselves so much with the tool that makes that ethical problem topical.

Stereotyping

African Americans are criminals. Latinos are gang members. Native Americans are alcoholics. Wheelchair-bound individuals are helpless. Gays are effeminate. Lesbians wear their hair short. Older adults need constant care. Anglos from the Southern states are rednecks. Homeless people are drug addicts. These prevalent stereotypes are perpetuated by images presented in the media. Stereotypical portrayals of ethnic, gender, physical characteristic, sexual preference and job-related cultural groups are a result of journalism professionals being lazy, ignorant or racist. As with the printing term from which the word comes, to stereotype is a short-hand way to describe a person with collective, rather than unique characteristics. It is easier and quicker for a photojournalist to take a picture of an angry African American during a riot than to take the time to explore in words and pictures the underlying social problems that are responsible for the civil disturbance. Critics complain that at best ignorance and at worse racism is the reason stereotypes persist. Racism may explain why mainstream media are slow to cover human catastrophes in remote sections of the world such as in Rwanda, Somalia and South-Central.

On April 29, 1992, four LAPD police officers were acquitted by an all-Anglo jury of unnecessarily beating Rodney King the year before. The surprising verdict sparked an orgy of violence, vandalism and looting never before seen in American history. More than 50 lives were lost, over a billion dollars in property damage was reported and hundreds of persons were arrested. On the cover of Newsweek magazine, readers were afforded a close-up picture of a young, angry African American man wearing a turned-around baseball cap and yelling while in front of a building engulfed in flames. Although dramatic, the colour picture illustrates a problem with the media: African Americans are more often than not shown as criminals to be feared. Research studies have shown that magazines and newspapers publish few photographs of African Americans, but when editors do select pictures that include African Americans, they are almost always concerned with crime, sports or entertainment. In fact, most people from diverse cultures are shown as their stereotype and not as ordinary people with everyday hopes and concerns.

Many readers form their opinions about individuals from cultural groups from the pictures they see in the media. Editors should make an assessment of the pictorial coverage of under-represented groups for their own newspaper or television station. If biases are found, photographers, reporters and editors should attend sensitivity training workshops in order to promote more fair and balanced images. For example, to break the stereotypical sports coverage of African Americans, show athletes with interests other than sports. And to avoid reporting errors or omissions, have culturally diverse avoid news-editorial staffs with experts knowledgeable about local and foreign issues and events.

Advertising/Editorial

Blurring

With names such as "advertorials" and "infomercials," advertisers mimic the production cues of print and screen journalists to persuade an unsuspecting viewer to purchase a product. With full-page ads in newspapers and magazines that resemble news-editorial pages and 30-minute commercials that look like talk shows, corporate executives rely on the credibility of the media to fool its audience of trusting viewers. Most consumers of the media can easily tell the difference between an advertisement and a news story. But sometimes the distinction is so subtle, only highly observant readers can tell the difference.

In 1992, the Benetton clothing company was criticized so severely for using news pictures in their print advertisements that the campaign was ended. One startling image—AIDS victim David Kirby on his deathbed surrounded by his grieving family—produced a firestorm of media attention. AIDS activists denounced the use of a family's tragedy to sell sweaters. Media critics were alarmed that the photograph spread across two pages in a magazine appeared at first glance to be a news-editorial image. An unsuspecting magazine reader is briefly fooled into noticing the powerful visual message because of the perception that the picture is a part of a news story. Once the green Benetton logo and "800" catalog ordering telephone number where a clothes catalogue can be ordered is noticed, it is too late. Advertising and journalism have been intentionally fused into the advertorial. From that moment on, the reader may be skeptical of all the rest of the pictures and stories in the magazine. Credibility—a priceless commodity—is reduced.

With the case of the Newsday cover of Tonya and Nancy, the decision to manipulate the cover image was not made solely for an illustrative reason—in a highly competitive, mostly street-sales environment, an eye-catching cover picture acts as an advertisement for the publication. If journalism professionals concede the cover or top half of a magazine or newspaper as belonging to the realm of advertising rather than news-editorial content, there will no longer be credibility for any other story, quotation or image within the pages of the publication.

Conclusion

In a rare exhibition of photo editing agreement, Newsweek and Time magazines presented a police mug shot picture of O.J. Simpson the same week on their covers. But the reaction from the public and media critics was vastly different. The controversial covers link all of the issues discussed above. Although the Newsweek cover image was altered (the top of the picture around his head was removed) to create a 3-dimensional, sensational effect, editors at Time were severely criticized for printing an artistic interpretation of the police picture in which O.J.'s features were blurred and darkened by computer manipulation. Typical of the response was NAACP's Benjamin Chavis who said the image made Simpson look more sinister, guilty and as "some kind of animal." Although labeled on the contents page as a "Photo-Illustration," the practice of turning objective photographs into interpretive works of art is considered unethical by many in the profession. The artist did not intentionally darken the photograph for racist reasons, but editors should have been aware that many readers would come to that conclusion.

Photography is undergoing an exciting and challenging time in its history. Currently, the photographic medium is in a hybrid or transitional period between traditional film and computer technologies. It is reasonable to predict that by the first decade of the next century, photojournalists will no longer use film in their cameras or developer in their trays. Print and screen media will also dramatically change as households are linked with fiber optic technology. Newspapers and televisions will be transformed into a medium that combines the best attributes of the printed page, telephone, television and computer. These stand-alone and portable teleputers (as some have called the new machine) will transform passive readers and viewers into active users with instantaneous links to text and images from sources anywhere in the world.

But no matter how the tools of journalism change, fundamental ethical concerns still apply. Displaying violent, sensational images for economic reasons, violating a person's privacy before the judicial process can function, manipulating news-editorial pictures to alter their content, stereotyping individuals into pre-conceived categories and blurring the distinction between advertising and editorial messages were journalism concerns in 1895, are important topics in 1995 and will be carefully considered issues, no doubt, in 2095. Professionals, academics and students owe it to their readers to be sensitive to unethical practices that demean the profession and reduce the credibility of journalism.

Therefore, it is imperative that whenever and wherever possible, ethical issues be discussed by all those concerned about the journalism profession.

FAKING IMAGES IN PHOTOJOURNALISM

That the camera cannot lie is true only in the sense that the images it captures must have existed in one form or another at some particular time. But it is not always clear if those images have been manipulated in some way to alter or to stage an event which never happened. We are familiar with historical photos that have been retouched to include or exclude political figures. We are less familiar with the potential of new technologies for falsifying images, particularly those that appear in newspapers and magazines. The following article introduces this topic and raises important ethical questions.

There were the huge printing shops with their sub-editors, their typography experts, and their elaborately equipped studios for the faking of photographs.

Photojournalism, photography that accompanies stories intended for newspaper and magazine readers, has a long and cherished tradition of truthfulness. The faking of photographs, either through stage direction by the photographer or through darkroom manipulation, unfortunately, also has a long tradition. As a result, Pulitzer Prize-winning images, photographs that have moved people to action, and pictures that have been hailed as beautiful humanistic documents filled with hope mud joy, have been questioned. Consequently, their impact has been diminished by charges of photographic faking. Such accusations are usually easily proven unsubstantiated and are the exception rather than the rule for photojournalism images. However, computer technology puts photographic faking on a new level of concern as images can be digitized and manipulated without the slightest indication of such trickery.

Early photographic history is filled with artists turned photographers who set-up situations with models and backdrops and made elaborate compositions from several negatives. In 1857 Oscar Gustave Rejlander produced a picture with a documentary quality, "Street urchins tossing chestnuts." The photograph showed a child who looked up at a chestnut suspended in the air. Stopping a moving object in mid-air was a technical feat impossible with the slow film and lenses in use at that time. Rejlander produced the effect through the use of a fine thread. In that same year, he also made the controversial "The Two Ways of Life," an elaborate story of a young man's decision to follow the good or evil way of life. Thirty separate negatives were combined to produce the single image.

Later, Rejlander denounced the process in a letter to H. P. Robinson, another early photographer known for his composite photographs. Rejlander wrote, "I am tired of photography-for-the-public, particularly composite photos, for there call be no gain and there is no honour only cavil and misrepresentation."

A curious and little mentioned photographic genre, spirit photography, had its beginning a decade later. Spirit photography, capturing on film a likeness of a deceased person, was proven through photographic experts as double exposure fakes. Nevertheless, many people, including Sir Arthur Conan Doyle, a strong advocate for the Spiritualism movement, believed in the truthfulness of the images. During World War I, many photographs were faked for propaganda purposes. For example, newspapers showed faked photographs of Kaiser Wilhelm cutting off the hands of babies. April Fool photographic fakes were popular in newspapers during the first half of this century. Curtis MacDougall in his book, *Hoaxes*, details several instances where newspapers published such images as giant sea creatures, Viking ships, and a man flying by his own lung power. The Madison, *Wisconsin Capital-Times* went so far as to publish a photographic composite of the Capitol dome collapsing in 1933. More serious fakes involved political campaigns. A 1928 campaign picture of Herbert Hoover and his running mate was faked because Hoover refused to pose with the vice-presidential candidate, Charles Curtis. *Life* magazine revealed a composite photograph of a Maryland Democrat running for office that looked like he was conferring with a Communist leaflet. He lost the election.

Three Famous photographs perhaps most troubling to the reputation of photojournalists and their photographs are reports that well-known and deeply moving photographs have been directed by the photographers. Three famous photographs, Robert Capa's moment of death of a Republican soldier during the Spanish Civil War, Arthur Rothstein's skull on parched South Dakota land, and Joe Rosenthal's raising of the American flag over Iwo Jima, have all been reported to be photographic fakes. Based on misunderstanding or professional jealousy, these three historical images reproduced more times than probably any other photographs, have a cloud of uncertainty that surrounds each photographer's reputation.

Published in *Life* magazine in 1937, Robert Capa's photograph shows in one instant the suddenness and loneliness of an anonymous soldier's death. It has been suggested that the photograph was either a chance occurrence by the photographer shooting blindly, or it was staged for the benefit of the camera.

Capa, whose motto was, "If your pictures aren't good you aren't close enough," would have been dismissed as a "one-shot wonder" had the "moment of death" photograph been the only image in this portfolio. However, Capa produced extraordinary war-time documents throughout his career. He photographed in China, on the beaches of Normandy, in Israel, and finally in Vietnam, where he was killed by a land mine. Capa consistently produced images with strong emotional impact and high technical expertise. He was not a photographer who needed to fake a photograph in order to enhance his career.

Arthur Rothstein, a documentary photographer for the Farm Security Administration during the American Dust Bowl era, was accused of photographic faking because he moved a skull he found on parched South Dakota pasture land ten feet. The skull was labeled a prop by Republican politicians who used the Rothstein pictures to attack the credibility of the Democratic administration. The Democrats, it was argued, were using photographs to make environmental conditions look worse than they actually were in order to pass controversial legislation through Congress. Rothstein was accused of traveling around the country with his suitcase, his camera, and his skull. He denied the charge and regretted the controversy for the rest of his career.

Rothstein produced several memorable photographic documents including the classic Dust Bowl photograph of a father walking through a storm with his two young sons. He received more than 50 photography awards and has written several books on the subject of photojournalism and documentary photography. Given such a reputation, it is difficult to imagine him packing a skull with his clothes and cameras.

Associated Press photographer, Joe Rosenthal, made three photographs a top Suribachi, a Japanese observation post on the island of Iwo Jima during World War II. His first picture became the most reproduced photograph in history and won for him a Pulitzer Prize. His third photograph became the source of accusations that the first picture had been set-up. The first picture is the image most remembered. It shows six soldiers erecting a large, American flag on a long, diagonally slanted flagpole. Rosenthal's third shot shows 18 soldiers smiling and waving for the camera under that same flag.

The confusion over the authenticity of the famous photograph resulted from Rosenthal's casual response to a correspondent back at Guam. The reporter congratulated Rosenthal on the image and then asked if it was posed. Thinking that the writer meant the third picture, Rosenthal admitted that it had been set-up. Speaking of the famous picture, he rightly argues that "Had I posed the shot, I would, of course, have ruined it. I would ... have made them turn their heads so that they could be identified for AP members throughout the country." Writing of the Rosenthal image, picture editor, Harold Evans in his book *Pictures on a Page,* notes that "no genius could have posed the picture if he had spent a year in a studio with lights and a wind machine." Lucky for photojournalism, Rosenthal did not carry a wind machine to the top of Iwo Jima.

Technological Threat to Integrity

There is currently a serious threat to the integrity of photojournalism images. Computer technology allows individuals to manipulate photographs to such an extent that alterations cannot be detected. As has been stated, such sleight-of-hand is not new. Those who believed in the Spiritualism movement believed in the photographs as well. Those who were unsophisticated as to the double exposure and composite tricks that could be accomplished by a darkroom technician were fooled by the April Fool and political photographs. Those who are cynical and perhaps professionally envious believe that Capa convinced a buddy to act as if he were being killed by a bullet in the head, Rothstein carried a skull in his suitcase, and Rosenthal directed the flag-raising photograph.

Computerized digital retouching involves more than suspicions about a photograph's authenticity. Companies such as Scitex, Hell Graphic Systems, and Crosfield have computers that can be used by newspaper, magazine, and book publishers to manipulate photographs that were originally intended to be classic, documentary accounts of real events.

The *A Day in the Life* books of America, Australia, and Canada have cover photographs that were manipulated by the computer. Likewise, the unsuccessful *Picture Week* magazine fused two different photographs in tabloid magazine style of Nancy Reagan and Raisa Gorbachev to portray a misleading attitude of friendliness. *National Geographic* magazine, long known for its reputation of photojournalism excellence, used the Scitex computer digitizer on two recent occasions. On a cover story of Egypt, pyramids were squeezed together to fit the cover's vertical format. A picture story on Poland contained a cover photograph that combined an expression on a man's face in one frame with a complete view of his hat in another picture. Both cover images were altered without a hint of possible detection and without a note to readers that such manipulation was performed.

Throughout photography's history, an unsuspecting public has been fooled by manipulated images. What is of concern to modern media watchers is the justifications used to alter images through computer technology—not tile fact that such alterations can be published without detection.

Rick Smolan, a producer of the *Day in the Life* books defends his use of the computer to alter the cover photographs. "We are very proud of the fact that we were able to use this technology to make the covers more dramatic and more impressive," Smolan said. Likewise, Rich Clarkson, director of photography at *National Geographic* when the pyramid and Poland covers; were faked, said he had no ethical problem with combining two photographs into a single cover picture, although "some publications could start abusing." Many journalists disagree with the practice. Jack Corn, director of photography for the *Chicago Tribune* says that such manipulation is "ethically, morally and journalistically horrible." Robert Gilka, former director of photography at *National Geographic* magazine says simply that significantly manipulating images is "like limited nuclear warfare. There arn't none."

Photographs, particularly those used as accurate and trustworthy accounts of a significant event by respected publications, are our best hedge against the threat of devious editors and special interest groups who want to change truth and history. If the manipulation of photographs is accepted for any image, the public will naturally doubt all photographs and text within all publications.

Before computers were popular, the famous photojournalist, W. Eugene Smith said, "Let truth be the prejudice." Truth is the guiding principle—not layout efficiency, not magazine cover eye-catching ability, not political persuasion, but truth. When truth is the prejudice, photographs, and the stories behind them, can be easily defended and are a source for humanistic concern and inspirations.

ROLE OF PHOTOJOURNALISM IN EDUCATION OF MASS COMMUNICATION

Julie Newton during Thursday's presentation made me think about the significance of the phrase she used to describe journalists with a camera. They're now called visual journalists. When I was a shooter (an awful term if ever there was) for the *Times-Picayune* in the 1970s and someone asked me what I did for a living, I would answer that I am a photographer for the newspaper. Ten years later we all started calling ourselves photojournalists. I resisted at first because it was a mouthful and it sounded haughty (and you still see the word hyphenated—an indication of the profession's schizophrenic nature. Another example is the name of the major organization for photojournalists—we are called news photographers). But big changes are afoot and Julie is ahead of us in using the term, visual reporter. But I see a lot of confusion in the photojournalism field as we shift from photojournalists to visual journalists.

Darkrooms will be eliminated. Darkrooms with their mysterious lighting, fixer smells, rushing water, and magical acts, will be eliminated. Consequently, that special place where we all initially fell in love with this marvelous medium will be manipulated—the lights will be turned on, the walls will be cleaned of odors, the plumbing will be removed, and the enlargers will be replaced with networked computer workstations where visual journalists will complete magical acts.

The reason I know this will happen is simple—only a photo student can use an enlarger—but anyone, everyone can use a computer. And not only is that concept positive and necessary to accept, it is inevitable because of economic, professional, technological, and sociological forces at work even as we speak.

Most newspapers made this switch five years ago. An immediate result, and discussed regularly on the NPPA listserve, is the relationship between the visual reporter, editor, and writer. There are indications that this shift in technology, because it increases the visibility of visual journalists in the newsroom, will lead to photographers giving assignments to writers. (Imagine a world where a visual reporter works on a story for a month and the writer has three hours to complete the piece).

And yet that shift leads to conflict because visual journalists—as professionals and students—are stereotyped by writers, editors, students and faculty members as journalists with their brains knocked out. The reason for the stereotype is because traditional photojournalism courses, textbooks, and magazine and newspaper photo departments stress camera operations, assignment completion, and printing issues—and not visual literacy, research and writing, political assertiveness, cultural and critical meaning, ethical and moral responsibilities, and sociological and psychological factors. When darkrooms are eliminated, photojournalists lose their hiding places and join the newsroom or the student computer lab. The technical first approach to photojournalism practice and education is exposed to the light and becomes subject to the criticism of hypocritical journalists and faculty members. It is important to consider that university photo departments, programmes, or sequences are not being eliminated solely because of budget cut-backs. Photo sequences are eliminated when photojournalism faculty members do not make the shift in their classes to visual reporting and the number of students in the programme declines to an unacceptable figure. It then becomes easy to select photojournalism as a target because chairs and deans don't ever get the message that photojournalism is more than using an eye and a finger.

A clue to a solution is in the phrase, visual reporter and how it expands the definition and job description of a student, staffer, and faculty member. It will be standing room only in photojournalism classes when we teach our students the fundamentals of visual communication—how to sense, select, and perceive a visual message—and how to work a camera, a computer, and the software, how to use database research methods, how to create informational graphics, how to combine words with your stories, and how to make layouts and designs for print and interactive multimedia. That's when students who never thought of themselves as visual journalists will sign up for your classes because they know that we will best teach them how to be prepared for what lies ahead.

TOWARDS ORGANIZATION OF ETHICAL PHOTOJOURNALISM

The Ethics of Photojournalism "Keeping it Real"

Photojournalism keeping it real: In the mid to late nineties the digital camera began to change photography. As was predicted the impact on photojournalism has been profound. Digital image capture has raised many ethical concerns in the journalism industry as a whole.

More often than not a press photographer has little control over how their images are used. However, they are the first to take the brunt of blame.

The purpose of this site is to address these issues of image manipulating and what is tantamount to a propaganda driven press creating stories and slanted editorials from the images of photojournalist rather than documenting the truth. News agencies in some instances have become a political arm of a government all unto itself. Creating or bending the news from images either modified taken out of context.

What we Do?

We as an organization inspect images published by the news outlets for signs of manipulation or misrepresentation, sometimes acting on tips from the public and even news insiders in order to bring these fraudulent representations to the light that presents a story primarily through the use of pictures.

Photojournalism is a particular form of photography (the collecting, editing, and presenting of images for publication or broadcast as news material) that creates images in order to tell a news story. It is now usually understood to refer only to still images, and in some cases to video used in broadcast journalism. Photojournalism is distinguished from other close branches of photography (such as documentary photography, street photography or celebrity photography) by the qualities of:

Relevance—the images have meaning in the context of a published chronological record of events.

Objectivity—the situation implied by the images is a fair and accurate representation of the events they depict.

Narrative—the images combine with other news elements, to inform and give insight to the viewer or reader.

Photojournalists must make photographic decisions instantly and be in complete command of their equipment, often while exposed to the same risks (natural or man made disasters, war, rioting, crime etc.) that are faced by participants and the copy collecting journalists. The fact that they often do not have the option to stand back or wait until the dangers of an event are over dictates they may take even more risks.

The Photojournalistic Approach to Ethics

In our opinion the only image manipulation acceptable in an image depicting news events (straight photojournalism).

CAREERS IN PHOTOJOURNALISM: A CASE STUDY

Getting Started in Photojournalism

Contemporary photojournalism, whether done with the traditional still camera or the more modern multimedia tools of computer and video camera, is still one of the more interesting "I-don't-work-in-an-office" jobs aspiring visual storytellers can pursue.

This profession also allows one to work from almost anywhere, whether that be one's hometown, one's own country, or from any particular location in the world. If photographers can get to the stories and content they want to cover, they can do this work from anywhere.

What qualities are most important for those who want to pursue such a career?

- *A desire to be "out in the world"*: The story-telling photographers do takes them into the community. That could be the local community where a photographer makes his or her home. It could also be the world community. The options are endless, depending on how far a field the photographer wants to work. But the key is that the story-telling photojournalists do, whatever tools they choose to use, are not at home in their studio or apartment. The work is out in the world with people. Unlike the world of fine art where the aim is for the photographer to tell *their* story to the world, in photojournalism the photographer/storyteller concentrates on the story of *other people*.
- *Technical proficiency*: Whether one is a documentary film-maker, a multimedia storyteller or still photography photojournalist, the tools today consist of electronic cameras and computers. Film and videotape are gone. Pictures are captured on digital media. The darkroom is gone. Today computers serve as the digital darkroom and as video editing machines.

  Photographers need to be willing to learn the essentials, buy the key gear they need, and then keep up with the evolving technological changes. New software, improved cameras, hard drives and computers come flying at working pros with increasing speed requiring upgrades and significant additional investment at least every 18 months, probably every 12 months.

- *Understanding of and a commitment to ethical standards*: With the vast degree of image manipulation visible in advertising, television commercials and the special effects in movies, it is easy to assume "anything goes" no matter which part of the visual world one works in today. Such is *not* the case for the photojournalist.
  Photographers who cover the world and its stories are much more in the mode of, "Record what you see, present what you saw." Yes, pictures and video are adjusted electronically to make this plain to the viewer. But the concept of not manipulating images to alter their meaning is still in play for the modern photojournalist.
- *Persistence*: This comes from a drive to get *the* story. Photojournalists, like writing journalists, are often told "no." The most successful journalists just don't accept the most recent no as the final answer. The best journalists press on without being obnoxious about it and just continue to pursue the story with the next phone call, the next request for an interview.

This same persistence comes into play when it comes to breaking into the business and then once in, to advancing up the ladder. Moving from one publication to another, one company to another or climbing the ranks to the "better" publications or video outlets takes time, energy and often, repeated visits to show your work.

Is formal education important?

The debate about whether or not a photographer needs a formal education goes back as far as the invention of photography. The best suggestion is for students to look at all the options and then choose the path that works for them.

- *Self-taught*: Throughout the history of art, students have learned their craft by taking on a strict regimen of work by themselves. They become artists or photographers by doing art and photography. For some, this is an effective method. The key is probably the term "strict regimen of work." The combination of technique plus artistic vision has to come from somewhere.

Professional sports photographer Brad Mangin notes, "Hard work and paying your dues is still a good way to separate yourself from the pack and get on everyone's radar as a good person to hire for a given job or freelance assignment." Says Mangin, "Being the son of an old-school basketball coach I was brought up with a philosophy that hard work and respect for the veterans were traits that would be rewarded in my future."

With the Internet, on-line courses, software manuals and a vast array of professional workshops, being self-taught may be more accessible that ever before. For those who learn best on their own, this might be the most effective method.

- *College training in photojournalism*: Many state universities and art institutes offer formal college degrees with photojournalism majors. The advantage here is a set of progressively challenging courses over time; instructors who act as coaches and mentors to take students to the next level; and an array of like-minded students who share a vision in which students can compare work and ideas. For students who like a focused, structured environment, a two to four year immersion in a formal programme might be the best solution.
- *College training in other subjects*: There is a thread in journalism that suggests one need not train in journalism or photojournalism *per se*. Using college to learn about the world through the study of other subjects is the recommended path. These voices insist photography and journalism can be learned later. In the beginning, they say study government, politics, international relations, sociology, anthropology, psychology, economics, English, foreign languages or any number of other subjects that will prepare one to work out in the world. The theory here is, if you can think and if you can write, you can probably find work if you're good.

Whatever, the approach, the key will be to assemble the necessary skills to be an effective story-teller with the kind of camera or current digital tools one aspires to use to tell the stories one wants to tell.

How important are multimedia and video?

Wherever one gets it, entry-level photographers can no longer just think of themselves as "just" still photographers. Still photographs are part of the content package that includes slide shows with music, recorded audio of the story's subjects, narrated audio, and eventually, video story-telling. One can begin with still and audio slide shows while in school. This will help carry a photographer into the video world.

Naples Daily News staff photographer Lexey Swall notes, "The Naples Daily News has gone to a 'web first' philosophy—meaning that the website is where we put the stories and photos the moment they are finished." She adds, "Then the web acts as a 'news service' for our print edition, where ideally, we will do more in depth coverage of a given story and hopefully not regurgitate what people have already read on the Web."

This approach is one sweeping the printed media industry as magazines and newspapers "move to the Web" which is now seen by managers as *the* new profit center for those companies that produce "content." At the Journal News in White Plains, New York Deputy Managing Editor for Presentation Larry Nylund, says "The list of qualifications we look for in a photojournalism applicant just got a lot longer."

Why?

"The photo department in now known as the multimedia department," Nylund says. "We are looking for talented people who can step in with the skills needed to tell visual stories in many different ways." The photographers in Nylund's department contribute to the newspaper, magazines, weekly tabloids, a television station and a Website. Photographers carry still and video cameras, laptops, cell phones. The company now has video and audio studios.

How does a candidate display his or her work?

This is the key element that allows the visual storyteller—whether still photographer, multimedia storyteller, documentary video filmmaker—to show at what level they are capable of working.

Still photographers should start building a collection of solid stand-alone single pictures. They should be technically proficient, display excellent colour correction skills on the part of the photographer and have complete caption information. Eventually these photographers will want to move beyond single pictures and take on longer stories and projects as their skills advance.

Documentary video filmmakers should begin with short story-telling projects, perhaps in the 5-10 minutes range. After honing their skills with projects of this length, they should expand their story-telling over time to projects in the 20-30 minutes range. Here solid skills of shooting, gathering audio and editing must be shown. For a portfolio on a DVD, students should have a 1-2 minutes "trailer" for any longer project. Editors will look at a summary such as this, which may get them interested in the longer piece. They probably will not commit themselves to a 20 minutes film unless they already know your work or you have won an award of some significance.

Multimedia storytellers can start with simple slide shows of still pictures set to music. As one's skills grow, learning to gather audio in the field is a necessity. This insures the audience can hear the voices of the subjects in the story. It also opens the door to more sophisticated and complex story-telling on the part of the photographer.

How important are captions?

For those showing still photographs accurate, correctly spelled caption information is still considered a must. This may go away as more projects are shown in a multimedia environment. However, for the foreseeable future hiring editors want clear, clean, communicative captions that are spell checked and grammar checked.

Recent errors such as the following are career killers:

- Having a caption on a photograph of a horse that refers to a circus clown. This is the wrong caption on the photo and suggests a lack of care on the part of the candidate.
- Having a project button on a portfolio that reads, "Inida"—and then having to explain this is "India", misspelled.
- Having the opening page of a Flash Website open with the words, "Sit requires Flash"—when actually, the

photographer was warning the viewer that the Website required Flash and was inviting the visitor to download it if they did not already have it.

How does one get internships?

Whatever one's chosen educational path, in the end photographers and visual storytellers have to be able to show they can produce work of sufficient quality to attract the attention of editors and hiring managers. That often comes down to a portfolio or video "reel" of one's best work. Students often put this together in school. However it happens, this is the key element those who hire want to see. Often editors are looking for the most talented potential intern they can find. On some occasions, that does not mean it will be the most polished photographer.

"I like work that shows originality of thought rather than what may be the most polished, says San Jose Mercury News Director of Photography Geri Migielicz. "I'd rather have an intern who is full of questions on the team than one who thinks they have the answers." She adds, "If the photo department is to be supportive of learning, you have to have critical thinkers and those who strive for original solutions. At times it means failing now rather than settling for safe. In the long run, the investment will pay off."

Besides class assignments and self-assigned projects, the entry-level photographer or video documentarian sometimes gets a chance to prove him or herself through internships or assistantships with professionals. Work with individual photographers or filmmakers is often like the age old apprenticeship experience where one turns oneself over to a master and learns by first watching, then doing. Magazine interns often work in the office and soon learn the culture of the modern magazine world. Initial work doing low-level tasks can evolve over time to taking on greater responsibility throughout the internship and eventually becoming an integral part of the publication's workflow. Students who want to shoot pictures or video and who want to see their work in front of an audience will seek internships where these opportunities exist. Newspapers often give student interns the same assignment and deadline responsibilities as staff photographers. Though he now shoots for Sports Illustrated and Major League Baseball, Mangin started in newspapers and still believes that gives new photographers great training. "It has always been my opinion that magazine editors who hire freelancers to shoot sports want to hire journalists who know how to tell stories with their photographs. This is why I always stress to get a start in newspapers where you can learn to become a complete journalist and prepare yourself for more opportunities in your future." Videographers at small televisions stations might learn the ropes in the newsroom or by editing. Before the end of the internship they can be shooting stories for broadcast if their skills are in place. While it takes a basic portfolio or reel to get hired, the aim is to add significant new material to the portfolio over the course of the internship.

What are the steps to an internship?

To get an internship photographers often find it helps to mount a campaign. For students, this is like taking on one extra self-designed course called, "Getting my first (or next) internship."

This means assembling a portfolio of excellent work and figuring out where you would like to intern, or where it would be most appropriate for you to intern based on your experience. In addition applicants will need a resume and a cover letter that introduces them and makes their case to be selected as an intern.

At the Palo Alto Weekly, Chief Photographer Norbert von der Groeben sees many photographers seeking their first internship. And he sees a lot basic mistakes, sometimes called "rookie errors" by professionals. Among these beginner errors are misspelling the name of the hiring editor. Worse yet is to get their gender wrong.

If a candidate is fortunate to get an interview with the boss, von der Groeben says appearance is the next hurdle. "Dress correctly for the interview" he says. "No jeans, T-shirts, gum or bottled water. Wear a nice clean shirt or blouse and slacks." This is so basic, even for beginners says von der Groeben, that he has been know to escort poorly dressed candidates straight out to the newspaper's parking lot, telling them to come back when they are REALLY (italics) ready to work—as a professional— at the paper.

How can I maximize the job interview opportunity?

Job candidates know they will be asked questions during an interview. Concord (N.H.) Monitor Photo Editor Dan Habib urges applicants to think about what they will be asked—and what they *want* to ask—during the interview. In the first instance, candidates should be able to speak about why they want to intern for this particular organization. Also, what can the intern candidate bring to this organization as an aspiring journalist or storyteller?

Having questions for the organization's interviewer is also smart. What is the daily routine of the job? Is it office bound or can interns get into the field? Is the work of interns published in print, on the Web or broadcast on the air? What were the duties of the previous intern? Habib encourages intern candidates to speak about their own needed areas of growth. This shows insight into the candidate's strengths and weaknesses and an ability to analyze their own work. Von der Groeben says, "If you are lacking sports or news photos in your portfolio be honest and say that you need to work on that and you want to learn. Make that a goal for the internship." How important is this process of the internship hunt? In Concord, Habib notes five of the last six people he has hired have interned at the paper at some point.

What are the intern "Do's" and "Dont's?"

Because journalism is a small industry where everyone knows everyone, even beginning interns must be on top of their game as best they can everyday. Simple honesty goes a long way, says von der Groeben. "Once you get the internship keep your commitment," says. "That means if you first get an internship at the Palo Alto Weekly and next day the Los Angeles Times offers you their internship, call the Palo Alto Weekly back and be honest." When someone is straightforward about a great circumstance like this, von der Groeben says chances are he will get behind the student taking the larger opportunity."

On the other hand, when interns try to worm their way out of what they have promised, that is another matter. "If you say you want to work weekends, don't change your mind once the internship gets going and ask for weekends off," says von der Groeben. "That makes everyone from the photo editor to the newest person on staff unhappy with you," he adds. "That can make for a very long summer." At the San Diego Union, Senior Editor for Visuals Robert York swears he has seen it all. He has several suggestions for candidates who land the internship.

"Never give anyone the finger in traffic while you're in a company car," says York. "Make double sure you don't give a retired navy admiral the bird. He's smart enough to figure out who you are and call your boss. It never ends well for you or your finger," he concludes. If as an intern the company gear suddenly goes missing, York counsels, "Never claim that the gear you lost was stolen by angry gypsy dwarves at the circus," he says. "If you want, we can provide you with a list of acceptable, staff-tested, far-fetched excuses. Surprisingly, angry gypsy dwarves didn't make the cut." And as a photo manager who has seen interns arrive late and leave early because the dog they brought on assignment with them needed special attention, York adds, "Never bring your dog to work." He flat out says, "Don't bring any pets to work. Don't bring them on assignments with you. Don't let them pee in the studio. It never ends well for you or the dog."

What about following-up?

Once the interview is over, smart candidates will follow-up in the subsequent weeks and months. Remember: Getting an internship or assistantship is a *campaign*. First, craft a handwritten thank you note to the interviewer expressing your appreciation for their time and the opportunity to interview with their organization.

Then at least everyone to three months, send an update of your work to the organization's hiring manager. Show them you are still interested in working for their organization. This will also allow you to show them new work as you grow and develop as a storyteller.

How do I get feedback?

A critical part of this process is for aspiring photographers to get as much feedback as possible. Students in class can do this with instructors and visiting professionals when they come to campus. Photographers without these possibilities should approach professionals whenever they can. E-mail and telephone requests work well. Seeing professionals at low-cost one-day workshops often allows one to hear from several pros at one event. Workshops that extend over a week or more allow in-depth analysis and review. It is not unusual at some time in a career to encounter a critique one might characterize as The Wood Chipper. That is, a photographer shows work and in a matter of minutes feels he or she has been chopped up and spit out of a C-shaped tube into a bin of tiny wood segments destined to be mulch. This happens so often to photographers at the start of their careers it should be considered an official rite of passage. Committed storytellers will know one critique is not *the* definitive word on one's life.

The question becomes, is this the last critique, as in the last one you had recently, or is this the Last Critique, as in you are planning to give up your aspirations to be a storyteller. The second option essentially guarantees the game is over. But if this kind of brutal review is just another in a series of moments of feedback along a career path, this photographer has a chance to persist and succeed. One of the best ways to get a critique and to start to build a relationship with a professional is through the NPPA mentorship programme. This one-year programme links photographers with veteran pros for dialogue and critique aimed to improve the photographer's skills and broaden their understanding of the industry. NPPA offers critique programmes for both still and video members.

How important are business skills?

Another leg of an aspiring visual storyteller's arsenal is some understanding of the marketplace. With so many photographers choosing the freelance path of the independent contractor today, often the ability to survive is based more on understanding marketing, copyright, business law, contracts and finance than on capturing an image. The most successful storytellers today understand how to create the content and how to market the result.

There is the capturing of the image, and there is the selling of the image. There is the making of a book and then the selling of the book. There is the making of the documentary film and there is the marketing of the film.

How about covering war?

Traditionally many journalists have jump started their career by finding a hot conflict zone offering an insurrection or civil war. With several months of gritty coverage a writer or photographer might make their reputation in a way that would take years if they worked their way up the ranks at home. Some photographers find this a fruitful path. However in the areas where full-blown armies are going at each other, the risks are substantial and may not be recommended for individual photographers without major organizational backing. Freelancer Max Becherer rotates in and out of the Middle East regularly with major news organizations. He notes, "Coming in to cover Iraq at this stage of things is extremely difficult and expensive. That is why only the largest organizations are able to even try to do it." An enterprising storyteller has to think about what new information they will capture as part of their being on this scene says Becherer. "If all you want to do is embed then the trail is well worn," he says. "As soon as you step off the plane you are in the battlefield. Actually being able to report on Iraqis or outside of the bases is a totally different ball game." Other locales of less intensity, but of no less journalistic importance, might be a better starting ground for the conflict zone novice.

What about compensation?

It has long been said that no one goes into journalism to get rich. While one might get rich, for the most part it does not happen. Most of the time people go into story-telling fields for other reasons.

Part of the issue here is that photojournalism and documentary video film-making have always attracted more people to them than there are formal jobs in the field. In short, this field is extremely competitive. But this has always been the case, going back to the earliest history of photojournalism. It looks like an easy, fun job. Fun it is, though not so easy. But many people are drawn to the field with varying degrees of skill and sophistication.

Clearly one cannot be stupid about money and expenses. One has to be sufficiently attentive to make a living. One must generate income above and beyond one's expenses. Starting out that might mean having a day job while one polishes journalistic skills. Actors and musicians know this process. It can work for photojournalists too. However with that in mind, people in journalism and story-telling often find the real compensation from this profession from the elements above and beyond just the paycheck. It might come from doing something different everyday. It might come from a range of travelling and having new experiences in different corners of the world—or in one's own community.

A storyteller might have a certain commitment to saving the oceans, to preserving the Amazon rainforest, to doing stories on refugees from conflict zones. Often storytellers set-up a balance in their life between these projects and more commercial work, with one funding the other. The resulting work is both profitable and meaningful for the storyteller. Those who will do well in the days ahead will mostly likely be those who combine their still photography efforts with multimedia presentation skills. Ideally, that will lead photographers to add video story-telling to their skill set. Photographers who have a solid understanding of the still camera, the computer and video story-telling are the photographers who will best set themselves up to prosper in the ever more emerging digital world. For those who love video, perhaps the highest compensation will come from getting their documentaries on television. Compared to other outlets, this can be one of the more lucrative venues for story-telling if one has that interest.

Conclusion

Seek to have the widest possible skill set. This includes work with a still camera, computer, audio and video tools. Be as complete a storyteller as possible with the range of tools available.

Special enhancements are equally valuable: Learn to write stories and proposals; learn one or more foreign languages; learn to compose music, an especially valuable skill as one moves into the multimedia and video world.

Storytellers should keep in mind they will be studying at least three topics as long as they pursue this career: (1) New technological developments, (2) the process of telling a story that communicates clearly, and (3) the copyright law. These are subjects that become the ordinary, on-going "homework" of the working professional.

Most likely creative people will have several if not many jobs over the course of their career. The days of being a photographer, a videographer, an editor or "just" one of anything are gone. Versatility combined with perseverance are the qualities that will keep storytellers working through this century.

Professional photojournalist Mark M. Hancock discusses photojournalism and the eccentricities associated with gathering images for daily newspapers.

I've been asked to explain photojournalism, news photography and my views on it a few times. Generally, this information is intended as an introduction for students considering a career in photojournalism or others unacquainted with this profession. Others who consider hiring me, freelance or otherwise, may also want to know more about my philosophy and work ethic. This information should answer most of those questions as well. This information should not be taken as absolute. It is a statement of my current *OPINION* about photojournalism, photojournalists, and news photographers as it applies to my present position and experience.

Note: "Photojournalist" is meant to apply to active, news/editorial photographers, whether they hold a specific degree in photojournalism or not. Terms such as "he, his," etc., are intended to be gender neutral.

What does it take to be a great journalist?

A great journalist cares about people and an ideal world. A great journalist can approach a topic as vast as the universe and make it simple and interesting to both Einstein and the new immigrant, who is trying to learn the language.

The written word has power. With skill, reporters can expose the dark deeds of the world and bring them into the light. However, journalism is limited to non-apathetic, monolinguistic people with some time to kill and a few neurons still firing. Enter photojournalism. It destroys almost all barriers. Justice can draw its sword in the time it takes an eye to scan an image. An image has no age, language or intelligence limits.

What is a photojournalist?

A journalist tells stories. A photographer takes pictures of nouns (people, places and things). A photojournalist takes the best of both and locks it into the most powerful medium available—a single frozen image. Photojournalists capture "verbs." This sounds simple, but a room of professional photographers was dumbfounded by this realization. Even after a full-length lecture with documentation and visual evidence, half of the photographers still had no clue what the difference was.

At the end of the presentation. One man said (he really did), "So, what's the difference between photography and photojournalism?" Luckily, two people (only two) turned to him and yelled, "Verbs!" Although photojournalists can take properly exposed and well-composed photographs all day long, they hunt verbs. They hunt them, shoot them and show them to their readers. Then, they hunt more. A photojournalist has thousands of pairs of eyes looking over his shoulder constantly. The readers are insistent: "What are they doing?" "What did you see?" and "What happened?" The readers wake PJs up at night. They keep PJs awake. The eyes always want to know what they missed. Readers cannot see what they missed with a noun. It works if the question is specific enough (what did the condemned building look like?), but most answers require verbs.

To tell a story, a sentence needs a subject, a verb and a direct object. News photos need the same construction. Photojournalists tell stories with their images. Also, words are always used in conjunction with photojournalist's images. The words below a photo are called a *cutline*. I write the cutlines that go with most of my images. At many newspapers, photographers provide names and nothing else. They don't write cutlines because they sometimes cannot write a lead (lede) graph for a story. They also may not be able to photograph a sentence (sports being the exclusion, and there are plenty of supporting images to prove my point in this genre as well). To be a photojournalist, we must understand the relationship between the image and these basic elements of language (all languages—worldwide).

The girl hits (or misses) the ball. There are no other options.

The girl is easy to photograph. The ball is easy to photograph. The verb is the hard part.

As a servant of the citizens, it is the photojournalist's OBLIGATION to capture the entire sentence involved in EVERY event. There are no excuses. It's hit or missed. Some photographers don't care. They have a picture of the bat. "Hey, that's what tried to hit the ball." They just don't get it. A photojournalist is a visual reporter of facts. The public places trust in its reporters to tell the truth. The same trust is extended to photojournalists as visual reporters. This responsibility is paramount to a photojournalist. At all times, we have many thousands of people seeing through our eyes and expecting to see the truth. Most people immediately understand an image. In today's world of grocery store tabloids and digital manipulation of images, the photojournalist must still tell the truth. The photojournalist constantly hunts for the images (or verbs), which tell of the day-to-day struggles and accomplishments of his community. These occurrences happen naturally. There is no need to "set-up" reality. There is no need to lie to a community that bestows its trust. In a nutshell: If a photojournalist isn't going to fake a fire or a street stabbing scene, why would he set-up "person A" giving "person B" an object (award, check, trophy etc.)? The photojournalist simply wants to hang around, be forgotten and wait for the right moment. Then, the hunt begins anew. Like the police officer or firefighter, the photojournalist's concern is his community even if that means sacrificing comfort or life. Many photojournalists die every year in the process of collecting visual information, which lets the public know of atrocities, dangers and the mundane.

What makes a photojournalist different from a potographer?

Photographers take pictures of nouns (people, places and things). Photojournalists shoot action verbs ("kicks," "explodes," "cries," etc.). Photojournalists do shoot some nouns. These nouns can be standard photos of people (portraits), places (proposed zoning areas or construction sites) and things (name it). However, the nouns we seek still must tell a story.

Assignments and image holes

Reporters and editors should knowhow I work (*i.e*: no set-ups, no nouns, no male bovine excrement). I have "holes" to fill each day. I track events in our community and anticipate what our readers expect to see. As a general rule, many daily newspapers expect three page one news images, and one to four inside B & W news/ business images, as well as two to nine Lifestyles images, and two to five Sports images. Metro papers expect more and have additional sections. Assignments are honoured on a first-come basis with exceptions. Once a section has its initial image quota, priority shifts to another section until each section is "safe." Then additional images are collected for future issues. Primarily, editorial news judgement is applied to image priority (murder is more important than other planned occurrences). However, unlike text-based reporters, visual reporters must be on location when events occur. Therefore, events with flexible times fall lower on a fixed priority scale, but have a greater overall editorial priority (and may bump other items under time restrictions).

- Additionally, anything with front page potential usually has priority over section front and inside images.
- Since this is a newspaper, here is the loose shooting priority.
- Breaking news (murders, hostages, natural disasters, major wrecks, etc.).
- General news (funerals, courts, perp walks, dignitary visits, etc.).
- Photo essays.
- Major feature events.
- Sporting events.
- Festivals.
- Educational events.
- Feature photos.
- Advertising (non-spec.).
- Illustrations.
- Mug shots.
- Spec. items.
- "Photo ops" and other garbage to make a singular reader happy.

A Note on Competition

Most photojournalists succumb to the vanity and competitive nature of contests. Unlike other journalism competitions, which separate stories by circulation, most photojournalists and photographers compete head-to-head with their best images. The winner takes all. Consequently, additional enthusiasm and effort goes toward potentially competitive images more than non-competitive images. The following items are generally non-competitive: set-ups ("grip and grins"), mug shots, lecturers ("talking heads"), building exteriors, theater performers/performances, advertising and product shots.

These are the monthly National Press Photographers Association categories:

(*a*) Spot news,
(*b*) General news,
(*c*) Sports (action and feature),

(*d*) Feature-single,
(*e*) Feature-multiple (photo essay), and
(*f*) Illustration (judged quarterly).

Graft and Gifts

All a photojournalist should require is unlimited access and documents. As the citizen's servant, a photojournalist can't accept anything other than water and an occasional cup of coffee during halftime of the sub-zero championship football game in the rain ("Why isn't this snow?"). If the photojournalist accepts gifts—any gifts—the photojournalist is perceived as corrupt and perpetuates the myth about the "evil media."

Consequently, everyone immediately offers them gifts and favours. Which PJs kindly turn down, and which, upon arrival at the newsroom, get chewed out for "not eating the old lady's darn cookie." Personally, I'll use event passes on days off since my presence costs nothing additional to the host. The organizer often makes money from my purchases and still may get into the newspaper because I bring my camera.

Coverage Zones

In newspapers, there are coverage zones. Larger papers have larger pieces of turf. This zone is created by physical circulation geography, area of influence upon the circulation area and predominant interests of the area. Outside of this area, the story must warrant leaving the community unattended by the photojournalist should breaking news occur. Traditionally, assigned events outside the circulation zone have included: spot news, general news (funerals, court cases, etc.), portions of photo essays, championship-level sporting events, and large events (fairs, festivals and exhibitions) with an expected participation or spectator draw from the circulation area.

Personal Views on the Job

This is not a "glam" job. A photojournalist is a servant (like a waitress or a sanitation worker). They're expected to be on the job around the clock to serve the public.

News never stops. Again, NEWS NEVER STOPS. You sleep when you can. You eat when you're done. You're never really off the clock.

Photojournalists are role models. They don't want to be, but they are.

At a mid-sized or small newspaper, a photojournalist can't have a night on the town and neglect his or her city. Everyone from the little takes to the senior citizens, from the street people to the debutantes, knows the photojournalist. The photojournalist is the visible portion of the newspaper.

Reporters can handle everything by phone. Editors can stay in their office and never talk to a soul. Press operators and graphic artists can go strait to the bar after work if they choose. However, the photojournalist must crawl through barnyard dung for one shoot and arrive at the annual celebrity gala an hour later.

I love this city and the people who make it the wonderful place it is. For the most part: houses don't catch fire, everyone looks out for each other, nobody goes to bed hungry, kids go to college and become CEOs (or photojournalists—that's a long, bizarre story), the arts flourish, the city leaders are respected, and red-light running is the biggest crime.

10

Public Relations and Journalism: Select Areas of Study

PR TOOLS IN JOURNALISM: COVERING SELECT AREAS OF STUDY

Public Relations Tools

The news release is the most important form of written communications used by a public relations professional, but not the only one. There are many other public relations tools that should be used when appropriate.

News releases may suffice for most news stories, but other, lengthier forms of communication can give in-depth coverage of an interesting news item. Feature articles, bylined articles, and emails may be written to provide human interest appeal, to explore topics and issues in more depth, to raise your organization's profile in the local community, or for other reasons.

Feature Articles

Feature articles, which explore a subject at length, are not constrained by the tight deadlines of regular news articles. Features may be submitted at any time, depending on the editor's needs. Features often stem from a regular news item. Imagine that the Linux operating system has been successfully implemented at a large organization in your community. This story is newsworthy, but begin to look for "the rest of the story." What difficulties did they experience in the transition, or what part did your organization play in their implementation? This could be the start of a feature article. More research and creativity will go into a feature story, but the must still be accurate. You will provide more facts, more statistics, more examples and anecdotes, and more analysis than in a news release. You can humanize and dramatize what may appear unexciting at first glance (a Linux implementation). You can openly focus on a particular angle or viewpoint, so long as you avoid outright advertising. Readers dislike advertorials masquerading as "articles," and no editor will accept an article that blatantly sells.

Another bonus is that editors are quite open to features, because they provide much needed content for filling an issue. When the feature is written by a reliable source and does not require payment (unlike a commissioned article), the article becomes a real asset. All writing needs to engage the reader. The first sentence or two must be compelling enough for the editor to read on. Features require a strong lead—something to hook your target audience. A headline or a photograph may help.

For a feature, you have a wide repertoire of leads to choose from. Some leads are designed to startle and shock, some will excite readers' curiosity, some will vividly describe a real or imagined scenario, and some will succinctly state the nature of the story. The body of the feature then unfolds in a logical sequence, and ends with a strong and memorable close. Every feature will be different, depending on the subject, the anticipated audience, and the skill of the writer. Reading features written by others in the Linux community is a good way to learn and pick up possible story ideas. You can direct a feature to the "feature editor" at a daily newspaper or your targetted trade magazines. Before going to the trouble of writing the article, you should pitch the idea to see if the publication has any interest at all. The pitch should include an outline, an estimated length (number of words), and a description of illustrations or photos you can supply. You could also include a selected portfolio of previously published articles about your organization.

The upfront consultation is invaluable. Since the editor knows their readership better than you do, they might suggest an angle of specific interest to their readers and indicate where this piece might fit in their publishing schedule. The more complete your package, the more seriously your work will be considered. Another possibility is to plant the story idea with the editor, and let the publication take care of writing the feature. In this case, you can supply expertise and interview subjects. Whatever your approach, keep in mind that the ultimate goal is to generate favourable coverage and visibility for your organization.

Bylined Articles

A by-line is the line showing the author's name at the beginning of an article. Basically, a bylined article is attributed to a source rather than being anonymous. Bylined articles can be any length, and they tend to based on opinion. They articulate views and opinions that are clearly the writer's own, without requiring objectivity. Issues, trends, and predictions regarding Linux and open source are ideal subjects for bylined articles. Moreover, forward-looking pieces are of high interest. Editors are always looking for "the next thing" to tell their readers about. Opinion articles are important to position your organization as the leader and trendsetter in your field. To be a guru is to be watched, quoted, respected, and followed. Editors like highlighting celebrated members of the community because they sell more issues.

Gauging the interest of the news media is very important. What's hot? What are they writing about? Check the topics listed in their editorial calendars. Try to match their interests to the activities of your organization in the community. Then start writing your opinion piece. Typically, the author of a bylined article should be your organization's designated spokesperson and acknowledged authority for the media. That might be you or a senior official. Sometimes a public relations professional will ghost-write the piece for the spokesperson, whose name will appear on the article. When this occurs, the article must closely reflect the spokesperson's views and ideas. In other words, he or she "owns" the ideas expressed in the article, not the writer.

An added bonus of bylined articles is that they can be adapted into speeches for possible speaking opportunities. Conversely, any speech can be written as a bylined article.

E-mail Writing

Another effective way to communicate to a targetted audience is through an email campaign. The effectiveness of a good e-mail should not be underestimated. Some fundraising experts, for example, can raise thousand of dollars with an effective e-mail campaign. Exceptional letters have obtained contracts, sold properties, and landed jobs.

E-mails can be targetted to a specific audience for much less than you would spend on a regular mail campaign. Every e-mail is an opportunity to effectively communicate to your target audience. For example, your organization might want to target recent graduates of local computer training courses with opportunities in their area. You will need to obtain the names and e-mail addresses of recent graduates from the institutions offering those programmes. Cooperation with their institution can often be established if you provide something in return, such as a reciprocal link on your website, a mention in your newsletter, or even free advertising.

Hopefully, your e-mail campaign will generate interest in your organization and your programmes. Be mindful of potentially spamming your intended audience—this could have a negative impact.

Miscellaneous Communications Tools

There are numerous other communication tools you can use in a public relations effort. Here are just a few suggestions:

- A speech at a Linux trade show.
- A presentation at a local training institution or career development conference.
- A brochure or flyer describing the work your company does.
- A white paper describing the benefits of your company's work, posted on your website.
- A newsletter or e-mail newsletter describing your organization's activities and achievements, aimed at current and prospective users.
- An advertisement placed in targetted magazines.
- Special events such as open houses and "media information" days.
- Regular tours of your facility.

The possibilities are limited only by your time, resources, and budget.

Typesetting

Typesetting involves the presentation of textual material in an aesthetic form on paper or some other media. Before the development of innovations such as the dot matrix, inkjet, and laserjet printers, printed material was produced in print shops.

In spite of centuries of innovation, the principle of printing remains the same: either a particular part of the page is marked or not marked with ink. This has remained true at the microscopic level even for halftone and four-colour printing. *Typesetting is the technology of deciding which parts of the paper should be marked, and printing is the technology of making the marks.* However, the two are not rigidly separated: for example, ink flows during the printing process, and type design has to take into account the dynamics of ink on paper. With early printing presses, individual letters and characters were on blocks (usually of metal, sometimes of wood), which would be assembled for each page. The setting of individual letters was rendered obsolete by hot-metal setting machines such as the Linotype machine.

The Computer Era

Computers are useful in automatically typesetting documents. Character-by-character computer-aided phototypesetting (now known as imagesetting) replaced systems such as Linotype in the 1980s, and was in turn rapidly rendered obsolete by modern systems which employ a raster image processor to render an entire page to a single high-resolution digital image which is then photoset. In the late 1980s desktop publishing on microcomputers became available, starting with the Apple Macintosh. Programmes like Adobe PageMaker and Adobe InDesign have not only popularized desktop publishing, but have also given more control to professional typesetters. The Text system is a widespread and powerful automatic typesetter.

Arranging Speaking Opportunities

Arranging possible speaking opportunities takes considerable effort and involves a long lead time. In most instances, you must be in contact with the conference organizers at least nine to ten months in advance of the show. You may even find that a sponsorship is required to be considered as a possible presenter.

First, do your research regarding relevant conferences that are being planned in your area in the months ahead. The website of the event organizer or of the conference itself is often a good place to start looking for information. Contact the organizers to find out their needs and application requirements for possible speakers.

Also, consider other venues in addition to trade shows focussing on Linux and open source. For example, you could offer your services as a speaker to human resources or computer training communities.

The key to successful participation is similar to pitching to the news media. You must understand your audience, you must have a compelling topic, and you must be ready and willing to impart your knowledge and experience of the industry. Most importantly, your presentation has to teach something to someone, and not just be a commercial for your organization or Linux. Give the audience the satisfaction of having really learned something from your presentation, and show organizers will want to have you as a presenter at their next show.

Getting Media Attention at Trade Shows

If you want publicity while exhibiting at a trade show, don't do what too many other organizations do. During the show, they wait patiently at their booth until they spot a reporter coming down the aisle. Then, if the reporter stops at its booth, the exhibitor moves in with the same tired pitch used on everybody else who walks by. If this has been your approach in the past, now is the time to change. Waiting until the show begins is already too late to capture the news media's attention. You should now understand that establishing strong news media relationships weeks or even months in advance can pay-off when the show begins.

Begin by finding out which news media will be covering the show. The best way to get that information is from the show's public relations department. Ask them if they can give you the names of print, broadcast, and online media they are targeting. This information is important to know, so that you don't pitch the same story ideas as the show organizers. If you discover the organizers are pitching an idea that fits well with your organization's objectives, ask if they could include your business as an example in their pitch.

Check the editorial calendars of both the publications that will be covering the show and other publications that might have an interest. (A computer magazine, for example, is a prime target for a large Linux conference.) Many publications will issue a special report before or after the show takes place. The report may be a section within an issue or even an entire special edition. If you cannot glean this information from the calendar, you should call the publication and ask. The special reports present ripe opportunities for media coverage. Pitch story ideas that may become part of the special report to your media contacts.

Prepare a compelling news release describing the most interesting thing that your organization will be doing at the show. Mention awards, impressive results, or endorsements by Linux experts—anything that will snag the media's attention. Include the line "For more information or to arrange an interview, contact:" as part of your contact information at the end. In devising your strategy to get media coverage at the show, always position your organization as "part of the solution," not as a mere attendee.

Planning for a Trade Show

Planning for trade shows needs to start at least a few months in advance. If you wish to have a significant presence at strategic or influential show, you should plan to set-up a booth, either on your own or with a key partner. Booth space is limited and must be reserved in advance. Usually a fee is involved, which varies according to square footage and location on the exhibition floor. Designing the portable booth can take a few months, so plan ahead.

Here are some tips for getting maximum benefit from your trade show appearances.

Before the Show

A major trade show requires considerable advance preparation and, if you aren't ready, can present a logistical nightmare. You must develop a solid plan and monitor your progress vigilantly.

1. *Evaluate and select trade shows carefully*: Participating in a show can require a major investment of time, money, and resources. Be tough in your evaluation of a show's worthiness. Are the attendees likely customers for your

organization? Exposure to a few hundred very qualified targets is better than exposure to thousands of generalists who are very unlikely to be interested in your business.

2. *Read the show manual*: Before you do anything, contact the organizers of the show to find the show's manual. Everything you need to know about the show should be there, including a proposed or final schedule, registration information and forms, floor plans, exhibit specifications, invitations for potential speakers, and other important details.
3. *Identify your goals*: Be specific about the things you want to accomplish as a result of your participation in the show. Do you want to increase visibility, gain exposure to a large number of customers who might be interested in your products, or check out the competition? Concrete goals are important to determine the value of the trade show to your organization.
4. *Define measurements of success:* For each goal, determine a way to measure its success. Make these measurements as specific as possible. You could plan to hand out 1000 brochures, obtain contact information for at least 200 prospects, and take a key editor out to lunch. These benchmarks will help you decide whether the show was worth the expense.
5. *Put your show plan in writing*: The plan should include a workable schedule, a comprehensive list of preparation activities, and an individual assigned for each task. You cannot leave things to chance, or else Murphy's Law (Whatever can go wrong, will go wrong.) will surely prevail!
6. *Develop a key message for your booth exhibit:* Like good advertising, a good exhibit clearly communicates one major message. This draws in more prospects to your booth than an unfocused cacophony of messages.
7. *Design an open, inviting booth*: An open booth design, with no tables obstructing access, invites attendees to come in. Your logo should be big enough to be seen from a good distance. Maximize "walking around" space by mounting brochure displays on walls. Use interesting graphics to draw people's attention. For demos, laptops and flat-

screen monitors are space-efficient. If space permits, provide comfortable chairs to encourage prospects to linger. A portable booth should be reasonably easy to set-up and take down.

8. *Advertise your show participation.:* Use tag lines such as: "see us at Booth 1525 at the Linux World Conference" in news releases and other communications leading up to the show (even if those releases are about something unrelated). Write a news release announcing show-related news. Invite editors to stop by the booth, or set-up appointments between them and your spokespeople.
9. *Order all necessary supplies, including brochures and giveaways*: If your marketing collateral needs to be updated or redesigned, take care of this early. You don't want to run the risk of having no brochures to hand out. Design forms for filling out prospect information—clear forms eliminate guesswork. Consider giveaways to generate attention and a sense of fun. These don't have to be expensive. Pens with your web address and a catchy slogan can be very effective.
10. *Design PowerPoint presentations and demos for the booth*: These will draw attendees to your booth and help them learn more about your business. Presentations will allow you to communicate information to many prospects at once.
11. *Create a unique identity for your booth staff*: Decide on the dress code for your staff. Matching blazers, T-shirts, or even boutonnieres will make your representatives easily identifiable.
12. *Train your exhibit staff before each show*: This is very important! Your staff needs to know what is expected of them. They need to be briefed on all new programmes and initiatives that should be emphasized. They must know how to run the demos and presentations, and they should know some basic trouble shooting. Nothing looks more unprofessional then demos that don't work.

During the Show

1. *Set-up a rotating booth schedule for your staff*: Your staff needs

breaks for lunch and relaxing. They will be more cheerful if they don't have stay at the booth all day long.

2. *Remind staff to record all prospect information:* Encourage your staff to record everything they can learn about a prospect's needs and experience with Linux. Stress the importance of getting phone numbers and e-mail addresses. (Creating an information form as suggested above will make this easier.)
3. *Encourage staff to greet people warmly and smile*: Amazingly, this is often forgotten. An inviting attitude can give a valuable first impression. The staff should avoid having their backs to the entrance, or taking phone calls while on duty. A friendly greeting to passersby may encourage them to stop rather than simply walk by. Staff who are uniformly courteous and helpful, knowledgeable about all aspects of the industry, and responsive to requests will make a very good impression.

After the Show

1. *Send requested literature immediately:* Send requested material within 24 hours. A quick response is your second opportunity to make a favourable impression. (Your performance in the booth is the first.)
2. *Include a teaser on the envelope or in the e-mail subject line:* Be sure to mention your organization's name and the name of the conference on the outside of the envelope or in the e-mail subject line, so they know your letter is not junk mail.
3. *Help your prospects take the next step:* Make sure your literature packages make responding easy for prospects by including your web address and information on the opportunities available to them.
4. *Keep track of your prospects:* Nothing signals the success of your trade-show effort better than having prospects purchase your products or having the media spotlight your efforts. Keep a record of the customers who found out about your products through the trade show. Use these results to demonstrate the show's return on investment.
5. *Analyze "lessons learned"*: After each show, evaluate what went well and what didn't. Critique each aspect of the

show and ask others for comments. Pay special attention to feedback regarding communication to prospective customers. The "lessons learned" will help improve your efforts in future shows.

Next, we will review the major topics we have covered in this guide to public relations. This final chapter will serve as a quick reference guide to the major elements of public relations. Use this guide to develop a successful public relations campaign.

11

News Values, Objectivity, Ethics, Standards and Rights: An Overview

NEWS VALUES

News values, sometimes called "news criteria," determine how much prominence a news story is given by a media outlet, and the attention it is given by the audience. A. Boyd states that: "News journalism has a broadly agreed set of values, often referred to as 'newsworthiness.... "News values are not universal and can vary widely between different cultures. In Western practice, decisions on the selection and prioritization of news are made by editors on the basis of their experience and intuition, although analysis by M. Galtung and M. Ruge showed that several factors are consistently applied across a range of news organizations. Some of these factors are listed below, together with others put forward by Schlesinger and Bell. According to Ryan, "there is no end to lists of news criteria." Among the many lists of news values that have been drawn up by scholars and journalists, some, like Galtung and Ruge's, attempt to describe news practices across cultures, while others have become remarkably specific to the press of certain (often Western) nations.

A variety of external and internal pressures influence journalists' decisions on which stories are covered, how issues are interpreted and the emphasis given to them. These pressures can sometimes lead to bias or unethical reporting. Achieving relevance, giving audiences the news they want and find interesting, is an increasingly important goal for media outlets seeking to maintain market share in a rapidly evolving market. This has made news organizations more open to audience input and feedback, and forced them to adopt and apply news values which will attract and keep audiences. The growth of interactive media and citizen journalism is fast altering the traditional distinction between news producer and passive audience and may in future lead to a deep-ploughing redefinition of what 'news' means and the role of the news industry

Conditions for News

- *Frequency*: Events which occur suddenly and fit well with the news organization's schedule are more likely to be reported than those which occur gradually or at inconvenient times of day or night. Long-term trends are not likely to receive much coverage.
- *Negativity*: Bad news is more newsworthy than good news.
- *Unexpectedness*: If an event is out of the ordinary it will have a greater effect than something which is an everyday occurrence.
- *Unambiguity*: Events whose implications are clear make for better copy than those which are open to more than one interpretation, or where any understanding of the implications depends on first understanding the complex background in which the events take place.
- *Personalization*: Events which can be portrayed as the actions of individuals will be more attractive than one in which there is no such "human interest."
- *Meaningfulness*: This relates to the sense of identification the audience has with the topic. "Cultural proximity" is a factor here—stories concerned with people who speak the same language, look the same, and share the pre-occupations as the audience receive more coverage than those concerned with people who speak different languages, look different and have different pre-occupations.
- *Reference to elite nations*: Stories concerned with global powers receive more attention than those concerned with less influential nations.
- *Reference to elite persons*: Stories concerned with the rich, powerful, famous and infamous get more coverage.
- *Conflict*: Opposition of people or forces resulting in a dramatic effect. Stories with conflict are often quite newsworthy.

- *Consonance*: Stories which fit with the media's expectations receive more coverage than those which defy them (and for which they are thus unprepared). Note this appears to conflict with unexpectedness above. However, consonance really refers to the media's readiness to report an item.
- *Continuity*: A story which is already in the news gathers a kind of inertia. This is partly because the media organizations are already in place to report the story, and partly because previous reportage may have made the story more accessible to the public (making it less ambiguous).
- *Composition*: Stories must compete with one another for space in the media. For instance, editors may seek to provide a balance of different types of coverage, so that if there is an excess of foreign news for instance, the least important foreign story may have to make way for an item concerned with the domestic news. In this way the prominence given to a story depends not only on its own news values but also on those of competing stories (Galtung and Ruge, 1965).
- *Competition*: Commercial or professional competition between media may lead journalists to endorse the news value given to a story by a rival.
- *Co-optation*: A story that is only marginally newsworthy in its own right may be covered if it is related to a major running story.
- *Prefabrication*: A story which is marginal in news terms but written and available may be selected ahead of a much more newsworthy story which has to be researched and written from the ground up.
- *Predictability*: An event is more likely to be covered if it has been pre-scheduled (Bell, 1991).
- *Time constraints*: Traditional news media such as radio, television and daily newspapers have strict deadlines and a short production cycle which select for items that can be researched and covered quickly.
- *Logistics*: Although eased by the availability of global communications even from remote regions, the ability to deploy and control production and reporting staff, and

functionality of technical resources can determine whether a story is covered (Schlesinger, 1987).

External Pressures

Many of these observed conditions for news can be explained as products of the way the news operation works e.g. budgetary or staffing constraints, or the suitability of the story for a particular production format; others by the way news judgements are shaped by the cultural background of the journalist, the collective norms of the organization and management policy directives.

Journalists may also be influenced by external pressures from the government or Establishment, manipulation by spin doctors, and, recently, a need to retain audience share in an increasingly fragmented and competitive market. Even the way audiences, journalists and pressure groups use language can determine how stories are written and interpreted, and the value they carry for both audience and news producer.

However, models of news evaluation based on these factors alone are incomplete; they explain how the news process works, not why it works. For instance, several of Galtung and Ruge's factors leave questions unanswered:

- Why is bad news stronger than good news?
- Why is the unexpected newsworthy?
- Why should scale influence an event's newsworthiness?
- Why is there a fascination for elite groups and people the audience may never meet?
- Why is human interest important in news?

Audience Perceptions of News

Conventional models concentrate on what the journalist perceives as news. But the news process is a two-way transaction, involving both news producer (the journalist) and the news receiver (the audience), although the boundary between the two is rapidly blurring with the growth of citizen journalism and interactive media. Little has been done to define equivalent factors which determine audience perception of news. This is largely because it would appear impossible to define a common factor, or factors, that generate interest in a mass audience. Basing his judgement on many years as a newspaper journalist Hetherington (1985) states that: "...anything which threatens people's peace, prosperity and well-being is news and likely to make headlines."

Venables (2005) suggests audiences may interpret news as a risk signal. Psychologists and primatologists have shown that apes and humans constantly monitor the environment for information that may signal the possibility of physical danger or threat to the individual's social position. This receptiveness to risk signals is a powerful and virtually universal survival mechanism.

A 'risk signal' is characterized by two factors, an element of change (or uncertainty) and the relevance of that change to the security of the individual. The same two conditions are observed to be characteristic of news. The news value of a story, if defined in terms of the interest it carries for an audience, is determined by the degree of change it contains and the relevance that change has for the individual or group. Analysis shows that journalists and publicists manipulate both the element of change and relevance ('security concern') to maximize, or some cases play down, the strength of a story. Security concern is proportional to the relevance of the story for the individual, his or her family, social group and societal group, in declining order. At some point there is a Boundary of Relevance, beyond which the change is no longer perceived to be relevant, or newsworthy. This boundary may be manipulated by journalists, power elites and communicators seeking to encourage audiences to exclude, or embrace, certain groups: for instance, to distance a home audience from the enemy in time of war, or conversely, to highlight the plight of a distant culture so as to encourage support for aid programmes.

Defining News Values

The practical constraints of the newsgathering process, the collective norms of the newsroom and manipulation by external pressure groups all affect the news value given to an event by the journalist and the way it is reported. The news value given to the story by the audience, its impact or interest, is determined by the degree of change it contains and the relevance of that change to the physical and social security of the individual or group. Major change, coupled with high relevance, gives the story a correspondingly high news value; little, or slow, change, together with low relevance, indicate low news value.

Some commentators (Harcup and O'Neill,) argue that as many stories are apparently manufactured, Galtung and Ruge's list of news values should be open to question. The dominance of celebrity and social news, the blurring of the boundary between news and reality shows and other popular culture, and the advent of citizen journalism may suggest that the nature of 'news' and news values are evolving and that traditional models of the news process are now only partially relevant.

OBJECTIVITY IN JOURNALISM

Objectivity is a significant principle of journalistic professionalism. Journalistic objectivity can refer to *fairness*, *disinterestedness*, *factuality* and *non-partisanship*, but most often encompasses all of these qualities. Advocacy journalism is one alternative to objective journalism.

Definitions

Journalists and the public often tend to identify objectivity in its absence. Few journalists would make a claim to total neutrality or impartiality. However, most strive toward a certain modicum of detachment from their own personal biases in their news work. In *Discovering the News* (1978), sociologist Michael Schudson argues that "the belief in objectivity is a faith in 'facts,' a distrust in 'values,' and a commitment to their segregation." In the United States, an objective story is typically considered to be one that steers a middle path between two poles of political rhetoric. The tenets of objectivity are violated to the degree to which the story appears to favour one pole over the other.

According to some, it refers to the prevailing ideology of newsgathering and reporting that emphasizes eyewitness accounts of events, corroboration of facts with multiple sources and "balance." It also implies an institutional role for journalists as a fourth estate, a body that exists apart from government and large interest groups. Others hold it should mean reporting things without bias, as if one just came to Earth from another planet and had no preconceived opinions about our behaviour or ways. This form of journalism is rarely practiced, although some argue it would lead to radical changes in reporting.

Still others hold it to mean that journalists should have something like a neutral point of view, not taking a stand on any issues on which there is some disagreement. Instead, journalists are simply to report "both sides" of an issue. Some even extend this standard to the journalist's personal life, prohibiting them from getting involved in political activities, which necessarily requires taking a stand. For example, Washington Post-executive editor Leonard Downie, Jr. has stated that the Post-maintains a code of ethics that forbids reporters and editors from all "political activities" except voting. Downie himself goes even further and "decided to stop voting when [he] became the ultimate gatekeeper for what is published in the newspaper."

Criticisms

Advocacy journalists and civic journalists criticize this last understanding of objectivity, arguing that it does a disservice to the public because it fails to attempt to find the truth. They also argue that such objectivity is nearly impossible to apply in practice—newspapers inevitably take a point of view in deciding what stories to cover, which to feature on the front page, and what sources they quote. Media critics such as Edward Herman and Noam Chomsky (1988) have described a propaganda model that they use to show how in practice such a notion of objectivity ends up heavily favouring the viewpoint of government and powerful corporations.

Another example of an objection to objectivity, according to communication scholar David Mindich (*Just the Facts: How "Objectivity" Came to Define American Journalism*, 1998), was the coverage that the major papers (most notably the New York Times) gave to the lynching of thousands of African Americans during the 1890s. News stories of the period often described with detachment the hanging, immolation and mutilation of men, women and children by mobs. Under the regimen of objectivity, news writers often attempted to balance these accounts by recounting the alleged transgressions of the victims that provoked the lynch mobs to fury. David Mindich argues that this may have had the effect of normalizing the practice of lynching.

Online Journalism

New forms of journalism, such as online journalism, further alter perceived notions of objectivity and balance due to the advantages of speed and content that can cause journalists to hasten their copy. If journalists are seen as gatekeepers for objective and verifiable information, then that role is surely threatened by a medium where people can access and use virtually any piece of information at will. It has been proposed to certify web based news with a news domain. Tim Berners-Lee, credited with the creation of the world wide web, has recently stated that he is worried that the Web is being used to spread misinformation:

> "On the web the thinking of cults can spread very rapidly and suddenly a cult which was 12 people who had some deep personal issues suddenly find a formula which is very believable. A sort of conspiracy theory of sorts and which you can imagine spreading to thousands of people and being deeply damaging."

Objectivity in online journalism can suffer as a direct result of these 'cults of thinking.' Tim Berners-Lee refers to the false rumours of the harmful effects of the MMR vaccine which spread across the web in the United Kingdom, which led to many children remaining unvaccinated.

Alternatives

Some argue that a more appropriate standard should be fairness and accuracy (as enshrined in the names of groups like Fairness and Accuracy in Reporting). Under this standard, taking sides on an issue would be permitted as long as the side taken was accurate and the other side was given a fair chance to respond. Many professionals believe that true objectivity in journalism is not possible and reporters must seek balance in their stories (giving all sides their respective points of view), which fosters fairness.

Notable departures from objective news work include the muckraking of Ida Tarbell and Lincoln Steffens, the New Journalism of Tom Wolfe and Hunter S. Thompson, the underground press of the 1960s and public journalism.

History

The term objectivity was not applied to journalistic work until the 20th century, but it had fully emerged as a guiding principle by the 1890s. A number of communication scholars and historians agree that the idea of "objectivity" has prevailed as a dominant discourse among journalists in the United States since the appearance of modern newspapers in the Jacksonian Era of the 1830s. The rise of objectivity in journalistic method is also rooted in the scientific positivism of the 19th century, as professional journalism of the late 19th century borrowed parts of its worldview from various scientific disciplines of the day.

Some historians, like Gerald Baldasty, have observed that "objectivity" went hand in hand with the need to make profits in the newspaper business by selling advertising. Publishers did not want to offend any potential advertising customers and therefore encouraged news editors and reporters to strive to present all sides of an issue. In a similar vein, the rise of wire services and other cooperative arrangements forced journalists to produce more "middle of the road" stories that would be acceptable to newspapers of a variety of political persuasions. Ben H. Bagdikian, especially in his book "The Media Monopoly" (1983) writes critically about the consequences of the rise of "objective journalism." (One sample can be found in an online excerpt: "Democracy and the Media"). Others have proposed a political explanation for the rise of objectivity, which occurred earlier in the United States than most other countries; scholars like Richard Kaplan have argued that political parties needed to lose their hold over the loyalties of voters and the institutions of government before the press could feel free to offer a non-partisan, "impartial" account of news events. This change occurred following the critical election of 1896 and the subsequent progressive reform era.

JOURNALISM ETHICS AND STANDARDS

Journalism ethics and standards comprise principles of ethics and of good practice as applicable to the specific challenges faced by professional journalists. Historically and currently, this subset of media ethics is widely known to journalists as their professional "code of ethics" or the "canons of journalism." The basic codes and canons commonly appear in statements drafted by both professional journalism associations and individual print, broadcast, and online news organizations.

> *"Every news organization has only its credibility and reputation to rely on."*
>
> —Tony Burman, editor-in-chief of CBC News

While various existing codes have some differences, most share common elements including the principles of—truthfulness, accuracy, objectivity, impartiality, fairness and public accountability—as these apply to the acquisition of newsworthy information and its subsequent dissemination to the public.

Like many broader ethical systems, journalism ethics include the principle of "limitation of harm." This often involves the withholding of certain details from reports such as the names of minor children, crime victims' names or information not materially related to particular news reports release of which might, for example, harm someone's reputation.

Evolution and Purpose of Codes of Journalism

The principles of Journalistic codes of ethics are designed as guides through numerous difficulties, such as conflicts of interest, to assist journalists in dealing with ethical dilemmas. The codes and canons provide journalists a framework for self-monitoring and self-correction as they pursue professional assignments.

Codes of Practice

While journalists in the United States and European countries have led in formulation and adoption of these standards, such codes can be found in news reporting organizations in most countries with freedom of the press. The written codes and practical standards vary somewhat from country to country and organization to organization, but there is a substantial overlap among mainstream publications and societies.

One of the leading voices in the U.S. on the subject of Journalistic Standards and Ethics is the Society of Professional Journalists. The Preamble to its Code of Ethics states:

> *...public enlightenment is the forerunner of justice and the foundation of democracy. The duty of the journalist is to further those ends by seeking truth and providing a fair and comprehensive account of events and issues. Conscientious journalists from all media and specialties strive to serve the public with thoroughness and honesty. Professional integrity is the cornerstone of a journalist's credibility.*

The Radio-Television News Directors Association, an organization exclusively centered on electronic journalism, maintains a code of ethics centering on—public trust, truthfulness, fairness, integrity, independence and accountability. RTDNA publishes a pocket guide to these standards.

Examples of journalistic codes of ethics held by international news gathering organizations may be found as follows:

- *British Broadcasting Corporation*: Editorial Guidelines.
- *Canadian Broadcasting Corporation*: Journalistic Standards and Practices.
- *Al Jazeera*: Code of Ethics.
- Code of Journalists of the Republic of Slovenia.

Common Elements

The primary themes common to most codes of journalistic standards and ethics are the following:

Objectivity

- Unequivocal separation between news and opinion. Editorials and op-eds are clearly separated from news pieces. News reporters and editorial staff are distinct.
- Unequivocal separation between advertisements and news. All advertisements must be clearly identifiable as such.
- Reporter must avoid conflicts of interests—incentives to report a story with a given slant. This includes not taking bribes and not reporting on stories that affect the reporter's personal, economic or political interests. See envelope journalism.
- Competing points of view are balanced and fairly characterized.

- Persons who are the subject of adverse news stories are allowed a reasonable opportunity to respond to the adverse information before the story is published or broadcast.
- Interference with reporting by any entity, including censorship, must be disclosed.

Sources

- Confidentiality of anonymous sources (see news source).
- Avoidance of anonymous sources if possible.
- Accurate attribution of statements made by individuals or other news media.
- Pictures, sound, and quotations must not be presented in a misleading context (or lack thereof). Simulations, reenactments, alterations, and artistic imaginings must be clearly labelled as such, if not avoided entirely.
- Plagiarism is strongly stigmatized and in many cases illegal (see copyright).

Accuracy and Standards for Factual Reporting

- Reporters are expected to be as accurate as possible given the time allotted to story preparation and the space available, and to seek reliable sources.
- Events with a single eyewitness are reported with attribution. Events with two or more independent eyewitnesses may be reported as fact. Controversial facts are reported with attribution.
- Independent fact-checking by another employee of the publisher is desirable.
- Corrections are published when errors are discovered.
- Defendants at trial are treated only as having "allegedly" committed crimes, until conviction, when their crimes are generally reported as fact (unless, that is, there is serious controversy about wrongful conviction).
- Opinion surveys and statistical information deserve special treatment to communicate in precise terms any conclusions, to contextualize the results, and to specify accuracy, including estimated error and methodological criticism or flaws.

Slander and Libel Considerations

- Reporting the truth is never libel, which makes accuracy very important.
- Private persons have privacy rights that must be balanced against the public interest in reporting information about them. Public figures have fewer privacy rights in U.S. law, where reporters are immune from a civil case if they have reported without malice. In Canada, there is no such immunity; reports on public figures must be backed by facts.
- Publishers vigorously defend libel lawsuits filed against their reporters, usually covered by libel insurance.

Harm Limitation Principle

During the normal course of an assignment a reporter might go about—gathering facts and details, conducting interviews, doing research, background checks, taking photos, video taping, recording sound—harm limitation deals with the questions of whether everything learned should be reported, and if so, how. This principle of limitation means that some weight needs to be given to the negative consequences of full disclosure, creating a practical and ethical dilemma. The Society of Professional Journalists' code of ethics offers the following advice, which is representative of the practical ideals of most professional journalists. Quoting directly:

- Show compassion for those who may be affected adversely by news coverage. Use special sensitivity when dealing with children and inexperienced sources or subjects.
- Be sensitive when seeking or using interviews or photographs of those affected by tragedy or grief.
- Recognize that gathering and reporting information may cause harm or discomfort. Pursuit of the news is not a license for arrogance.
- Recognize that private people have a greater right to control information about themselves than do public officials and others who seek power, influence or attention. Only an overriding public need can justify intrusion into anyone's privacy.

- Show good taste. Avoid pandering to lurid curiosity.
- Be cautious about identifying juvenile suspects or victims of sex crimes.
- Be judicious about naming criminal suspects before the formal filing of charges.
- Balance a criminal suspect's fair trial rights with the public's right to be informed.

Presentation

Ethical standards should not be confused with common standards of quality of presentation, including:

- Correctly spoken or written language (often in a widely spoken and formal dialect, such as Standard English).
- Clarity.
- Brevity (or depth, depending on the niche of the publisher).

Self-Regulation

In addition to codes of ethics, many news organizations maintain an in-house Ombudsman whose role is, in part, to keep news organizations honest and accountable to the public. The Ombudsman is intended to mediate in conflicts stemmsing from internal and or external pressures, to maintain accountability to the public for news reported, and to foster self-criticism and to encourage adherence to both codified and uncodified ethics and standards. This position may be the same or similar to the public editor, though public editors also act as a liaison with readers and do not generally become members of the Organization of News Ombudsmen.

An alternative is a news council, an industry-wide self-regulation body, such as the Press Complaints Commission, set up by UK newspapers and magazines. Such a body is capable perhaps of applying fairly consistent standards, and of dealing with a higher volume of complaints, but may not escape criticisms of being toothless.

Ethics and Standards in Practice

As with other ethical codes, there is a perennial concern that the standards of journalism are being ignored. One of the most controversial issues in modern reporting is media bias, especially on political issues, but also with regard to cultural and other issues. Sensationalism is also a common complaint. Minor factual errors are also extremely common, as almost anyone who is familiar with the subject of a particular report will quickly realize.

There are also some wider concerns, as the media continue to change, for example that the brevity of news reports and use of soundbites has reduced fidelity to the truth, and may contribute to a lack of needed context for public understanding. From outside the profession, the rise of news management contributes to the real possibility that news media may be deliberately manipulated. Selective reporting (spiking, double standards) are very commonly alleged against newspapers, and by their nature are forms of bias not easy to establish, or guard against.

This section does not address specifics of such matters, but issues of practical compliance, as well as differences between professional journalists on principles.

Standards and Reputation

Among the leading news organizations that voluntarily adopt and attempt to uphold the common standards of journalism ethics described herein, adherence and general quality varies considerably. The professionalism, reliability and public accountability of a news organization are three of its most valuable assets. An organization earns and maintains a strong reputation, in part, through a consistent implementation of ethical standards, which influence its position with the public and within the industry.

Genres and Ethics

Advocacy journalists—a term of some debate even within the field of journalism—by definition tend to reject "objectivity", while at the same time maintaining many other common standards and ethics. Creative non-fiction and Literary journalism use the power of language and literary devices more akin to fiction to bring insight and depth into often book-length treatment of the subjects about which they write. Such devices as dialogue, metaphor, digression and other such techniques offer the reader insights not usually found in standard news reportage. However, authors in this branch of journalism still maintain ethical criteria such as factual and historical accuracy as found in standard news reporting. Yet, with brilliant prose, they venture outside the boundaries of standard news reporting in offering richly detailed accounts. One widely regarded author in the genre is Joyce Carol Oates, as with her book on boxer Mike Tyson.

New Journalism and Gonzo journalism also reject some of the fundamental ethical traditions and will set aside the technical standards of journalistic prose in order to express themselves and reach a particular audience or market segment.

Tabloid journalists are often accused of sacrificing accuracy and the personal privacy of their subjects in order to boost sales. Supermarket tabloids are often focussed on entertainment rather than news. A few have "news" stories that are so outrageous that they are widely read for entertainment purposes, not for information. Some tabloids do purport to maintain common journalistic standards, but may fall far short in practice. Others make no such claims.

Some publications deliberately engage in satire, but give the publication the design elements of a newspaper, for example, The Onion, and it is not unheard of for other publications to offer the occasional, humorous articles appearing on April Fool's Day.

Relationship with Freedom of the Press

In countries without freedom of the press, the majority of people who report the news may not follow the above described standards of journalism. Non-free media are often prohibited from criticizing the national government, and in many cases are required to distribute propaganda as if it were news. Various other forms of censorship may restrict reporting on issues the government deems sensitive.

Variations, Violations and Controversies

There are a number of finer points of journalistic procedure that foster disagreements in principle and variation in practice among "mainstream" journalists in the free press. Laws concerning libel and slander vary from country to country, and local journalistic standards may be tailored to fit. For example, the United Kingdom has a broader definition of libel than does the United States.

Accuracy is important as a core value and to maintain credibility, but especially in broadcast media, audience share often gravitates toward outlets that are reporting new information first. Different organizations may balance speed and accuracy in different ways. The New York Times, for instance, tends to print longer more detailed, less speculative, and more thoroughly verified pieces a day or two later than many other newspapers. 24-hour television news networks tend to place much more emphasis on getting the "scoop." Here, viewers may switch channels at a moment's notice; with fierce competition for ratings and a large amount of airtime to fill, fresh material is very valuable. Because of the fast turn-around, reporters for these networks may be under considerable time pressure, which reduces their ability to verify information.

Laws with regard to personal privacy, official secrets, and media disclosure of names and facts from criminal cases and civil lawsuits differ widely, and journalistic standards may vary accordingly. Different organizations may have different answers to questions about when it is journalistically acceptable to skirt, circumvent, or even break these regulations. Another example of differences surrounding harm reduction is the reporting of preliminary election results. In the United States, some news organizations feel that it is harmful to the democratic process to report exit poll results or preliminary returns while voting is still open. Such reports may influence people who vote later in the day, or who are in western time zones, in their decisions about how and whether or not to vote. There is also some concern that such preliminary results are often inaccurate and may be misleading to the public. Other outlets feel that this information is a vital part of the transparency of the election process, and see no harm (if not considerable benefit) in reporting it.

Taste, Decency and Acceptability

Audiences have different reactions to depictions of violence, nudity, coarse language, or to people in any other situation that is unacceptable to or stigmatized by the local culture or laws (such as the consumption of alcohol, homosexuality, illegal drug use, scatological images, etc.). Even with similar audiences, different organizations and even individual reporters have different standards and practices. These decisions often revolve around what facts are necessary for the audience to know.

When certain distasteful or shocking material is considered important to the story, there are a variety of common methods for mitigating negative audience reaction. Advance warning of explicit or disturbing material may allow listeners or readers to avoid content they would rather not be exposed to. Offensive words may be partially obscured or bleeped. Potentially offensive images may be blurred or narrowly cropped. Descriptions may be substituted for pictures; graphic detail might be omitted. Disturbing content might be moved from a cover to an inside page, or from daytime to late evening, when children are less likely to be watching.

There is often considerable controversy over these techniques, especially concern that obscuring or not reporting certain facts or details is self-censorship that compromises objectivity and fidelity to the truth, and which does not serve the public interest.

For example, images and graphic descriptions of war are often violent, bloody, shocking and profoundly tragic. This makes certain content disturbing to some audience members, but it is precisely these aspects of war that some consider to be the most important to convey. Some argue that "sanitizing" the depiction of war influences public opinion about the merits of continuing to fight, and about the policies or circumstances that precipitated the conflict. The amount of explicit violence and mutilation depicted in war coverage varies considerable from time to time, from organization to organization, and from country to country.

Reporters have also been accused of indecency in the process of collecting news, namely that they are overly intrusive in the name of journalistic insensitivity. War correspondent Edward Behr recounts the story of a reporter during the Congo Crisis who walked into a crowd of Belgian evacuees and shouted, "Anyone here been raped and speaks English?"

Campaigning in the Media

Many print publications take advantage of their wide readership and print persuasive pieces in the form of unsigned editorials that represent the official position of the organization. Despite the ostensible separation between editorial writing and news gathering, this practice may cause some people to doubt the political objectivity of the publication's news reporting. (Though usually unsigned editorials are accompanied by a diversity of signed opinions from other perspectives.)

Other publications and many broadcast media only publish opinion pieces that are attributed to a particular individual (who may be an in-house analyst) or to an outside entity. One particularly controversial question is whether media organizations should endorse political candidates for office. Political endorsements create more opportunities to construe favouritism in reporting, and can create a perceived conflict of interest.

Investigative Methods

Investigative journalism is largely an information-gathering exercise, looking for facts that are not easy to obtain by simple requests and searches, or are actively being concealed, suppressed or distorted. Where investigative work involves undercover journalism or use of whistleblowers, and even more if it resorts to covert methods more typical of private detectives or even spying, it brings a large extra burden on ethical standards.

Anonymous sources are double-edged—they often provide especially newsworthy information, such as classified or confidential information about current events, information about a previously unreported scandal, or the perspective of a particular group that may fear retribution for expressing certain opinions in the press. The downside is that the condition of anonymity may make it difficult or impossible for the reporter to verify the source's statements. Sometimes sources hide their identities from the public because their statements would otherwise quickly be discredited. Thus, statements attributed to anonymous sources may carry more weight with the public than they might if they were attributed.

The Washington press has been criticized in recent years for excessive use of anonymous sources, in particular to report information that is later revealed to be unreliable. The use of anonymous sources increased markedly in the period before the 2003 invasion of Iraq.

Science Issues

The mainstream press is often criticized for poor accuracy in reporting science news. Many reporters are not scientists, and are thus not familiar with the material they are summarizing.

Technical information is also difficult to contextualize for lay audiences, and short-form reporting makes providing background, context, and clarification even harder. Food scares are an example of the need for responsible science journalism, as are stories connected with the safety of medical procedures.

Examples of Ethical Dilemmas

One of the primary functions of journalism ethics is to aid journalists in dealing with many ethical dilemmas they may encounter. From highly sensitive issues of national security to everyday questions such as accepting a dinner from a source, putting a bumper sticker on one's car, publishing a personal opinion blog, a journalist must make decisions taking into account things such as the public's right to know, potential threats, reprisals and intimidations of all kinds, personal integrity, conflicts between editors, reporters and publishers or management, and many other such conundra. The following are illustrations of some of those:

- The Pentagon Papers dealt with extremely difficult ethical dilemmas faced by journalists. Despite government intervention, The *Washington Post*, joined by *The New York Times*, felt the public interest was more compelling and both published reports. (The cases went to the Supreme Court where they were merged and are known as *New York Times* Co. v. United States, 403 U.S. 713).
- *The Washington Post* also once published a story about a listening device that the United States had installed over an undersea Soviet cable during the height of the cold war. The device allowed the United States to learn where Soviet submarines were positioned. In that case, Post Executive Editor Ben Bradlee chose not to run the story on national security grounds. However, the Soviets subsequently discovered the device and, according to Bradlee, "It was no longer a matter of national security. It was a matter of national embarrassment." However, the U.S. government still wanted *The Washington Post* not to run the story on the basis of national security, yet, according to Bradlee, "We ran the story. And you know what, the sun rose the next day."

- The Ethics Advice Line, a joint venture, public service project of Chicago Headline Club Chapter of the Society of Professional Journalists and Loyola University Chicago Center for Ethics and Social Justice, provides some examples of typical ethical dilemmas reported to their ethical dilemma hotline and are typical of the kinds of questions faced by many professional journalists.

A partial listing of questions received by *The Ethics Advice Line*:

- Is it ethical to make an appointment to interview an arsonist sought by police, without informing police in advance of the interview?
- Is lack of proper attribution plagiarism?
- Should a reporter write a story about a local priest who confessed to a sex crime if it will cost the newspaper readers and advertisers who are sympathetic to the priest?
- Is it ethical for a reporter to write a news piece on the same topic on which he or she has written an opinion piece in the same paper?
- Under what circumstances do you identify a person who was arrested as a relative of a public figure, such as a local sports star?
- Freelance journalists and photographers accept cash to write about, or take photos of, events with the promise of attempting to get their work on the AP or other news outlets, from which they also will be paid. Is that ethical?
- Can a journalist reveal a source of information after guaranteeing confidentiality if the source proves to be unreliable?

DEFAMATION

In law, defamation (also called calumny, libel, slander, and vilification) is the communication of a statement that makes a false claim, expressly stated or implied to be factual, that may give an individual, business, product, group, government or nation a negative image. Slander refers to a malicious, false, and defamatory statement or report, while libel refers to any other form of communication such as written words or images. Most jurisdictions allow legal actions, civil and/or criminal, to deter various kinds of defamation and retaliate against groundless criticism. Related to defamation is public disclosure of private facts which arises where one person reveals information which is not of public concern, and the release of which would offend a reasonable person. "Unlike libel, truth is not a defence for invasion of privacy."

False light laws are "intended primarily to protect the plaintiff's mental or emotional well-being." If a publication of information is false, then a tort of defamation might have occurred. If that communication is not technically false but is still misleading then a tort of false light might have occurred.

History

In the later Roman jurisprudence, from which many of modern laws descend, verbal defamations are dealt within the edict under two heads. The first comprehended defamatory and injurious statements made in a public manner (*convicium contra bonos mores*). In this case, the essence of the offense lay in the unwarrantable public proclamation. In such a case the truth of the statements was no justification for the unnecessarily public and insulting manner in which they had been made. The second head included defamatory statements made in private, and in this case the offense lay in the imputation itself, not in the manner of its publication. The truth was therefore a sufficient defense, for no man had a right to demand legal protection for a false reputation. Even belief in the truth was enough, because it took away the intention which was essential to the notion of injuria.

The law thus aimed at giving sufficient scope for the discussion of a man's character, while it protected him from needless insult and pain. The remedy for verbal defamation was long confined to a civil action for a monetary penalty, which was estimated according to the significance of the case, and which, although vindictive in its character, doubtless included practically the element of compensation. But a new remedy was introduced with the extension of the criminal law, under which many kinds of defamation were punished with great severity. At the same time increased importance attached to the publication of defamatory books and writings, the *libri* or *libelli famosi*, from which we derive our modern use of the word libel; and under the later emperors the latter term came to be specially applied to anonymous accusations or pasquils, the dissemination of which was regarded as particularly dangerous, and visited with very severe punishment, whether the matter contained in them were true or false.

Types of Torts

Slander and Libel

The common law origins of defamation lie in the torts of slander (harmful statement in a transitory form, especially speech) and libel (harmful statement in a fixed medium, especially writing but also a picture, sign, or electronic broadcast), each of which gives a common law right of action.

"Defamation" is the general term used internationally, and is used in this article where it is not necessary to distinguish between "slander" and "libel." Libel and slander both require publication. The fundamental distinction between libel and slander lies solely in the *form* in which the defamatory matter is published. If the offending material is published in some fleeting form, as by spoken words or sounds, sign language, gestures and the like, then this is slander. If it is published in more durable form, for example in written words, film, compact disc (CD), DVD, blogging and the like, then it is considered libel." The debate whether Internet blogs or Bulletin Boards are publishers is the key subject being addressed, where as an Internet based community is more akin to conversations in a bar or pub, with content being written as an on-going dialog which is generally not edited or regulated such as in the publishing industry. "out-law.com" (August 8th, 2008).

Criminal Defamation

Many nations have criminal penalties for defamation in some situations, and different conditions for determining whether an offense has occurred. ARTICLE 19, Global Campaign for Free Expression, has published global maps charting the existence of criminal defamation law across the globe. The law is used predominantly to defend political leaders or functionaries of the state. In Britain, the Italian anarchist Errico Malatesta was convicted of criminal libel for denouncing the Italian state agent

Ennio Belelli in 1912. In Canada, though the law has been applied on only six occasions in the past century, all of those cases involve libellants attached to the state (police officers, judges, prison guards). In the most recent case, Bradley Waugh and Ravin Gill were charged with criminal libel for publicly accusing six prison guards of the racially motivated murder of a black inmate.

Defences

Even if a statement is derogatory, there are circumstances in which such statements are permissible in law.

Truth

In many legal systems, adverse public statements about legal citizens presented as fact must be proven false to be defamatory or slanderous/libel. Proving adverse, public character statements to be true is often the best defense against a prosecution for libel and/or defamation. Statements of opinion that cannot be proven true or false will likely need to apply some other kind of defense. The use of the defense of justification has dangers, however; if the defendant libels the plaintiff and then runs the defense of truth and fails, he may be said to have aggravated the harm.

Another important aspect of defamation is the difference between fact and opinion. Statements made as "facts" are frequently actionable defamation. Statements of opinion or pure opinion are not actionable. In order to win damages in a libel case, the plaintiff must first show that the statements were "statements of fact or mixed statements of opinion and fact" and second that these statements were false. Conversely, a typical defense to defamation is that the statements are opinion. One of the major tests to distinguish whether a statement is fact or opinion is whether the statement can be proved true or false in a court of law. If the statement can be proved true or false, then, on that basis, the case will be heard by a jury to determine whether it is true or false. If the statement cannot be proved true or false, the court may dismiss the libel case without it ever going to a jury to find facts in the case.

In some systems, however, notably the Philippines, truth alone is not a defense. Some U.S. statutes preserve historical common law exceptions to the defense of truth to libel actions. These exceptions were for statements "tending to blacken the memory of one who is dead" or "expose the natural defects of one who is alive." It is also necessary in these cases to show that there is a well-founded public interest in the specific information being widely known, and this may be the case even for public figures. Public interest is generally not "that which the public is interested in", but rather "that which is in the interest of the public."

Privilege and Malice

Privilege provides a complete bar and answer to a defamation suit, though conditions may have to be met before this protection is granted.

There are two types of privilege in the common law tradition:

(*a*) "Absolute privilege" has the effect that a statement cannot be sued on as defamatory, even if it were made maliciously; a typical example is evidence given in court (although this may give rise to different claims, such as an action for malicious prosecution or perjury) or statements made in a session of the legislature (known as 'Parliamentary privilege' in Commonwealth countries).

(*b*) "Qualified privilege" may be available to the journalist as a defense in circumstances where it is considered important that the facts be known in the public interest; an example would be public meetings, local government documents, and information relating to public bodies such as the police and fire departments. Qualified privilege has the same effect as absolute privilege, but does not protect statements that can be proven to have been made with malicious intent.

Other Defences

Defences to claims of defamation include:

- *Truth* is an absolute defence in the United States as well as in the common law jurisdictions of Canada. In some other countries it is also necessary to show a benefit to the public good in having the information brought to light.

- *Statements made in a good faith and reasonable belief that they were true* are generally treated the same as true statements; however, the court may inquire into the reasonableness of the belief. The degree of care expected will vary with the nature of the defendant: an ordinary person might safely rely on a single newspaper report, while the newspaper would be expected to carefully check multiple sources.
- *Privilege* is a defense when witness testimony, attorneys' arguments, and judges' decisions, rulings, and statements made in court, or statements by legislators on the floor of the legislature, or statements made by a person to their spouse, are the cause for the claim. These statements are said to be privileged and cannot be cause for a defamation claim.
- *Opinion* is a defense recognized in nearly every jurisdiction. If the allegedly defamatory assertion is an expression of opinion rather than a statement of fact, defamation claims usually cannot be brought because opinions are inherently not falsifiable. However, some jurisdictions decline to recognize any legal distinction between fact and opinion. The United States Supreme Court, in particular, has ruled that the First Amendment does not require recognition of an opinion privilege.
- *Fair comment on a matter of public interest,* statements made with an honest belief in their truth on a matter of public interest (official acts) are defenses to a defamation claim, even if such arguments are logically unsound; if a reasonable person could honestly entertain such an opinion, the statement is protected.
- *Consent* is an uncommon defense and makes the claim that the claimant consented to the dissemination of the statement.
- *Innocent dissemination* is a defense available when a defendant had no actual knowledge of the defamatory statement or no reason to believe the statement was defamatory. The defense can be defeated if the lack of knowledge was due to negligence. Thus, a delivery service cannot be held liable for delivering a sealed defamatory letter.

- Claimant is *incapable of further defamation*—e.g., the claimant's position in the community is so poor that defamation could not do further damage to the plaintiff. Such a claimant could be said to be "libel-proof," since in most jurisdictions, actual damage is an essential element for a libel claim. Essentially, the defense is that the person has a bad reputation before the libel, hence there was no further damages by the statement.

In addition to the above, the defendant may claim that the allegedly defamatory statement is not actually capable of being defamatory—an insulting statement that does not actually harm someone's reputation is prima facie not libelous. Also, the public figure doctrine, also called the absence of malice rule, may be used as a defense.

Public Figure Doctrine (Absence of Malice)

Special rules apply in the case of statements made in the press concerning public figures, which can be used as a defense. A series of court rulings led by *New York Times Co. v. Sullivan*, 376 U.S. 254 (1964) established that for a public official (or other legitimate public figure) to win a libel case, the statement must have been published knowing it to be false or with reckless disregard to its truth, (also known as actual malice). Under United States law, libel generally requires five key elements. The plaintiff must prove that the information was published, the plaintiff was directly or indirectly identified, the remarks were defamatory towards the plaintiff's reputation, the published information is false, and that the defendant is at fault.

The estimates that 95 per cent of libel cases involving news stories do not arise from high-profile news stories, but "run of the mill" local stories like news coverage of local criminal investigations or trials, or business profiles. Media liability insurance is available to newspapers to cover potential damage awards from libel lawsuits.

Defamation and Feedom of Speech

Defamation laws may come into tension with freedom of speech, leading to censorship or chilling effects where publishers fear lawsuits, or loss of reputation where individuals have no effective protection against reckless or unfounded allegations. Article 10 of the European Convention on Human Rights permits restrictions on freedom of speech which are necessary for the protection of the reputation or the rights of others.

Jurisdictions resolve this tension in different ways, in particular in determining where the burden of proof lies when unfounded allegations are made. The power of the internet to disseminate comment, which may include malicious comment, has brought a new focus to the issue.

There is a broader consensus against laws which *criminalize* defamation. Human rights organizations, and other organizations such as the Council of Europe and Organization for Security and Co-operation in Europe, have campaigned against strict defamation laws which criminalize defamation. The European Court of Human Rights has placed restrictions on criminal libel laws because of the freedom of expression provisions of the European Convention on Human Rights. One notable case was Lingens v. Austria (1986).

Defamation Laws by Jurisdiction

Europe:

England: Modern libel and slander laws as implemented in many but not all Commonwealth nations, in the United States, and in the Republic of Ireland, are originally descended from English defamation law. The history of defamation law in England is somewhat obscure. Civil actions for damages seem to have been relatively frequent so far back as the reign of Edward I (1272-1307), though it is unknown whether any generally applicable criminal process was in use. The first fully-reported case in which libel is affirmed generally to be punishable at common law was tried during the reign of James I. From that time we find both the criminal and civil remedies in full operation.

English law allows actions for libel to be brought in the High Court for any published statements which are alleged to defame a named or identifiable individual or individuals in a manner which causes them loss in their trade or profession, or causes a reasonable person to think worse of him, her or them. Allowable defenses are justification (the truth of the statement), fair comment (whether the statement was a view that a reasonable person could have held), and privilege (whether the statements were made in Parliament or in court, or whether they were fair reports of allegations in the public interest). An offer of amends is a barrier to litigation. A defamatory statement is presumed to be false unless the defendant can prove its truth. Furthermore, to collect compensatory damages, a public official or public figure must prove actual malice (knowing falsity or reckless disregard for the truth). A private individual must only prove negligence (not using due care) to collect compensatory damages. In order to collect punitive damages, all individuals must prove actual malice.

Scotland: In Scots law, as in other jurisdictions which base themselves on the civil law tradition, there is no distinction between libel and slander, and all cases are simply defamation. The equivalent of the defence of justification is "veritas."

Germany: In German law, there is no distinction between libel and slander. Germany is a leader in Europe in enforcement of its defamation law, and lawsuits are increasing. The relevant sections of Germany's law are §90 (Denigration of the President of State), §90a (Denigration of the State and its Symbols), §90b (Unconstitutional denigration of the Organs of the Constitution), §185 ("insult"), §186 (Defamation of character), §187 (Defamation with deliberate untruths), §188 (Political defamation with increased penalties for offending against paras 186 and 187), §189 (Denigration of a deceased person), §190 (Defamation by means of a non-proven criminal conviction), §192 ("insult" with true statements), §193 (Claim to defamation by rightful interests), §194 (The Application for a criminal prosecution under these paragraphs), §199 (Cases of exchange of verbal abuse), and §200 (Method of proclamation). Paragraph 188 has been criticized for allowing certain public figures additional protection against criticism.

United States

The origins of US defamation law pre-date the American Revolution; one famous 1734 case involving John Peter Zenger established some precedent that the truth should be an absolute defense against libel charges. (Previous English defamation law had not provided this guarantee.) Though the First Amendment of the U.S. Constitution was designed to protect freedom of the press, for most of the history of the United States, the Supreme Court neglected to use it to rule on libel cases. This left libel laws, based upon the traditional common law of defamation inherited from the English legal system, mixed across the states. The 1964 case *New York Times Co. v. Sullivan,* however, dramatically changed the nature of libel law in the United States by establishing that public officials could win a suit for libel only if they could demonstrate publishers' "knowledge that the information was false" or that it was published "with reckless disregard of whether it was false or not." Later Supreme Court cases dismissed the claim for libel and forbade libel claims for statements that are so ridiculous to be clearly not true, or are involving opinionated subjects such as one's physical state of being. Recent cases have addressed defamation law and the internet.

Defamation law in the United States is much less plaintiff-friendly than its counterparts in European and the Commonwealth countries, due to the enforcement of the First Amendment. In the United States, a comprehensive discussion of what is and is not libel or slander is difficult, because the definition differs between different states, and under federal law. Some states codify what constitutes slander and libel together into the same set of laws. Criminal libel is rare or non-existent, depending on the state. Defenses to libel that can result in dismissal before trial include the statement being one of opinion rather than fact or being "fair comment and criticism." Truth is always a defense.

Most states recognize that some categories of statements are considered to be defamatory *per se,* such that people making a defamation claim for these statements do not need to prove that the statement was defamatory.

Slander Per Se

The four (4) categories of slander *per se* are: (*i*) accusing someone of a crime; (*ii*) alleging that someone has a foul or loathsome disease; (*iii*) adversely reflecting on a person's fitness to conduct her business or trade; and (*iv*) imputing serious sexual misconduct (especially the chastity of a woman). Once again, all you would have to prove is that someone had published the statement to a third party. No proof of special damages is required.

Singapore

Singapore has perhaps the world's strongest libel laws. The country's leaders have clearly indicated to the public that libel, as they choose to define it from time-to-time, on the Internet will not be tolerated and that those they deem responsible will be severely punished. On March 6, 1996, the government made providers and publishers liable for the content placed on the Internet. Even the owners of cybercafes may be held liable for libelous statements posted or possibly viewed in their establishments.

In 2001, a Singapore bank was fined SG$2 million (approx. 1 million euros or 1 million US$ at the time) for accidentally publishing a mildly libelous statement during the heated discussion of a takeover bid. The mistake was corrected very quickly, and there was no intent to do harm. In fact, it was reported that no harm seems to have been done. Nevertheless, the offended parties were awarded SG$1 million each. Apparently confirming the stringency of Singapore's defamation law, *Business Times* declined to report on the matter because one of the libelled parties objected.

Australia

Australian law tends to follow English law on defamation issues, although there are differences introduced by statute and by the implied constitutional limitation on governmental powers to limit speech of a political nature established in *Lange v. Australian Broadcasting Association* (1997). Since the introduction of the uniform defamation laws in 2005 the distinction between slander and libel has been abolished.

A recent judgement of the High Court of Australia has significant consequences on interpretation of the law. On 10 December 2002, the High Court of Australia handed down its judgement in the Internet defamation dispute in the case of *Gutnick v. Dow Jones*. The judgement, which established that Internet-published foreign publications that defamed an Australian in his or her Australian reputation could be held accountable under Australian libel law, has gained worldwide attention and is often (although inaccurately, see for example *Berezovsky v. Forbes* in England) said to be the first of its kind; the case was subsequently settled. Slander has been occasionally used to justify (and with some success) physical reaction, however usually the punishment for assault is only slightly reduced when there is evidence of provocation. Among the various common law jurisdictions, some Americans have presented a visceral and vocal reaction to the *Gutnick* decision. On the other hand, the decision mirrors similar decisions in many other jurisdictions such as England, Scotland, France, Canada and Italy.

Controversial uniform legislation was passed in Australia in 2005 severely restricting the right of corporations to sue for defamation (see, e.g., *Defamation Act 2005* (vic), s 9). The only corporations excluded from the general ban are those not for profit or those with less than 10 employees and not affiliated with another company.

Canada

As is the case for most Commonwealth jurisdictions, Canada follows English law on defamation issues (although the law in the province of Quebec has roots in both the English and the French tradition). At common law, defamation covers any communication that tends to lower the esteem of the subject in the minds of ordinary members of the public. Probably true statements are not excluded, nor are political opinions. Intent is always presumed, and it is not necessary to prove that the defendant intended to defame. In *Hill v. Church of Scientology of Toronto* (1995), the Supreme Court of Canada rejected the *actual malice* test adopted in the US case *New York Times Co. v. Sullivan*. Once a claim has been made, the defendant may avail him or herself to a defense of justification (the truth), fair comment, or privilege. Publishers of defamatory comments may also use the defense of innocent dissemination where they had no knowledge of the nature of the statement, it was not brought to their attention, and they were not negligent.

In Quebec, defamation was originally grounded in the law inherited from France. To establish civil liability for defamation, the plaintiff must establish, on a balance of probabilities, the existence of an injury, a wrongful act, and of a causal connection between the two. A person who has made defamatory remarks will not necessarily be civilly liable for them. The plaintiff must further demonstrate that the person who made the remarks committed a wrongful act. Defamation in Quebec is governed by a reasonableness standard, as opposed to strict liability; a defendant who made a false statement would not be held liable if it was reasonable to believe the statement was true.

Religious Law

Related Torts: Some jurisdictions have a separate tort or delict of "verbal injury," "intentional infliction of emotional distress," "ourageousness", or "convicium," involving the making of a statement, even if truthful, intended to harm the claimant out of malice; some have a separate tort or delict of "invasion of privacy" in which the making of a true statement may give rise to liability: but neither of these comes under the general heading of "defamation." Some jurisdictions also have the tort of "false light", in which a statement may be technically true, but so misleading as to be defamatory. There is also, in almost all jurisdictions, a tort or delict of "misrepresentation", involving the making of a statement which is untrue even though not defamatory; thus if a surveyor states that a house is free from the risk of flooding, he or she has not defamed anyone, but may still be liable to someone who purchases the house in reliance on this statement. Other increasingly common claims similar to defamation in U.S. law are claims that a famous trademark has been diluted through tarnishment, see generally trademark dilution, "intentional interference with contract," and "negligent misrepresentation."

Criminal laws prohibiting protests at funerals, sedition, false statements in connection with elections, and the use of profanity in public, are also often used in contexts similar to criminal libel actions. The boundaries of a court's power to hold individuals in "contempt of court" for what amounts to alleged defamatory statements about judges or the court process by attorneys or other people involved in court cases is also not well established in many common law countries.

FREEDOM OF THE PRESS

Freedom of the press consists of constitutional or statutory protections pertaining to the media and published materials. With respect to governmental information, any government distinguishes which materials are public or protected from disclosure to the public based on classification of information as sensitive, classified or secret and being otherwise protected from disclosure due to relevance of the information to protecting the national interest. Many governments are also subject to sunshine laws or freedom of information legislation that are used to define the ambit of national interest.

Basic Principles and Criteria

The Universal Declaration of Human Rights states: "Everyone has the right to freedom of opinion and expression; this right includes freedom to hold opinions without interference, and impart information and ideas through any media regardless of frontiers."

This philosophy is usually accompanied by legislation ensuring various degrees of freedom of scientific research (known as scientific freedom), publishing, press and printing the depth to which these laws are entrenched in a country's legal system can go as far down as its constitution. The concept of freedom of speech is often covered by the same laws as freedom of the press, thereby giving equal treatment to media and individuals.

Besides legal definitions, some non-governmental organizations use other criteria to judge the level of press freedom around the world:

- Reporters without Borders considers the number of journalists murdered, expelled or harassed, and the existence of a state monopoly on TV and radio, as well as the existence of censorship and self-censorship in the media, and the overall independence of media as well as the difficulties that foreign reporters may face.
- The Committee to Protect Journalists (CPJ) uses the tools of journalism to help journalists by tracking press freedom issues through independent research, fact-finding missions, and firsthand contacts in the field, including local working journalists in countries around the world. CPJ shares information on breaking cases with other press freedom organizations worldwide through the International Freedom of Expression Exchange, a global e-mail network. CPJ also tracks journalist deaths and detentions. CPJ staff applies strict criteria for each case; researchers independently investigate and verify the circumstances behind each death or imprisonment.
- Freedom house likewise studies the more general political and economic environments of each nation in order to

determine whether relationships of dependence exist that limit in practice the level of press freedom that might exist in theory. So the concept of independence of the press is one closely linked with the concept of press freedom.

Status of Press Freedom Worldwide

Worldwide Press Freedom Index

Every year, Reporters without Borders establishes a ranking of countries in terms of their freedom of the press. The worldwide press freedom index list is based on responses to surveys sent to journalists that are members of partner organizations of the RWB, as well as related specialists such as researchers, jurists and human rights activists. The survey asks questions about direct attacks on journalists and the media as well as other indirect sources of pressure against the free press, such as pressure on journalists by non-governmental groups. RWB is careful to note that the index only deals with press freedom, and does not measure the quality of journalism.

In 2003, the countries where press was the most free were Finland, Iceland, the Netherlands and Norway. In 2004, apart from the above countries, Denmark, Ireland, Slovakia, Portugal and Switzerland were tied at the top of the list, followed by New Zealand and Latvia. The country with the least degree of press freedom was North Korea, followed by Burma, Turkmenistan, People's Republic of China (mainland only), Vietnam, Nepal and Iran.

Non-Democratic States

According to Reporters without Borders, more than a third of the world's people live in countries where there is no press freedom. Overwhelmingly, these people live in countries where there is no system of democracy or where there are serious deficiencies in the democratic process.

Freedom of the press is an extremely problematic concept for most non-democratic systems of government since, in the modern age, strict control of access to information is critical to the existence of most non-democratic governments and their associated control systems and security apparatus. To this end, most non-democratic societies employ state-run news organizations to promote the

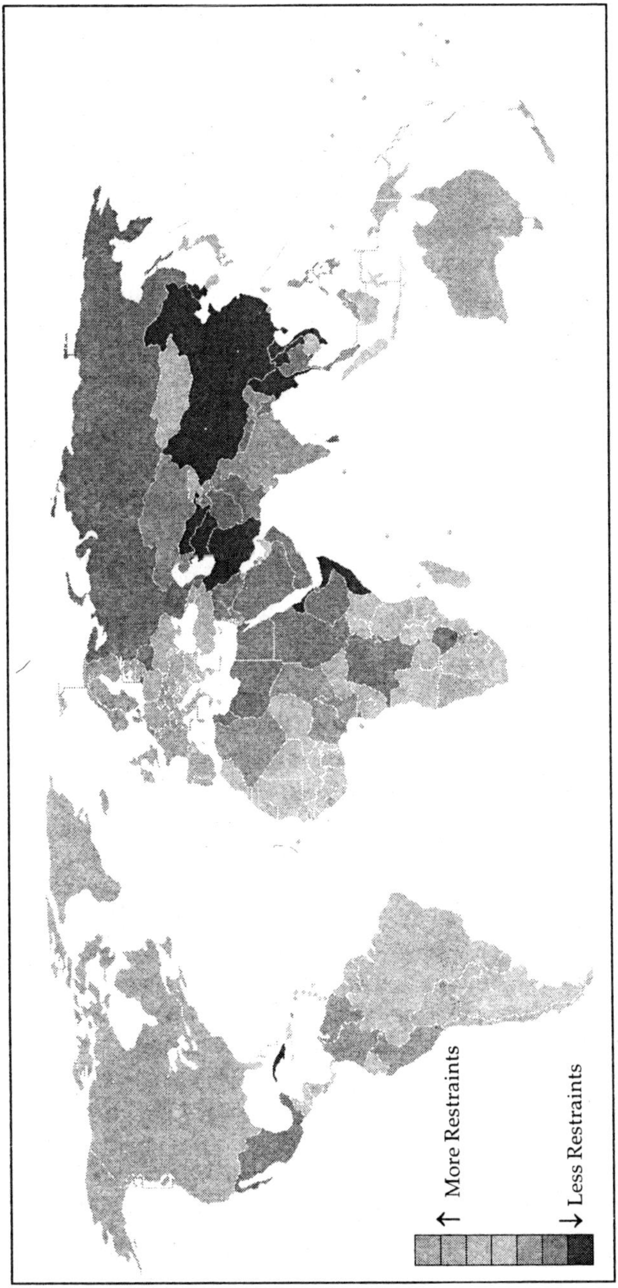

Freedom of the Press worldwide according to Reporters without Borders.

propaganda critical to maintaining an existing political power base and suppress (often very brutally, through the use of police, military, or intelligence agencies) any significant attempts by the media or individual journalists to challenge the approved "government line" on contentious issues. In such countries, journalists operating on the fringes of what is deemed to be acceptable will very often find themselves the subject of considerable intimidation by agents of the state. This can range from simple threats to their professional careers (firing, professional blacklisting) to death threats, kidnapping, torture, and assassination.

Reporters without Borders reports that, in 2003, 42 journalists lost their lives pursuing their profession and that, in the same year, at least 130 journalists were in prison as a result of their occupational activities. In 2005, 63 journalists and 5 media assistants were killed worldwide.

- The Lira Baysetova case in Kazakhstan.
- In Nepal, Eritrea and China (mainland only), journalists may spend years in jail simply for using the "wrong" word or photo.
- The Georgiy R. Gongadze case in Ukraine (information needed, spammer removed information).

According to the Press Freedom Index for 2007, Iran ranked 166th out of 169 nations. Only three other countries—Eritrea, North Korea and Turkmenistan—had more restrictions on news media freedom than Iran. The government of Mahmoud Ahmadinejad and the Supreme National Security Council had imprisoned 50 journalists in 2007 and had all but eliminated press freedom. RWB has dubbed Iran the "Middle East's biggest prison for journalists."

Regions Closed to Foreign Reporters

- Chechnya, Russia
- Jaffna, Sri Lanka
- Myanmar, Burma
- Papua, Indonesia
- Waziristan, Pakistan
- Tibet, People's Republic of China.

History

England

The Glorious Revolution of 1688 in England established parliamentary sovereignty over the Crown and, above all, the right of revolution. A major contributor to Western liberal theory was John Locke. Locke argued in Two Treatises of Government that the individual placed some of his rights present in the state of nature in trusteeship with the sovereign (government) in return for protection of certain natural individual rights. A social contract was entered into by the people.

Until 1694, England had an elaborate system of licensing. No publication was allowed without the accompaniment of a government-granted license. Fifty years earlier, at a time of civil war, John Milton wrote his pamphlet Areopagitica. In this work Milton argued forcefully against this form of government censorship and parodied the idea, writing "when as debtors and delinquents may walk abroad without a keeper, but unoffensive books must not stir forth without a visible jailer in their title." Although at the time it did little to halt the practice of licensing it would be viewed later a significant milestone in press freedom.

Milton's central argument was that the individual is capable of using reason and distinguishing right from wrong, good from bad. In order to be able to exercise this ration right, the individual must have unlimited access to the ideas of his fellow men in "a free and open encounter." From Milton's writings developed the concept of the open marketplace of ideas, the idea that when people argue against each other, the good arguments will prevail. One form of speech that was widely restricted in England was seditious libel, and laws were in place that made criticizing the government a crime. The King was above public criticism and statements critical of the government were forbidden, according to the English Court of the Star Chamber. Truth was not a defense to seditious libel because the goal was to prevent and punish all condemnation of the government.

John Stuart Mill approached the problem of authority versus liberty from the viewpoint of a 19th century utilitarian: The individual has the right of expressing himself so long as he does not harm other individuals. The good society is one in which the greatest number of persons enjoy the greatest possible amount of happiness. Applying these general principles of liberty to freedom of expression, Mill states that if we silence an opinion, we may silence the truth. The individual freedom of expression is therefore essential to the well-being of society.

Mill's application of the general principles of liberty is expressed in his book On Liberty: "If all mankind minus one, were of one opinion, and one, and only one person were of the contrary opinion, mankind would be no more justified in silencing that one person, than he, if he had the power, would be justified in silencing mankind."

Nazi Germany

The dictatorship of Adolf Hitler largely suppressed freedom of the press through Joseph Goebbels' Propaganda Ministry. As the Ministry's name implies, propaganda did not carry the negative connotations that it does today (or did in the Allied countries); how to manuals were openly distributed by that same ministry explaining the craft of effective propaganda. The Ministry also acted as a central control-point for all media, issuing orders as to what stories could be run and what stories would be suppressed. Anyone involved in the film industry—from directors to the lowliest assistant—had to sign an oath of loyalty to the Nazi Party, due to opinion-changing power Goebbels perceived movies to have. (Goebbels himself maintained some personal control over every single film made in Nazi Europe.) Journalists who crossed the Propaganda Ministry were routinely imprisoned or shot as traitors.

India

The Indian Constitution, while not mentioning the word "press", provides for "the right to freedom of speech and expression" [Article 19(1), a]. However, this right is subject to restrictions under subclause (2), whereby this freedom can be restricted for reasons of "sovereignty and integrity of India, the security of the State, friendly relations with foreign States, public order, preserving decency, preserving morality, in relation to contempt of court, defamation, or incitement to an offence." Laws such as the Official Secrets Act and Prevention of Terrorism Act (PoTA) have been used to limit press freedom. Under PoTA, person could be detained for up to six months for being in contact with a terrorist or terrorist group. PoTA was repealed in 2006, but the Official Secrets Act 1923 continues.

For the first half-century of independence, media control by the state was the major constraint on press freedom. Indira Gandhi famously stated in 1975 that All India Radio is "a Government organ, it is going to remain a Government organ..." With the liberalization starting in the 1990s, private control of media has burgeoned, leading to increasing independence and greater scrutiny of government. Organizations like Tehelka and NDTV have been particularly influential, *e.g.* in bringing about the resignation of powerful Haryana minister Venod Sharma.

Italy: Russia: United States

John Hancock was the first person to write newspapers in the British colonies in North America published "by authority," that is, under license from and as the mouthpiece of the colonial governors. The first regularly published newspaper was the Boston News-Letter of John Campbell, published weekly beginning in 1704. The early colonial publishers were either postmasters or government printers, and therefore unlikely to challenge government policies.

The first independent newspaper in the colonies was the New-England Courant, published in Boston by James Franklin beginning in 1721. A few years later, Franklin's younger brother, Benjamin, purchased the Pennsylvania Gazette of Philadelphia, which became the leading newspaper of the colonial era.

During this period, newspapers were unlicensed, and able freely to publish dissenting views, but were subject to prosecution for libel or even sedition if their opinions threatened the government. The notion of "freedom of the press" that later was enshrined in the United States Constitution is generally traced to the seditious libel prosecution of John Peter Zenger by the colonial governor of New York in 1735. In this instance of jury nullification, Zenger was acquitted after his lawyer, Andrew Hamilton, argued to the jury (contrary to established English law) that there was no libel in publishing the truth. Yet even after this celebrated case, colonial governors and assemblies asserted the power to prosecute and even imprison printers for publishing unapproved views.

During the American Revolution, a free press was identified by Revolutionary leaders as one of the elements of liberty that they sought to preserve. The Virginia Declaration of Rights (1776) proclaimed that "the freedom of the press is one of the greatest bulwarks of liberty and can never be restrained but by despotic governments." Similarly, the Constitution of Massachusetts (1780) declared, "The liberty of the press is essential to the security of freedom in a state: it ought not, therefore, to be restrained in this commonwealth." Following these examples, the First Amendment to the United States Constitution restricted Congress from abridging the freedom of the press and the closely associated freedom of speech.

John Locke's ideas had inspired both the French and American revolutions. Thomas Jefferson wanted to unite the two streams of liberalism, the English and the French schools of thought. His goal was to create a government that would provide both security and opportunity for the individual. An active press was essential as a way of educating the population. In order to be able to work freely, the press must be free from control by the state. Jefferson was a person who himself suffered great calumnies of the press. Despite this, in his second inaugural address, he proclaimed that a government that could not stand up under criticism deserved to fall.

Jefferson said: "No experiment can be more interesting than that we are now trying, and which we trust will end in establishing the fact, that man may be governed by reason and truth. Our first object should therefore be, to leave open to him all avenues of the truth."

In 1931, the U.S. Supreme Court decision in *Near v. Minnesota* used the 14th Amendment to apply the freedom of the press to the States. Other notable cases regarding free press are:

- *New York Times Co. v. United States*: The Supreme Court upheld the publication of the Pentagon Papers.
- *New York Times Co. v. Sullivan*: The Court decided that in order for written words to be libel, it must be, first of all, false.

Notable Exceptions

- In 1798, not long after the adoption of the Constitution, the governing Federalist Party attempted to stifle criticism by means of the Alien and Sedition Acts. (It was notable that the Sedition Act made criticism of Congress, and of the President, a crime, but not criticism of the Vice-President. Jefferson, a non-Federalist, was Vice-President at the time the Act was passed.) These restrictions on freedom of the press proved very unpopular in the end and worked against the Federalists, leading to the party's eventual demise. Thomas Jefferson was among those who opposed the Acts, and did so vehemently, and he was elected President in the election of 1800. Jefferson then pardoned most of those convicted under the Acts. He made it a principle not to ask what they had done, but only whether they had been charged under the Acts. In his first Inaugural Address in 1801 he reiterated his longstanding commitment to freedom of speech and of the press: "If there be any among us who would wish to dissolve this Union or to change its republican form, let them stand undisturbed as monuments of the safety with which error of opinion may be tolerated where reason is left free to combat it."

- The Espionage Act of 1917 and the Sedition Act of 1918, which amended it, imposed restrictions on the free press during wartime. It carried fines of $10,000 and up to 20 years imprisonment for people publishing "... disloyal, profane, scurrilous, or abusive language about the form of government of the United States or the Constitution of the United States, or the military or naval forces of the United States..." In Schenck v. United States (1919), the Supreme Court upheld the laws, setting the "Clear and present danger" standard. Congress repealed both laws in 1921, and *Brandenburg v. Ohio* (1969) revised the "Clear and present danger" test to the "Imminent lawless action" test, which is less restrictive.
- 1988: *Hazelwood v. Kuhlmeier*: The Supreme Court upheld that the principal of a school has the right to review and block controversial articles of a school paper funded by the school and published in the school's name.
- In the United States in 2005, interpretation of the Bipartisan Campaign Reform Act may consider political statements as being the equivalent of campaign donations. Because access to Internet statements are weakly controlled, the

campaign value of statements is not known in advance and a high ultimate value may trigger large fines for violations. This particularly threatens Internet statements by individuals, and ambiguous definitions of membership in *the press* make the possible effects ambiguous.

- 2008: Wikileaks was forcefully censored by the United States. Wikileaks was given only hours notice "by e-mail" prior to the hearing. Wikileaks pre-litigation California council Julie Turner attended the start of hearing in a personal capacity but was then asked to leave the court room. After appeal, however, all the court of appeals threw out the case, restoring access to Wikileaks.

Implications of New Technologies

Many of the traditional means of delivering information are being slowly superseded by the increasing pace of modern technological advance. Almost every conventional mode of media and information dissemination has a modern counterpart that offers significant potential advantages to journalists seeking to maintain and enhance their 'freedom of speech.' A few simple examples of such phenomena include:

- *Terrestrial television versus satellite television*: Whilst terrestrial television is relatively easy to manage and manipulate, satellite television is much more difficult to control as journalistic content can easily be broadcast from other jurisdictions beyond the control of individual governments. An example of this in the Middle East is the satellite broadcaster Al Jazeera. This Arabic language media channel operates out of the 'relatively liberal' state of Qatar, and often presents views and content that are problematic to a number of governments in the region and beyond. However, because of the increased affordability and miniaturisation of satellite technology (*e.g.* dishes and receivers) it is simply not practicable for most states to control popular access to the channel.
- *Web-based publishing (e.g., blogging) vs. traditional publishing*: Traditional magazines and newspapers rely on physical resources (*e.g.* offices, printing presses) that can easily be

targetted and forced to close down. Web-based publishing systems can be run using ubiquitous and inexpensive equipment and can operate from any global jurisdiction. To get control over web publications, nations and organizations are using Geolocation and Geolocation software.

- *Voice over Internet protocol (VOIP) vs. conventional telephony*: Although conventional telephony systems are easily tapped and recorded, modern VOIP technology can employ sophisticated encryption systems to evade central monitoring systems. As VOIP and similar technologies become more widespread they are likely to make the effective monitoring of journalists (and their contacts and activities) a very difficult task for governments.

Naturally, governments are responding to the challenges posed by new media technologies by deploying increasingly sophisticated technology of their own (a notable example being China's attempts to impose control of through a state run internet service provider that controls access to the Internet) but it seems that this will becomes an ever increasingly difficult task as journalists continue to find new ways to exploit technology and stay one step ahead of the generally slower moving government institutions that attempt to censor them.

Organizations for Press Freedom

- ARTICLE 19.
- The Committee to Protect Journalists.
- Electronic Frontier Foundation.
- International Freedom of Expression Exchange.
- Internationale Medienhilfe.
- International Press Institute.
- OSCE Representative on Freedom of the Media.
- Reporters without Borders.
- World Association of Newspapers.
- World Press Freedom Committee.
- Worldwide Governance Indicators.
- Student Press Law Centre.

Glossary of Terms

Access Channel: One of the three cable channels designed for use by the public, government, or education.

Acculturation: In a media context, the tendency of reporters or other media professionals to adopt the ideas and attitudes of the groups they cover or with which they have a great deal of contact.

Advertising Agency: A company that handles both the creative and the business side of an advertising campaign for its clients.

Agenda Building: The ways the media decide what is newsworthy.

Agenda-Setting Effect: The influence of the mass media created by emphasizing certain topics, thus causing people to perceive those same issues as important.

Alphabet: A group of letters used to symbolize each of the sounds that make up a word.

AM: *Amplitude Modulation* of radio waves.

Ambient Sound: Unintelligible background noise found in and generally unique to an audio environment.

Amp. Ampere: Unit of electrical measure equal to one volt sent through a resistance of one ohm. Also: one watt divided by one volt.

Amphenol Connector: A threaded connector sometimes used for unbalanced microphone lines.

Amplified: Any electronic device used to increase the level or power of signals applied to it.

Aperture: Any electronic device used to increase the level or power of signals applied to it.

Arbitron: The professional research organization that measures radio audiences.

ASA: *American Standards Association*. A unit measuring the sensitivity of photographic emulsions. The higher the ASA number, the more sensitive the emulsion.

ASCAP: *American Society of Composers, Authors and Publishers.*

Assemble Edit: A video editing procedure which records new video, audio, and control track information simultaneously without reference to any signal already on the tape.

Astroturfing: Fake "grassroots." Any attempt by an individual or organization to use websites or comments posted to website—published under false or misleading identities—to create an impression of grassroots support for something, usually in the individual's or organization's interest.

Attack time: The response time of an automatic gain control circuit to rapidly increasing signals.

Audio: Sound.

Audit Bureau of Circulations (ABC): An organization formed by advertisers and publishers in 1914 to establish ground rules for counting circulation data.

Authoritarian Theory: The prevailing belief that a ruling elite should guide the intellectually inferior masses.

Automatic Gain Control: Electronic circuit designed to keep signals at an acceptable level by amplifying signals that are too low and attenuating or reducing signals that are too high.

Available Light: Light from a natural source or commonly used lamp, as opposed to light added to a scene by using special photographic or television lights.

AWG: *American Wire Gauge.* A unit of measure of the cross sectional diameter of wire. The higher the number, the thinner the wire. Ordinary lamp wire is 18 AWG.

Back Focus: The distance from the rear element of a lens to the image plane.

Background Light: Any light used to illuminate the background of a set or scene, but not intended to illuminate the subject.

Backlight: Light striking a subject from the direction opposite to the camera. Generally used to highlight the subject and set it apart from the background.

Balanced Line: A cable carrying two equal signals of opposite polarity on separate conductors, both surrounded by a grounded shield.

Bandwidth: The amount of audio or radio spectrum required or used by a signal or waveform.

Banner Ads: Type of advertising found on web pages.

Barn Door: A metal flap or group of metal flaps attached to the front of a lamp housing to prevent light from spilling outside a desired area.

Base Light: An even, diffuse, light filling a setting with sufficient light to keep shadows from key or back lights from being too dark.

Base Video: A video signal that is not combined with a carrier to place it in the radio frequency spectrum. Normally has an amplitude of one volt peak to peak across an impedance of 75 ohms.

Bayonet Mount: A lens mount, or electrical connector which engages by means of interlocking fingers and cams and permits attachment with only a relatively small amount of twisting action.

Beta Format: A group of videotape formats similar to U-matic used with half inch colour videocassette recorders and players.

Betacam: A component broadcast system using half-inch tape and cases similar to those for the Beta format.

Beware Surveillance: A media function that occurs when the media inform the public of short-term, long-term, or chronic threats.

Bidirectional Microphone: A microphone designed to pick up sound on two sides of the microphone along the same axis, but reject sound from any other direction.

Billboard: The sound-recording industry trade publication that tabulates record popularity.

Block Booking: A policy of major film studios that required theater owners to show several of a studio's low-quality films before they could receive the same studio's top-quality films.

Blog: Derivative of "weblog." A series of entries to an online journal, posted in some chronological order. Sometimes used, incorrectly, by writers to describe discussion forums or even all websites not affiliated with offline publishers. A blog can be written by an individual or a group. It can allow comments to entries or not.

Bloom: A loss of picture detail and increase in size of bright portions of a video picture seen when too much light is allowed to strike a pickup tube or when the signals controlling a tube allow it to be overdriven.

BMI: *Broadcast Music Incorporated.* A music licensing service.

BNC *Connector*: A connector with a bayonet lock used with coaxial video cable.

Boom Microphone: Any microphone, but usually a unidirectional or shotgun microphone, attached to a pole or boom to keep the microphone near an audio source but outside of the field of view.

Brightness Control: A control used to adjust the illumination of view finders, monitors, and receivers, but not affecting signal levels from cameras or other picture sources.

Broad: A light with a long bulb perpendicular to the direction in which the light is aimed, designed to throw an even light with an indistinct shadow.

Broadband: Increased bandwidth for Internet connections, which speeds up downloads.

Browsers: Type of software that lets individuals search for content on the World Wide Web.

Burn: Part of a pickup tubes that has a depletion of charge evidence by a negative image of the picture source causing the depletion. This condition is temporary unless the tube is turned off and allowed to cool before the problem is corrected.

Burst: A gated 3.58 megahertz signal immediately following horizontal sync and used as a reference in controlling the hue, or phase, of colour signals.

Business-to-Business Advertising: Advertising directed not at the general public but at other businesses.

Cable: A term generally referring to a broadband distribution system using wire rather than over-the-air broadcast.

Camera Cap: A cap screwed or mounted onto the front of a camera in place of the lens to protect the camera pickup tube from light or dirt when the lens is not in place.

Campaign: In advertising, a large number of ads that stress the same theme and appear over a specified length of time.

Cannon: A three-pin connector used with balanced audio lines for line and mic level audio signals. Also known as an XL or XLR connector.

Capacitor: An electrical device which stores energy as an electrostatic charge. Often used as a component in filter circuits.

Capstan: The spindle that actually drives tape across head assemblies.

Cardioid Microphone: A somewhat unidirectional microphone with a heart-shaped pickup pattern.

Carriage Fee: Fee paid by cable systems to carry a cable network.

Carrier: The RF signal which is modulated by a video or audio signal for broadcast transmission.

Categorical Imperative: Ethical principle that states people should behave as they would wish all others to behave.

Catharsis: A release of pent-up emotion or energy.

Catharsis Theory: A theory that suggests viewing aggression will purge the viewer's aggressive feelings.

CATV: *Community Antenna Television.* Broadband distribution system using coaxial cable rather than over-the-air broadcast.

CCD: *Charge-coupled device.* In television, the device that senses light coming through the lens and translates it into electrical impulses (replacing the pickup tube).

CCU: *Camera control unit.*

CD: *Compact disk.* Laser disk with five inch diameter, which may contain video, audio, or data in digital format.

CD ROM: *Compact disk* with digital data used with a computer as *"read-only memory."*

Cease-and-Desist Order: A Federal Trade Commission order notifying an advertiser that a certain practice violates the law; failure to comply with a cease-and-desist order can result in fines being levied against the advertiser.

CG: *Character Generator.*

Channel: The pathway by which a message travels from sender to receiver.

Character Generator: A small computer used to generate titles and other text electronically without the use of a camera.

Characteristic Impedance: The apparent resistance to an alternating current shown by a wire or electronic device.

Chroma: The characteristic of a colour which refers to its saturation or intensity. Also the colour pattern of the television signal.

Chroma Key: A key based on the chroma saturation and hue of portions of a picture, rather than on the luminance, or brightness. A specific hue is replaced by one picture source, while the rest of the picture is replaced by another picture source. A chroma key is an external key.

Chrominance: The colour portion of the television signal.

Circulation: The total number of copies of a publication delivered to newsstands, vending machines and subscribers.

Citizen Journalism: AKA "grassroots journalism." The collecting and publication of timely, unique, non-fiction information by individuals without formal journalism training or professional affiliation. Examples include the publication of cell phone photos from a breaking news scene, blog reports covering local government meetings and discussion forums reporting results from international competitions.

Clock Hour: Radio format that specifies every element of the programme.

C-Mount Lens: A lens with a standard one-inch threaded mount assembly that is screwed into the camera body, as opposed to a bayonet or "m" mount.

CMS: *Content management system*. The computer software, housed on your site's Web server, that manages the publication of content to your website. Popular examples include Blogger, Wordpress, Typepad, Drupal and Geeklog.

Coaxial Cable: A cable having a center conductor surrounded by insulation and a grounded shield.

Colour Killer: A circuit designed to detect the presence of burst in a television signal and deactivate the colour circuits if the burst signal is low or absent.

Commercial Television: Television programmes broadcast by local stations whose income is derived from selling time on their facilities to advertisers.

Communist Theory: Theory of the press that holds the media should promote the goals of the ruling political party.

Compatible: Meeting all of the electronic requirements for signals and levels necessary to interface devices to achieve desired results.

Comprehensive Layout: The finished model of a print ad.

Computer-Assisted Reporting (CAR): Skills involved in using the Internet to aid reporting.

Concept Testing: A type of feedback in which a one or two-paragraph description for a new series is presented to a sample of viewers for their reactions.

Condenser Microphone: A microphone using a power supply (usually a battery) to maintain a charge across two plates which modulate a voltage when the distance between them changes.

Confidence Dead: A video head separate from the normal record/ play head found on some videotape recorders and used to monitor the actual recorded signal on the videotape during recording.

Consent Order: Federal Trade Commission order in which the advertiser agrees to halt a certain advertising practice without admitting any violation of the law.

Consumer Advertising: Advertising directed at the general public.

Contrast: The difference in illumination between the brightest and darkest parts of a scene or picture.

Contrast Control: A control used to change the amplitude of the video signal in view finders receivers, and monitors, but not affecting the output of cameras or other video sources.

Control Track: A reference signal recorded on videotape and used to control the path of the video heads across the tape on playback.

Controlled Circulation: A type of circulation in which publications are sent free or distributed to a select readership, such as airline passengers or motel guests.

Convergence: The blending of communication technologies.

Conversational Currency: Topic material presented by the media that provides a common ground for social conversations.

Cookie: A line of text recorded on a reader's computer when that reader requests content from a specific web domain, either an entire Web page or just an element on a web page. The cookie includes the name of the domain, a unique visitor number and values for whatever other variables the visited domain wishes to set. The cookie can be read only by a server from the domain that set the cookie. Cookies can be used to track unique visitors to a website, to maintain shopping carts in e-commerce stores and keep visitors logged in to discussion forums and blogs.

Copy: Headlines and message in an ad.

CPM: Cost per thousand impressions (M being the Roman numeral for 1,000). In advertising, the rate than an advertiser will pay a publishers to have his ad displayed on 1,000 page views. Or, the revenue from advertising that a publishers will receive for every 1,000 page views served.

Creative Boutique: Advertising organization that specializes in the creative side of advertising.

Credibility: The trust that the audience holds for media that perform surveillance functions.

Credits: Listings of all those involved in making a programme, usually appearing at the end of a television programme or film.

Critical/Cultural Approach: Analytical technique that examines power relationships in society and focuses on meanings people find in texts.

Critical Focus: The plane in front of a focussed lens in which the image will be precisely in focus on the film or pickup tube.

Crowd Sourcing: A subset of grassroots journalism. A process in which readers submit individual reports that are collected into a larger data set for use in reporting a story. Examples include damage reports in earthquakes as well as watchdog efforts to track various elected officials' stands on an issue. Also known as "distributed news reporting."

Crystalization: The sharpening and elaboration of a vaguely held attitude or predisposition.

CU: *Close-up.*

Cultivation Analysis: An area of research that examines whether television and other media encourage perceptions of reality that are more consistent with media portrayals than with actuality.

Culture: Common values, behaviours, attitudes, and beliefs that bind a society together.

Cume: The total audience size (number of viewers) for a programme or series of programmes over several showings. Repeat viewers are not counted.

Cut: The instantaneous transition from one picture or audio source to another.

Cutaway: A shot interposed at an edit point to prevent the appearance of a jump cut at the edit point.

Cycle: In all-news radio, the amount of time that elapses before the programme order is repeated.

Cyclorama: A seamless background, blending into the floor and usually lit from behind. Used to eliminate any background detail from a set.

DA: *Distribution Amplifier.*

dB: *Decibel.* A unit used to compare the relative levels of electrical signals on a logarithmic scale. The formula for the calculation is db=10(log(P2/P1)), or db=20(log(E2/E1)).

Decoding: The activity in the communication process by which physical messages are translated into a form that has eventual meaning for the receiver.

Defamation: The act of harming the reputation of another by publishing false information.

Demo: A demonstration tape used to sell a musical performer or group.

Demodulation: The process of separating a signal from its carrier frequency.

Depth of Field: The range of distances in front of the lens in which objects appear to be in acceptable focus.

Depth of Focus: The range of distances from the rear of the lens to the face of the pick-up tube in which acceptable focus can be achieved.

Developmental Journalism: Type of journalism, practiced by many Third World countries, that stresses national goals and economic development.

Developmental Theory: The assumption that government uses media to further national, economic, and social goals.

Digital Technology: A system that encodes information—sound, text, data, video—into a series of on and off pulses that are usually denoted as zeros and ones.

Digital Television (DTV): Television signals consisting of binary signals that allow for improved picture quality.

Digital Videodisk (DVD): A disk that stores audio, movies, video, and graphics in digital format that is compatible with DVD players and home computers.

DIN: (1) A standard for film sensitivity similar to ASA. Not Direct Current. An electrical current that does not change polarity. (2) A type of multi-pin connector.

Direct Action: An ad that contains a direct response item (such as a toll-free number) that allows advertisers to see results quickly.

Direct Broadcast Satellite (DBS): A system in which a home TV set receives a signal directly from an orbiting satellite.

Disintermediation: The process of delivering a product or service directly to the consumer.

Dissolve: The gradual change from one picture to another, allowing the pictures to be superimposed during the transition.

Distortion: Any undesirable alteration in an audio or video signal.

Distribution Amplifier: An amplifier with essentially unity gain used to distribute control and picture signals to equipment in a television system.

Distribution System: The actual cables that deliver the signals to subscribers.

Distributors: Sector of media industry that takes products from manufacturers and delivers them to retailers.

Dolly: A wheeled device attached to a tripod to allow smooth movement of a camera.

Double Feature: Practice started by theaters in the 1930s of showing two feature films on the same bill.

Dub: To copy by playing back on one machine and recording on another.

Duct Tape: A shiny adhesive tape designed for holding metal heating and cooling ducts, but also commonly used as a substitute for gaffers tape, a general purpose tape used in television and film.

Dummy: Rough version of a magazine that is used for planning how final version will look.

Dynamic Microphone: A microphone which uses a magnet moving in a coil of wire to generate an electrical signal.

Dysfunction: Consequence that is undesirable from the point of view of the welfare of society.

E to E: *Electronics to Electronics*. Refers to the normal record mode in a videotape recorder in which the recorder output is connected to the recorder input and cannot show the actual signal recorded on tape. Some videotape recorders have special confidence heads which allow direct tape monitoring during recording.

E-Book: Digital version of a book, which can be read by using a computer or a special reader.

Edit: In television, to record from any programme source altering the duration or temporal sequence of events using a recorder specifically designed to do this efficiently and cleanly, maintaining continuity of sync and proper timing relationships between signals at edit points.

Editorial Policies: Guidelines the print media follow to persuade the public on certain issues or to achieve specific goals.

EFP: *Electronic Field Production.*

EIA: *Electrical Industries Association.*

EIAJ: *Electrical Industries Association of Japan.* Universal standard for video recording in black and white on half inch reel-to-reel videotape recorders. The standard involves a tape speed of 7½ inches per second with a sixty-minute capacity using a seven inch reel. There is only one audio channel.

Eight-Pin: A common rectangular connector generally used between television monitors and videotape recorders combining all of the cable connections necessary for record and playback functions into a single connector.

Electret: A type of condenser microphone.

Electronic Field Production (EFP): Production of a television programme or programme segment by recording material on location with a single camera and editing this material to make the finished product.

Electronic News Gathering (ENG): Producing and airing field reports using small, lightweight portable TV equipment.

E-Mail: Electronic messages sent from computer to computer.

Encoding: The activity in the communication process by which thoughts and ideas from the source are translated into a form that may be perceived by the senses.

Equal Opportunities Rule: Part of the Communications Act of 1934; Section 315 allows bona fide candidates for public office to gain access to a broadcast medium during political campaigns.

Equalization: Changing the relative balance of frequencies in an audio or video signal.

Equalizing Pulses: A series of sync pulses within the horizontal interval which determine the starting point for the first scan line of each field of video.

Establishing Shot: A shot used to introduce a scene, including a relatively wide angle of view and showing the relationships between objects, settings, and people in the scene.

Evaluation: Research done to measure the effectiveness of an advertising or a public relations campaign.

Experiment: A research technique that stresses controlled conditions and manipulates variables.

F Connector: A small threaded connector used with coaxial cable in the RF distribution of television signals.

Fade: The gradual change from one picture or sound source to another. Usually to or from black (video) or silence (audio).

Fairness Doctrine: Now defunct FCC doctrine that required broadcast stations to provide various points of view on a controversial issue.

Federal Communications Commission (FCC): A regulatory agency, composed of five individuals appointed by the president, whose responsibilities include broadcast and wire regulation.

Feedback: The responses of the receiver that shape and alter subsequent messages from the source.

Fidelity: A subjective appraisal of the amount of distortion in the reproduction and transmission of signals.

Field Experiment: An experiment that is conducted in a natural setting as opposed to a laboratory.

Field: One scan from the top to the bottom of the television frame, tracing alternate horizontal lines and taking one sixtieth of a second to complete.

Fill Light: Light used to fill in shadows left by key light and keep the contrast range of a scene within the capabilities of the recording medium.

Film Chain: An equipment grouping including a dedicated camera, super 8 mm and 16 mm projectors, dual dissolving 35 mm slide projectors, and a special rotating mirror assembly (multiplexer) which transmits the images from one of the projectors to the dedicated camera.

Filter: A flat piece of glass or gelatin with no optical properties other than to control the colour or intensity of light.

First Amendment: The first amendment of the Bill of Rights, stating that Congress shall make no law abridging the freedom of speech, or of the press.

Flag: The horizontal shift observed at the top of the screen when a timing error occurs due either to skew and tension problems on playback or to slight timing errors at an edit point created in the editing process.

Flare: An undesired image, or overall haziness of an image caused by undesired reflections of light from surfaces within the lens itself.

Flat Response: The reproduction or transmission of a signal with very little deviation from the original amplitude of the signal over its entire frequency range. Deviations in amplitude are expressed in db, plus or minus.

Flat: A framed upright panel, usually 4 × 8 feet or larger, used to simulate a wall or wall section in a television set.

Flood Light: Any light throwing a broad, even illumination in a circular pattern with diffused shadows.

Flutter: A form of signal distortion caused by rapid fluctuations in the speed of a tape crossing a head assembly.

Flying Erase Head: An erase head mounted on the rotating video head drum in advance of the record/playback head.

FM: *Frequency Modulation* of radio waves.

Focal Length: The distance from the optical center of a lens to the focal plane.

Focal Plane: The plane perpendicular to the lens axis at which parallel rays striking the lens are converged to a point.

Focus: To cause a sharp image from a lens to be projected onto the focal plane (in the case of a camera) or onto a screen (in the case of a projector). Also to adjust the electron beam converging circuits in a television monitor for maximum sharpness as they strike the surface of the picture tube.

Focus Group: A group of 10 to 15 people led by a moderator that discusses predetermined topics.

Foot Candle: The amount of light produced by a standard candle at a distance of one foot. The most common unit of measure for incident light used in film and television work.

Format Wheel: Visual aid that helps radio programmers plan what events happen during a given time period.

Format: Consistent programming designed to appeal to a certain segment of the audience.

Formative Research: Advertising research done before developing a campaign.

Frame: A complete television picture consisting of two interlaced fields of video. The frame rate for NTSC television is thirty frames per second.

Framing: The general way a news medium treats a topic.

Franchise: An exclusive right to operate a business in a given territory.

Free Marketplace of Ideas: Press philosophy that endorses the free flow of information.

Free-Link Exchange: Web advertising technique in which one company exchanges free ad space with another.

Freeze Frame: The continuous repetition of a single frame of video. It is technically not possible for helical videotape recorders to display freeze frames, since they read only one field of video on each pass across the videotape.

Frequency: The rate of repetition of an electrical or audio signal, expressed in Hertz (cycles per second).

Fresnel: A special light-weight lens used in focussing beams of light. Originally used in lighthouses, now also used in high quality studio and theatrical lights.

Full-Service Agency: An ad agency that handles all phases of advertising for its clients.

Functional Approach: A methodology that holds something is best understood by examining how it is used.

Fuse: A device designed to interrupt an electrical circuit in the event of an overload of that circuit.

Gaffer: The crew member principally responsible for transporting, maintaining, and setting up lighting equipment.

Gaffer's Tape: A strong adhesive tape used in film and television production.

Gag Rules: Judicial orders that restrict trial participants from giving information to the media or that restrain media coverage of events that occur in court.

Gain: Degree of amplification. The difference between the signal level at the input of a device and the level at the output, usually expressed in dB.

Gatekeepers: Individuals who decide whether a given message will be distributed by a mass medium.

Generation: The number of duplication processes by which a videotape is removed from the live source. The original recording is first generation, while a copy of an original recording is second generation, and so on.

Genloc: To reference a signal generator to a signal normally external to and separate from the system controlled by the signal generator. The purpose is to bring a system, such as a studio, into proper timing with an external source, such as a live remote camera, so that special effects as wipes, keys, and dissolves can be done using the external source in combination with internal sources.

Golden Mean: Ethical principle that states moderation is the key to virtue.

Gramophone: A "talking machine" patented in 1887 by Emile Berliner that utilized a disk instead of a cylinder.

Grip: The crew member principally responsible for the transportation, maintenance and mounting of the camera.

Ground: A connection to the chassis or a common return path, or an actual connection to the earth in an electrical device.

Hard News: Timely stories with significance for many people.

Head End: The antenna and related equipment of the cable system that receives and processes distant television signals so that they can be sent to subscribers' homes.

Head Gap: The space between the poles of a head. Good frequency response is dependent on proper width of the head gap. Dirt or oxide particles clogging a head can cause reduced signal level and distortion of the signal.

Head: The uppermost portion of a tripod or pedestal which provides for the ability to pan and tilt the camera.

Head Room: The space between the top of a subject's head and the top of the video frame.

Heavy Metal: Counterculture musical trend of the 1960s-1970s, characterized by a vaguely threatening style and heavy use of amplification and electronic equipment.

Hegemony: Dominance of one entity over another.

Helical: Like a helix. Specifically, the geometric pattern formed by a rotating video head in relation to videotape moving across the rotating head assembly. Thus, referring to any videotape recorder using a rotating head assembly that reads a complete field of video on each pass across the tape. These include all EIAJ, U-matic, Beta, and VHS formats as well as one-inch SMPTE types A, B and C.

Hertz: Cycle per second.

Heterodyne: A system used for recording colour video signals at a reduced frequency.

Hicklin Rule: A long-standing obscenity standard based upon whether a book or other item contains isolated passages that might deprave or corrupt the mind of the most susceptible person.

High Level: Audio signal intended to attain a maximum, or peak, level of zero *db*, or one volt at six hundred ohms impedance. (0.775 volts rms.)

Hiss: The background noise generated in an audio system which is internally generated by microphones, amplifiers, and tape.

Hits: Requests for any single file on a web server. A hit can be a request for a web page or any element of that page, such as an image, a stylesheet or an external javascript. Therefore, "hits" is a meaningless statistic for measuring web traffic. A large number of hits on a website might mean that a site uses a lot of images or scripts on its pages, rather than that many people visit the site. "Unique visitors" over a defined period should be used to measure a site's popularity instead.

Horizontal Hold: An adjustment on viewfinders, monitors, and receivers to make the frequency of the horizontal sweep circuits to the horizontal sync pulse from an incoming signal.

Horizontal Sync: That portion of the sync signal that controls the horizontal timing (and therefore horizontal location) of each line of picture.

House Drop: The section of the cable that connects the feeder cable to the subscriber's TV set.

HTML: *Hypertext Markup Language.* A language in which content is formatted to display as a web page. It is a subset of XML. Web pages no longer need to be written in HTML. Most modern web browsers can display an XML document as a web page if the document's web server specifies a style sheet for the browser to use when rendering the XML document.

Hue: Shade of colour, determined in television by the phase angle between a colour and the colour subcarrier or colour burst reference signal.

Hum: Unwanted low frequency audio noise caused by improperly shielded or improperly grounded audio cables and circuits.

Human Interest: News value that emphasizes the emotional, bizarre, offbeat, or uplifting nature of a news story.

Hypertext: Digital navigational tool that links one electronic document to another.

IBOC (*In-Band, On-Channel*)**:** Digital radio broadcasting system that is also compatible with current analog radio.

Ideology: Particular set of beliefs or ideas.

Impedance Matching: The use of a transformer or other device to alter the impedance of a device to equal the impedance of another device. Minimum distortion and loss of signal can be achieved only where the output transmitting a signal, the cable carrying the signal, and the input receiving the signal all have the same impedance.

Impedance: The apparent resistance to an alternating current shown by a wire or electronic device.

Incident Light: Light striking a subject, as opposed to light reflected by a subject. Usually measured in film and television by light meters calibrated in foot candles.

Independents: Radio or TV stations unaffiliated with any network.

Indirect Action Ad: Advertisement that works over the long run to build a company's image.

Information Gathering: Phase of a public relations campaign where pertinent data are collected.

Injunction: A court order that requires an individual to do something or to stop doing something.

Insert Edit: A video or audio edit made with reference to pre-recorded control track so synchronization is maintained and the insert can be ended without visible disruption of the picture.

Insert: A shot or sequence inserted into a television programme used to illustrated a subject.

Instrumental Surveillance: A media function that occurs when the media transmit information that is useful and helpful in everyday life.

Interlace: The process of combining the two video fields into frames by writing only even-numbered lines in one field and only odd-numbered lines in the other.

Internal Sync: Synchronizing signals generated by a camera, recorder, or other picture source without reference to or need of external synchronizing signals.

Internet Addiction: Condition in which a person spends too much time on the Internet, cannot control his or her Internet use, and neglects social responsibilities to spend time online.

Interpersonal Communication: A method of communication in which one person (or group) interacts with another person (or group) without the aid of a mechanical device.

Investigative Reports: News reporting that requires extraordinary efforts to gather information about matters of public importance.

IRE: *Institute of radio engineers*. NOW IEEE. Also a unit of measure of video amplitude. One IRE unit is equal to 1/140 volt, peak to peak. The composite video signal is composed of sync, from -40 to 0 IRE and video, from 0 to 100 IRE. Black is normally set at between 7.5 IRE and 10 IRE.

Jazz Journalism: Journalism of the Roaring Twenties that was characterized by a lively style and a richly illustrated tabloid format.

Jazz: A form of popular music that emerged during the Roaring Twenties and was noted for its spontaneity and disdain of convention.

Joint Venture: Method of movie financing in which several companies pool resources to finance films.

Joint-Operating Agreement (JOA): An agreement, intended to preserve editorial competition, in which two newspapers merge their business and printing operations but maintain separate newsrooms.

Jump Cut: An edit made without regard to the thirty degree rule, which results in a visual discontinuity as subjects appear to "jump" on screen.

Key Light: The primary illumination for a scene, generally giving the impression of a natural light source and throwing the darkest and most defined shadows in a scene.

Key: A video special effect in which the level of a video signal is used as a switch which allows selective substitution of picture information from one source with picture information from a different source. Luminance keyers use the amplitude of the monochrome portion of the signal, while chroma keyers use the amplitude of a specific colour or hue. Most printed material is inserted into video using luminance keys, while picture information is inserted using chroma keys.

Keystone: The effect of projecting an image onto a surface that is not perpendicular to the axis of the projecting lens. Parallel lines tend to converge in the direction where the surface is closer to the lens.

Kinetoscope: The first practical motion picture camera and viewing device, developed by William Dickson in 1889.

Lag: The tendency in some camera pick-up tubes to retain an image after it is no longer presented to the tube. This effect is most evident when a relatively bright image is replaced by a darker field of view and is aggravated when a bright image is stationary in the field of view for an extended period of time before it is replaced.

Latent Image: The image retained by a pick-up tube after the source of that image is removed. If a latent image is present on a pick-up tube when a camera is turned off, the image may be permanently fixed on the tube.

Lavalier: A microphone worn on the body and held in place either with a lanyard worn around the neck or a clip fastened to clothing. The frequency response of a lavalier microphone is skewed toward the higher frequencies to compensate for the low frequency sound transmitted directly to the microphone by contact with the body.

Lens Hood: Also lens shade. A cone fastened to the front end of a lens to keep incident light from striking the lens elements and causing lens flare.

Libel Per Quod: Written material that becomes libelous under certain circumstances.

Libel Per Se: Falsely written accusations (such as labelling a person a "thief" or a "swindler") that automatically constitute libel.

Libel: Written defamation that tends to injure a person's reputation or good name or that diminishes the esteem, respect, or goodwill due a person.

Libertarian Theory: The assumption that all human beings are rational decision makers and that governments exist to serve the individual.

Limited Partnership: Method of movie financing in which a number of investors put up a specified amount of money for a film.

Limiter: An amplifier designed to limit or compress signals over a desired level, thus reducing the chances of distortion and keeping the range of signal levels within the range that can be recorded. Unlike an automatic gain control, a limiter does not augment or boost low levels.

Line Level. In audio, a signal with a peak power of about one milliwatt at an impedance of 600 ohms, or zero dBm: This is equivalent to a voltage of .775 volts rms. Also know as "high level" or "auxiliary level."

Linkage: The ability of the mass media to join different elements of society that are not directly connected by interpersonal channels.

Live: Not prerecorded. Occurring at the same instant as it is seen or recorded.

Live Card: A card, usually about 11 × 14, used in television to display text or graphics to a camera.

Live on Tape: Unedited. Recorded exactly as occurring with no compression of time or alteration of any sequence of events.

Long Shot: A shot including a relatively wide view of an overall scene, often used as an establishing shot.

Low Level. Microphone Level: An audio signal with a maximum level of about minus fifty dB, relative to line level, or 2.45 millivolts at 600 ohms impedance.

Lux: The amount of light produced by a standard candle at a distance of one meter.

Machine-Assisted Interpersonal Communication: A method of communication involving one or more persons and a mechanical device (or devices) with one or more receivers.

Macro Analysis: A sociological perspective that considers the functions performed by a system (*e.g.*, mass media) for the entire society.

Mainstreaming: In cultivation analysis, the tendency of differences to disappear among heavy-TV-viewing people, apparently because of cultural and social factors.

Management by Objectives (MBO): Management technique that sets observable, measurable goals for an organization to achieve.

Marketing: Developing, pricing, distributing, and promoting an idea, a good, or a service.

Mass Communication: The process by which a complex organization, with the aid of one or more machines, produces and transmits public messages that are directed at large, heterogeneous, and scattered audiences.

Mass Media: The channels and the institutions of mass communication.

Master: A control uniformly governing the outputs of a number of other controls.

Matching Transformer: A transformer used to alter the impedance of a signal source to match the input impedance of another device. A common use of matching transformers is to change the characteristic impedance of a 75 ohm coaxial antenna cable to 300 ohms to match the antenna input of a television set.

Media Buying Service: An organization that specializes in buying media time to resell to advertisers.

Media Vehicle: A single component of a mass medium, for example, a newspaper or TV network.

Mediamark Research Inc. (MRI): Company that measures magazine readership.

Medium Shot (MS): A shot showing a single subject, rather than an overall scene, but not in detail. For example, a shot of a person including the body from the waist to slightly above the top of the head.

Message: The actual physical product in the communication process that source encodes.

Message Research: Pretesting messages in an ad campaign.

Mic Mouse: A soft foam pad or holder for a microphone which is placed on a stage or studio floor. The mic mouse holds the microphone very near the floor without allowing it to touch. The purpose is to eliminate the effect of sound waves bouncing off the floor and interferring with sound waves transmitted directly to the microphone.

Microanalysis: A sociological perspective that considers the functions performed by a system (e.g., mass media) for the individual.

Mixer: An electronic device for combining the outputs of several sound sources, with separate control over the volume or quality of each.

Modem: Device that allows computers to communicate *via* phone lines.

Modulation: The process of varying the instantaneous amplitude, frequency, or phase of a carrier signal in response to the waveform of an information-bearing signal.

Motion Picture Patents Company (MPPC): An organization formed by the nine leading film and film equipment manufacturers in 1908 for the purpose of controlling the motion picture industry.

Mp3: Digital method of encoding sound files on the Internet.

Mpaa Rating System: The G, PG, PG-13, R, NC-17 rating system for movies administered by the Motion Picture Association of America.

Muckrakers: Term coined by Theodore Roosevelt to describe the reform movement undertaken by leading magazines in the 1890s; corrupt practices of business and government were exposed to the general public by crusading members of the press.

Multiplexer: A device which uses a movable mirror to select images from one of several optical sources for transmission to the dedicated camera in a film chain.

National Advertiser: Advertiser who sells a product all across the country.

National Public Radio (NPR): A non-commercial U.S. radio network.

Network: An organization composed of interconnecting broadcasting stations that cuts costs by airing the same programmes.

Neutral Density Filter: A filter having no effect on colour and no optical effect on the lens to which it is attached, but which reduces the overall amount of light reaching the lens. A one power filter reduces transmission by half, or by one f-number. A two power filter reduces transmission by two f-numbers.

Newsgroups: Section of the Internet devoted to message boards that are organized according to topic.

Newshole: The amount of space available each day in a newspaper for news.

Nickelodeon: A popular name for the many penny arcades and amusement centers that emerged around the beginning of the 20th century and specialized in recordings and film.

Noise: In communication, anything that interferes with the delivery of a message.

Non-commercial Television: Television programmes broadcast by those stations whose income is derived from sources other than the sale of advertising time.

Non-duplication Rule: FCC rule passed in 1965, stating that an AM-FM combination may not duplicate its AM content on its FM channel for more than 50 per cent of the time.

Nose Room: The space between the nose of a subject's head in profile and the edge of the video frame the subject is facing.

NTSC: *National Television Systems Committee*: Referring to any standard for signals devised by that body, such as NTSC colour bars or NTSC sync. The television system used in the United States, Canada, Japan, Central America, and a number of other countries. The NTSC system has 525 interlaced horizontal lines and 30 frames per second. Look for countries using NTSC.

Nuvicon: A type of video pick-up tube used in inexpensive colour television cameras.

Observational Learning: A form of education in which individuals learn by observing the actions of others.

Octave: A doubling of frequency. Almost all audio devices have a sound frequency range of from four to ten octaves. A piano, with 88 keys, has a range of seven and a third octaves. A video signal has a range of almost twenty octaves.

Ombudsperson: An individual in a media organization assigned to handle complaints from audience members.

Omnidirectional Microphone: A microphone which picks up sound equally well from all directions.

One-Hundred Eighty Degree Rule: A rule of visual continuity which states that when dealing with two or more subjects, shots may only be cut together if they are taken from the same side of a line drawn through the subjects. Used to maintain proper direction on the screen.

One-Stops: Individuals who sell records to retail stores and jukebox operators who are not in a position to buy directly from the record company.

Open Source Reporting: A method in which reporters, or readers working as reporters, make their source list and gathered information public while they are working on their report, instead of merely revealing selected information from their newsgathering available in a traditional report at the conclusion of the project.

Open Source Software: Software for which the uncompiled source code of the programme is freely available for users to see and modify. Open source software is typically made available to users for free, under the General Public License [GPL].

Operating Policies: Guidelines that cover the everyday problems and situations that crop up during the operation of a media organization.

Optical Viewfinder: A camera viewfinder which has no electronics and therefore cannot reflect the actual picture being transmitted from the camera. Optical viewfinders for inexpensive television cameras are rangefinder viewfinders which are separate from the camera lens system and show a picture slightly different from that seen by the camera. The difference is most troublesome for subjects close to the camera where the angle of difference, or parallax, is greatest.

Original: Usually first generation audio or videotape from which a master is made.

Paid Circulation: A type of circulation in which the reader must purchase a magazine through a subscription or at a newsstand.

PAL. *Phase Alternating Line*: The television system used in western Europe, China, and most of the rest of the world. The PAL system has 625 interlaced lines and 25 frames per second. Look for countries using PAL.

Pan: A camera movement in which the camera is rotated in the horizontal axis. The proper commands are "pan right" and "pan left."

Panel Study: A research method in which data are collected from the same individuals at different points in time.

Parabola: A parabolic dish used to reflect sound waves, concentrating them on a microphone, allowing sound to be picked up from greater distances than with even a normal unidirectional or shotgun microphone.

Paradigm: A model used for analysis.

Parallax: The difference in view caused by looking at a scene from two slightly different locations.

Parasocial Relationship: A situation whereby audience members develop a sense of kinship or friendship with media personalities.

Pass-Along Audience: That portion of a magazine's total audience composed of individuals who pick up copies of a magazine while at the doctor's office, at work, while travelling, and so on.

Patch Bay: Patch panel. A control panel where all the video and audio lines used in a studio are brought together and terminated in connectors allowing any combination of lines to be wired together as desired by patching in short lengths of cable.

Patch Cord: A short cable with connectors used to interconnect lines in a patch panel. Any audio or video cable used for temporary connections.

Payola: Bribes of gifts and money paid to DJs by record companies in order to gain favourable airplay for their releases.

Pay-per-View (PPV): A system that allows cable TV subscribers to pay a one-time fee to view one specific programme or movie.

Peak to Peak: Literally, encompassing the entire waveform from the most negative part to the most positive. One of two ways to measure signal amplitude, the other being *rms* (root mean square). Peak to peak measurements are usually more meaningful in video, while *rms* is more meaningful in audio.

Pedestal: A camera support generally restricted to studio use having a single elevator column mounted on a tricycle base.

Penny Press: The mass-appeal press of the early 19th century.

Persistence of Vision: Quality of the human eye that enables it to retain an image for a split second after the image has disappeared.

Phase: The difference, expressed in degrees, between two signals. In colour television, the angle between the burst reference signal and any colour or hue.

Phi Phenomenon: Tendency of the human perceptual system to perceive continuous motion between two stationary points of light that blink on and off; basis for the illusion of motion in motion pictures.

Phone Jack: An audio connector generally used with unbalanced lines and intercom systems. Phone jacks may have a single conductor with ground (unbalanced lines) or two conductors with shield (intercom systems and stereo headphones).

Phonograph: A "talking machine" developed by Thomas Edison in the late 1870s; the hand-cranked device preserved sound on a tinfoil-wrapped cylinder.

Photoflood: Any of a number of lamps designed for still photography that throw an even, diffuse light. They may be designed to fit into a dish reflector or have internal reflectors. Since they are ordinary tungsten bulbs, they tend to lose output power and change colour temperature with age, making them unsuitable for colour television.

Photojournalism: Journalism in which written text is secondary to photographs in news stories.

Pickup: A technique of financing a motion picture.

Pick-up Tube: A light-sensitive electron tube which is scanned by an electron beam to convert an image focussed on the face of the tube into an electronic signal.

Pilot Testing: A process that involves showing a sample audience an entire episode of a show and recording their reactions.

Pilot: The first episode of a projected television series.

Pixel: The smallest indivisible area of a computer display that can be addressed.

Plumbicon: A pick-up tube used in almost all tube-type broadcast colour cameras.

Policy Book: At radio and TV stations, a book that spells out philosophy and standards of operation and identifies practices that are encouraged or discouraged.

Political Press: Newspapers and magazines of the 1790-1820 era that specialized in publishing partisan political articles.

Polysemic: Having many meanings.

Pop: Microphone distortion caused by speaking certain consonants (especially "p") into a microphone placed too close to the mouth.

Portal: The first page a person sees when opening an Internet browser.

Portapak: A brand name for a battery-operated portable video camera and recorder combination.

Positioning: In advertising, stressing the unique selling point of a product or service to differentiate it from the competition.

Pot: Potentiometer. A variable resistor used to control the level of a signal.

PPC: *Pay per click.* An advertising system, such as Google's AdWords/AdSense, where advertisers pay publishers each time a reader clicks on their ads, and only when the ads are clicked on.

Preamp: An amplifier used to increase signal levels prior to additional processing.

Presence: The ambient sound found in and unique to a recording location.

Primary Audience: That portion of a magazine's total audience made up of subscribers or those who buy it at the newsstand.

Primary Demand Ad: Advertisement that promotes a specific product category, such as milk.

Prime-Time Access Rule: Rule adopted in 1970 intended to expand programme diversity by barring network programmes from the 7:30-8:00 P.M. (E.S.T.) time slot.

Printing On Demand: One-at-a-time printing of books that exist in a digital database.

Prior Restraint: An attempt by the government to censor the press by restraining it from publishing or broadcasting material.

Proc Amp: *Processing amplifier*. Separates the video signal into sync and picture components to allow limited adjustment of pedestal, gain, and some other aspects of the picture and recombination with internally generated sync signals.

Profile: Side view, especially of a person.

Prominence: News value that stresses the importance of the person involved in the event.

Prosocial Behaviour: A general term used by researchers to describe behaviours that are judged desirable or worthwhile under the circumstances.

Protocol: A common language accepted by computer programmers.

Proximity Effect: An overemphasis of low-frequency tones caused by speaking too close to a unidirectional microphone.

Proximity: News value based on the location of a news event.

Public Journalism: The philosophy that newspapers should try to solve civic problems as well as report the news.

Publicity: The placing of stories in the mass media.

Publics: The various audience served by public relations.

Publishers: Segment of the print media industry responsible for the creation of content.

Quad: Broadcast videotape recorder having four rotating video heads, each of which reads only 17 horizontal lines of picture per pass over the tape. Quad recorders use two-inch videotape.

Quartz-Halogen: The light of choice in colour television, designed to maintain correct colour temperature and uniform output throughout its life. Provides much higher output than conventional tungsten light of the same power consumption and has a life up to one hundred times that of common tungsten photographic lights. These lamps are sensitive to shock and handling and should never be touched with bare hands.

Rack Jobbers: Individuals who service record racks located in variety and large department stores by choosing the records to be sold in each location.

Radio Frequency (RF): That part of the frequency spectrum in which it is possible to radiate (transmit) electromagnetic waves. Any part of the broadcast band, including radio and television.

Radio Mic: *Transmitter mic or wireless mic.* A microphone connected to a small radio transmitter, used in situations where cables would be cumbersome or impossible to use. FCC regulations are stringent in the use of transmitter microphones.

Rate Base: Number of buyers guaranteed by a magazine and used to compute advertising rates.

Rating: (1) The percentage of the total potential television homes tuned to a specific programme. Because the rating is based on total television homes, including those that are not watching any television, the totaling one sixteeth of a second to complete.

(2) The ratio of listeners to a particular radio station to all people in the market; the ratio of viewers of a particular TV programme to the number of households in the market equipped with TV.

RCA Pin Plug: A small connector used with unbalanced single conductor shielded audio cables to interconnect home entertainment audio products. Also used as high level inputs and outputs on some video recorders and audio mixers. Also called a *phone plug*.

Receiver: Any device capable of demodulating an RF signal, such as a radio, tuner, or television set.

Recorder: Any device that converts an electronic signal to a magnetic pattern in the oxide coating of a magnetic tape.

Reel-to-Reel: Any audio or videotape format which uses tape packaged on open reels which must be threaded manually, rather than enclosed in a cassette or cartridge.

Reflected Light: Light reaching the camera after being reflected by a subject. Measured in candles per square foot.

Reflector Flood: A sealed floodlight with a self-contained reflector.

Reflector Spot: A sealed spotlight with a self-contained reflector.

Reinforcement: Support of existing attitudes and opinions by certain messages.

Release Time: The response time of an automatic gain control circuit to rapidly decreasing signal levels.

Remote: A production at a location other than a television studio using a special effects generator and other equipment associated with multiple-camera studio facilities.

Resolution: The degree to which fine detail can be recorded or displayed. In film, measured in pairs of light and DARK lines per millimeter. In television, measured in lines per scan. Thus, the horizontal resolution of a television camera would be measured by the number of discernible vertical lines that could be displayed across the width of the screen.

Resonance: In cultivation analysis, the situation in which a respondent's life experiences are reinforced by what is seen on TV, thus reinforcing the effect of TV content.

Retail (local) Advertiser: Business that has customers in only one trading area.

Retailers: Segment of the media industry responsible for selling media products to the consumer.

Revenue Sharing: Process by which video stores share movie rental fees with movie companies.

RF Modulator: A device used to convert a signal to a form similar to that transmitted by an over-the-air broadcast so the output can be used by standard receivers.

RF Splitter: A passive device used to distribute radio frequency signals to two or more receivers.

RF: *Radio frequency*.

Riser: A platform on which talent sit or stand, used to raise the talent to a level more suited to coverage by the television camera.

rms: *Root mean square*. A measure of the effective level of an audio signal or alternating current.

Roll-off: The gradual reduction of frequencies above or below a certain point. Filters which roll off the bass frequencies are often included in unidirectional microphones to compensate for proximity effect.

ROM: *Read only memory*. Computer memory that can be read, but cannot be overwritten by the host computer.

Rough Layout: Early version of a print ad.

Rover: A brand name for a battery-operated portable video camera and recorder combination.

rpm: *Revolutions per minute.*

RSS: A method for syndicating website content to another website or online application, such as a news reader. *"Rich Site Summary"* or *"Really Simple Syndication."* It is a text file, marked up in XML, that includes formatted headlines, summaries and URLs for articles, blog entries or discussion topics on a website.

Safe Area: In television graphics or film shot for television, the area which is almost certain to be displayed on any television set. About 80 per cent of the scanned area.

Satellite News Gathering (SNG): Using specially equipped vans and trucks to transmit live stories from any location *via* satellite.

Saticon: A television pick-up tube used mostly in industrial television and electronic news gathering.

Scanned Area: In television graphics, the area on a slide or live card which is to be scanned by the television camera. This area is about 25 per cent larger than the safe area.

Scrim: A wire mesh used to reduce and soften the light from a light.

SECAM. Sequential Colour with Memory: The colour television system developed in France using 25 frames per second and 625 horizontal lines. Look for countries using SECAM.

SEG: *Special Effects Generator*. The device in television used to switch between and combine various picture sources. Also called a switcher.

Selective Demand Ad: Ad that stresses a particular brand.

Self-determination: Ethical principle that states that human beings deserve respect for their decisions.

Sensitivity: The ability of a device, such as a camera or microphone, to sense intelligible information and convert it into a usable electronic signal.

Sequence: The importance or weightiness of a news story.

Servo: An electronic circuit used to control the speed of a motor which drives a videotape recorder head assembly drum, which must be controlled with great precision.

Share: The percentage of the total television sets in use that are tuned to a specific programme.

Share of the Audience: The ratio of listeners to a particular radio station to the total number of listeners in the market; the ratio of the number of households watching a particular TV programme to the number of households watching TV at that time.

Shield: The outer metal portion of a shielded or coaxial cable, normally grounded, to protect conductors from interference.

Shield Laws: Legislation that defines the rights of a reporter to protect sources.

Shock Mount: A support for a microphone which used rubber of foam supports to isolate the mic from vibrations which can appear as low frequency rumble in the audio.

Shotgun Microphone: A unidirectional microphone with a narrow pick-up pattern.

Shovelware: Publishing stories from one media, usually a print newspaper, in another, usually a website, without substantially altering the content. Newspaper websites without online original content, such as blogs, mid-day updates, discussions and video, are derisively called "shovelware."

Sibilance: An undesired hissing sound resulting from over emphasis of high-frequency sound in the reproduction of "s" and "z" sounds in speech. Reduced by equalization or use of a windscreen.

Signal Generator: A device used to generate electronic test signals and, in television, the drive and synchronizing signals used to control and time components in a television system.

Signal to Noise Ratio: The difference in amplitude between unintelligible noise and the maximum signal output of a device.

Skew: In television, the tendency of a picture to hook at the top of the television screen and the control found on some videotape recorders which adjusts tape tension in order to correct this picture problem.

Slander: Spoken defamation. (In many states, if a defamatory statement is broadcast, it is considered libel, even though technically the words are not written. Libel is considered more harmful and usually carries more serious penalties than does slander.)

Slave: In some editing systems, the record machine, or the machine on which the edited tape is compiled.

Sliding Scale: An arrangement between a motion picture exhibitor and a distributor that details how much box office revenue will be kept by the movie theater.

Slow Motion: Playback of a film or videotape at a speed slower than the speed at which it was recorded. This is impossible to do in all but a few specialized videotape recorders without sacrificing picture stability.

SMPTE: *Society of Motion Picture and Television Engineers*. An organization devoted to the standardization of equipment and practices.

SMPTE Leader: The leader with the eight second count-down commonly used in film.

SMPTE Type A, B or C: The standards for one inch videotape recorders. Type C is the preferred standard for broadcast one inch videotape.

Social Responsibility Theory: The belief that the press has a responsibility to preserve democracy by properly informing the public and by responding to society's needs.

Social Utility: The media function that addresses an individual's need to affiliate with family, friends, and others in society.

Socialization: The ways an individual comes to adopt the behaviour and values of a group.

Sock Puppetry: An attempt by a web writer to make a site look more popular than it is by posting comments under multiple aliases. Reference comes from comedians who wear a sock puppet on one hand to carry two sides of a conversation by themselves. Can be considered a form of "astroturfing."

Soft News: Features that rely on human interest for their news value.

Source: Any piece of equipment which transmits information to another piece of equipment. Usually referring to devices attached to the input ports of audio mixing consoles, special effects generators, or recorders.

Spam: The electronic equivalent of junk mail.

Special Effects Generator or (SEG): The device in television used to switch between and combine various picture sources.

Splitter: A passive device used to distribute RF signals.

Spotlight: A light having a narrow beam that casts well-defined shadows.

Status Conferral: A process by which media attention bestows a degree of prominence on certain issues or individuals.

Stimulation Theory: A theory that suggests viewing violence will actually stimulate an individual to behave more violently.

Storyboard: A series of drawings depicting the key scenes in a TV ad.

Strategic Planning: Management technique that sets long-range, general goals.

Streaming Video: Method of sending TV over the Internet.

Style Sheet: A set of instructions to a web browser on how to display various elements on a web page. Style sheets can declare font styles, image positioning, page layout and mouse behaviour across a web page.

Subcarrier: The 3.58 megahertz signal used in generating and controlling the hue of NTSC colour television signals.

Subsidiary Rights: Rights given by a publisher to others, allowing them to reproduce certain content.

Superimposition: The adding or mixing of two video signals to produce and image with two or more pictures visible simultaneously. Used when a keyer is not available to add graphics to video. Sometimes used to refer to a key.

Surveillance: The news and information function of the mass media.

Survey: A technique of gathering data that typically uses a questionnaire.

Switcher: Also special effects generator or SEG. The device in television used to switch between and combine various picture sources.

Sync Defeat: A switch on videotape recorders that use the composite video signal at the video input to control the internal timing of the recorder which interrupts that control function, allowing the recorder to control timing functions without reference to the incoming video signal.

Sync: Any of the signals used to generate and control a television picture, but, specifically, the portion of the composite video signal from zero to minus forty IRE units consisting of vertical and horizontal timing pulses and equalizing signals to maintain the proper relationship of the two fields of video making up each frame.

Synthesizer: A device used to generate video signals without a camera, used in the production of graphics.

Tabloid: A heavily illustrated publication usually half the size of a normal newspaper page.

Tactical Planning: Management technique that sets short-range, specific goals.

Take: The instantaneous transition from one picture source to another. A cut.

Target Audience: In advertising, the segment of the population for whom the product or service has an appeal.

Target Voltage: The voltage applied to the pick-up tube which determines the sensitivity of the tube to light.

TBC: *Time base corrector.*

Technological Determinism: The theory that contends technology drives historical change.

Telephoto Lens: Any lens with a focal length significantly greater than the standard focal length for the format in which it is to be used. The standard length for 35 mm still cameras and one inch television cameras is 50 mm.

Text: Object of analysis in the critical/cultural approach.

Thirty-Degree Rule: A principle of visual continuity which states that the relative angle of view of any two similarly framed shots of the same subject which are to be cut together should vary by at least thirty degrees.

Tilt: A camera movement in which the camera is rotated in the vertical axis. The commands are "tilt up" and "tilt down."

Time Base Corrector: A highly specialized device with the primary function of making the unstable video output of a videotape recorder conform to the rigid timing of a signal generator, allowing videotape to be used as a picture source in combination with other sources driven by the signal generator.

Time Shifting: Recording programmes and playing them back at times other than when they were aired.

Timeliness: News value that stresses when an event occurred.

Titles: Graphic information appearing at the beginning of a programme, generally including the title, author, producer, writer, director, and major personalities.

Tracking Control: The control used to maintain alignment of the video head with the tracks of video information on a tape.

Tracking Head: The magnetic head that writes and reads a sixty hertz pulse on videotape. During playback this pulse is used to maintain proper alignment of the video heads with the tracks of video information on a tape.

Tracking Studies: Study that examines how ads perform during or after a campaign.

Trespass: Illegal entry onto another's property.

Troll: A person who posts to an online forum or blog to provoke a hostile response from other readers.

T-Stop: Similar to an f-stop, this is a number which indicates the effective aperture opening of a lens after compensation is made for the amount of light lost due to internal absorption and reflection. The T-number is always larger than the corresponding f-number.

T-Stop: The size of the aperture in a lens, given in f-numbers. The lower the f-number, the more light passes through the lens. It is the ratio of the lens focal length to the actual diameter of the aperture opening.

Tuner: The demodulator section of a radio, television set, or videotape recorder.

UHF: *Ultra High Frequency*. Radio frequencies from 300 to 3,000 megahertz.

UHF Connector: A threaded video connector used with coaxial cable.

U-Matic: The standard format for 3/4 inch videocassette recorders. This format has a maximum record/play time of one hour and two discrete audio channels.

Unbalanced Line: A cable with a single signal-carrying conductor and a grounded shield.

Underground Press: A type of specialized reporting that emerged in the mid- to late 1960s, with emphasis on politically liberal news and opinion, and cultural topics such as music, art, and film.

Unique Visitors: Originally, the number of unique IP addresses from which requests for content were made a web server over some defined period of time (usually per day, week or month). Due to the use of proxy servers, a more accurate count of unique visitors can be made by setting cookies to each site visitor and recording how many unique cookie identities visited the site over a period.

Uses-and-Gratifications Model: A model proposing that audience members have certain needs or drives that are satisfied by using both non-media and media sources.

Utility: Ethical principle that stresses the greatest good for the greatest number.

Variety: The entertainment industry trade publication.

V-Chip: A device installed in a TV set that restricts the reception of violent or objectionable material.

Vectorscope: A special type of oscilloscope designed to display the saturation and hue of chroma signals in a polar pattern. This device is essential in the evaluation of colour signals when aligning colour picture sources or matching and timing colour sources in a television system.

Veil of Ignorance: Ethical principle that argues that everyone should be treated equally.

Vertical Hold: A control on television monitors, view-finders, and receivers used to control the frequency of the vertical oscillator and allow the vertical sweep circuits to lock to the vertical sync component of an incoming video signal.

Vertical Interval Editing: Use of a videotape recorder which is capable of recording and erasing video field by field (has a "flying" erase head) and employs vertical interval switching at the edit point.

Vertical Interval Switching: Switching based on circuits that delay switching from one picture source to another until the picture source being switched to is between fields, or in the vertical interval.

Vertical Interval: The period of time between the last line of a field and the first line of the next field.

VHF: The *"very-high-frequency"* band of the electromagnetic spectrum; channels 2 through 13 on the TV set.

VHS: A half inch videocassette format using the "M" wrap tape path. Not compatible with the BETA format.

Video: The picture portion of a television signal, sometimes referred to as "composite video" when both picture and sync signals are present.

Videocassette: A container holding both the feed and take-up reels which is inserted into a videotape recorder and threaded automatically.

Vidicon: A type of television pickup tube common in inexpensive cameras and still used to some extent in broadcast cameras.

Volt: The standard unit for measuring the difference of potential between two points in an electronic circuit.

VTR: *Videotape recorder.*

VU: *Volume unit*. Unit of measure of complex waveforms such as audio signals.

Watt: Unit of electrical power equal to one volt across a resistance of one ohm, or one volt at a current of one ampere.

Waveform Monitor: A specialized oscilloscope designed to display the video waveform with great stability and high resolution. Essential in determining and setting correct levels for the luminance (monochrome) and sync portions of the composite video signal and useful in evaluating critical timing relationships.

Web Page: A hypertext page contained within a website.

Website: A set of hypertext pages linked to each other that contain information about a common topic.

Wide Angle: Any lens with a focal length significantly less than the standard length for the format in which it is used. For 35 mm still cameras and one inch television cameras, the standard length is 50 mm.

Wide Shot (WS): A picture showing a subject in the context of the surroundings to establish the relationship between the subject and the surroundings.

Wind Screen: A thin soft foam cover for microphones which reduces the noise made by wind striking the microphone.

Wipe: The transition between television picture sources in which each picture source is displayed on only a portion of the screen, that portion being determined by an electronically generated pattern which can be sized and positioned using a special effects generator.

World Wide Web (WWW): A network of information sources that uses hypertext to link one piece of information to another.

Wow: The slow fluctuation in speed of a transport mechanism which results in low frequency instability and distortion in playback of an audio or video tape.

XL: Also **XLR** or cannon. A three-pin audio connector used with balanced lines in microphone and line level audio applications.

XML: *Extensible mark-up language.* A way of organizing text information by labelling it with specified variables in a fixed format.

Yellow Journalism: Sensationalized journalism, appearing during the 1890s, noted for its emphasis on sex, murder, popularized medicine, pseudoscience, self-promotion, and human-interest stories.

Zoned Edition: Newspaper that has special sections for specific geographic areas.

Zoom Lens: A lens with a variable focal length.

Zoom Ratio: The ratio of the longest focal length to the shortest focal length of a zoom lens.

Zoom: To change the focal length of a zoom lens.

Bibliography

"America from the Great Depression to World War II: Black-and-white photographs from the FSA-OWI, 1935–1945." Prints and photographs division, Library of Congress.

"Dave Barry," *The Miami Herald*.

"Flag Raising on Iwo Jima," News Photographer, *January, 1980,* p. 13.

"In Praise of Insensitive Reporters" by Jack Schafer, *Slate,* April 17, 2007.

"Inside Story: The Graduates"—The Independent.

"Internet Author, Stephen L. Rush (Applied Quantum Politics)."

"Totem Column," *Time,* November 10, 1941.

"Photo Portfolio Success" by John Kaplan. A great resource for preparing portfolios for photojournalism, fine art, weddings and much more.

A New Mechanism for Improved Media Representation and Public Participation in Development.

Allan M. Siegal and William G. Connolly. The New York Times Manual of Style and Usage: The Official Style Guide Used by the Writers and Editors of the World's Most Authoritative Newspaper, (2002).

An Introduction to a History of Woodcut, Arthur M. Hind, P. Houghton Mifflin Co. 1935 (in USA), reprinted Dover Publications, 1963.

Anderson, Gary, Video Editing and Production: A Professional Guide—Knowledge Industries, 1984.

Andrea Sutcliffe. New York Public Library Writer's Guide to Style and Usage, (1994).

Anonymous Sources/American Journalism Review.

Arthur Rothstein, *"The Picture that Became a Campaign Issue,"* Popular Photography, *September, 1961,* pp. 42-43, 79.

Arthur Rothstein, Documentary Photography, *Focal Press, Boston, 1986,* p. 93.

Article 10 of the European Convention on Human Rights.

ASMP Website (American Society of Media Photographers) (http://www.asmp.org/)—Often focused on good business practices and the latest information about the copyright law, topics all photographers need to follow.

Barker, Martin (with Julian Petley) (2001), *"On the problems of being a 'trendy travesty'" In: M. Barker and J. Petley (eds)* Ill effects: the media/violence debate. *(2nd ed.) London: Routledge,* pp. 202-224.

BBC News, reporting the comments of Professor Michael Geist, July 31, 2006.

Bell A. (1991), The Language of News Media. *Oxford: Blackwell.*

Bensinger, Charles—The Video Guide, 3rd edition, Sams Publisher, 1982.

Bensinger, Charles—Video as a Second Language: How to Make a Video Documentary—VTR Publishers, 1979.

Bill Number S. 193, *Broadcast Decency Enforcement Act of 2005 (Introduced in Senate) from Congressional THOMAS DB.* Retrieved on April 11, 2005.

Bill Walsh, The Elephants of Style: A Trunkload of Tips on the Big Issues and Gray Areas of Contemporary American English.

Boyd, A. (1994), Broadcast Journalism,Techniques of Radio and TV News. Oxford: Focal.

British Press Photographers Association; Hong Kong Press Photographers Association; Northern Ireland Press Photographers Association; (Swedish) Pressfotografernas Klubb; (Norwegian) Fotojournalisten.

Broadcast News, Reporting and Production—by White, Ted and Meppen, Macmillan Press, 1984.

Bryan A. Garner. The Winning Brief: 100 Tips for Persuasive Briefing in Trial and Appellate Court (1999).

Buck Ryan and Michael O'Donnell. The Editor's Toolbox: A Reference Guide for Beginners and Professionals, (2001).

Bundeskriminalamt (Federal Police) Yearly Statistics 2006.

C. Wright Mills, The Mass Society, Chapter in the Power Elite, 1956.

Cable rantings boost ratings—USATODAY.com.

Center for Visual Computing Invasion of Privacy.

CFJ—Centre de Formation des Journalistes.

Citation from *The Encyclopedia of World History Sixth Edition,* Peter N. Stearns (general editor), 2001 The Houghton Mifflin Company, at Bartleby.com.

Clifton C. Edom, Photojournalism, Wm. C. Brown Company Publishers, Dubuque, Iowa, 1976, p. 31.

Combs, Roberta. *Christian Coalition of America,* Washington Weekly Review, June 17, 2006.

Common Law Privacy Torts.

Crisell, Andrew (2002), An Introductory History of British Broadcasting. (2nd ed.) London: Routledge.

Crisis of Conscience—Perspectives on Journalism Ethics. Hausman, Carl. New York, Harper Collins, 1992.

Curtis MacDougall, Hoaxes, The MacMillan Company. New York, 1040.

Curtis MacDougall, News Pictures Fit to Print, *Journalistic Services, Inc., Stillwater, Oklahoma, 1971,* pp. 118-119.

Eden, Clifton C., *Photojournalism*: Principles and Practices, 2nd ed., Wm.C. Brown 1980.

Editorial Photographers (http://www.editorialphoto.com/). This organization also focusses on education, business practices and monitoring the changes in the copyright law.
Ethics and Journalism, Sanders, Karen. London, Sage Publications, 2003.
FALSE LIGHT by Professor Edward C. Martin—Cumberland School of Law, Samford University.
Feinberg, Milton—*Techniques of Photojournalism paper*. Books Demand UMI.
Fifth Review of the Radio Industry, FCC Media Bureau, undated.
Fontaine, Jean-Paul. L'aventure du livre: Du manuscrit medieval a nos jours. Paris: Bibliotheque de l'image, 1999.
Fowler, Nathaniel Clark. (1913), *The Handbook of Journalism*: All about Newspaper Work. Facts and Information of Vital Moment to the Journalist and to all who would enter this calling. New York: Sully and Kleinteich.
Fred Ritchin, *"Photography's New Bag of Tricks,"* The New York Times Magazine, November 4, 1984, p. 49.
Free News Release (*http://www.free-news-release.com*).
From Latin: libellus *("little book") ("Webster's 1828 Dictionary, Electronic Version." Christian Technologies, Inc.* (1828). Retrieved on 2006-12-31.
Galtung, J. & Ruge, M. Holmboe (1965), *The Structure of Foreign News*. The Presentation of the Congo, Cuba and Cyprus Crises in Four Norwegian Newspapers, *Journal of Peace Research*, Vol. 2, pp. 64-91; *online edition (JSTOR access required).*
George Orwell, 1984, *Harcourt Brace and World, Inc.*, New York, 1949, p. 43.
Good News, Bad News—Journalism Ethics and the Public Interest (Critical Studies in Communication and in the Cultural Industries) by Jeremy Iggers (New York, Westview Press, 1998).
Harcup T. and O'Neill D. (2001), What is News? Galtung and Ruge Revisited *Journalism Studies*, Vol. 2, No. 2, p. 277.
Harold Evans, Pictures on a Page, *Holt, Rinehart and Winston*, New York, 1978, pp. 145-148.
Hartley, J.: *"Mass Communication", In: O'Sullivan; Fiske (eds.):* Key Concept in Communication and Cultural Studies (Routledge, 1997).
Helmet Gernsheim, *The History of Photography*, McGraw-Hill Book Company, New York, 1969.
Herman, Edward and Noam Chomsky. (1988), *Manufacturing Consent*: The Political Economy of the Mass Media. New York: Pantheon.
Hetherington A. (1985), *News, Newspapers and Television*. London: Macmillan, p. 40.
Hicks, Wilson—*Words and Pictures: An Introduction to Photojournalism*—Ayer Co. Pub.
House of Lords—Berezovsky v. Michaels and Others Glouchkov v. Michaels and Others (Consolidated Appeals).

How the Other Half Lives complete text and photos online.

How to write a press release, incl. template (*http://www.andreas.com/faq-pressrelease.html*).

Huffman, James, L. (2003), A Yankee in Meiji Japan: The Crusading Journalist. Lanham, Maryland: Rowman & Littlefield.

IRIS 2006-10:2/1: Ilia Dohel, Office of the OSCE Representative on Freedom of the Media. Report on Achievements in the Decriminalization of Defamation.

John Dunbar, *"Lawyer says FCC Ordered Study Destroyed"*, Associated Press, September 14, 2006.

John Dunbar, *[Senator says media study suppressed "Senator says media study suppressed"]*, Associated Press, September 18, 2006.

Journalism and Mass Communications, Washington and Lee University.

Journalism Ethics—A Reference Handbook (Contemporary Ethical Issues) edited by Elliot D. Cohen and Deni Elliott (Abc-Clio, 1998).

Kaplan, Richard (2002), Politics and the American Press: The Rise of Objectivity, 1865-1920. New York: Cambridge University Press.

Letter from the Editor—Barron's Online.

Levy, Steven: Hackers: Heroes of the Computer Revolution (*Anchor Press/ Doubleday*, 1984).

Libel on The Internet: An International Problem.

Life, July 12,1937, p. 19.

Linda Jorgensen. Real-World Newsletters (1999).

M.L. Stein, Susan Paterno, and R. Christopher Burnett, *The Newswriter's Handbook Introduction to Journalism* (2006).

Mackay, H.; O'Sullivan T.: *The Media Reader: Continuity and Transformation* (Sage, 1999).

Mark Levin. The Reporter's Notebook : Writing Tools for Student Journalists (2000).

Master E.S., Alan Shestack, Philadelphia Museum of Art, 1967.

McQuail, D. (1994), *Mass Communication Theory*. London: Sage.

McQuail, D.: *McQuail's Mass Communication Theory* (fifth edition) (Sage, 2005).

Media Ethics and Accountability Systems. New Brunswick, NJ: Transaction Publishers, 2000. Originally published in French, translated in Armenia, Brazil, Greece, Italy, Korea, Portugal, Romania & Turkey. Arabic & Chinese translations in progress.

Media studies? Do yourself a favour—forget it—*The Guardian*.

Merriam-Webster Online Dictionary.

Millerson, Gerald,—Video Camera Techniques, Focal Press, 1983.

Mindich, David T.Z. 1998, Just the Facts: How "Objectivity" Came to Define American Journalism. New York: New York University Press.

Missouri School of Journalism: A Brief History of the Missouri School of Journalism.

Moores, Shaun (1993), *Interpreting Audiences: The Ethnography of Media Consumption*. London: Sage.

Murphy v. LaMarsh (1970), 73 W.W.R. 114.

National Geographic, February, 1982 and April, 1982.

News values. IT and citizen journalism. URL accessed June 26, 2008.

Newsweek Retracts Guantanamo Story.

NPPA Website (http://www.nppa.org/)—Has articles and services to help new talent break into the business, including the Mentor Programme, the Portfolio Critique Programme and the Job Information Bank (JIB).

NY Times Advertisement.

PACE Resolution 1577 (2007): *Towards decriminalisation of defamation*.

Philip Gerard, Creative Nonfiction: Researching and Crafting Stories of Real Life (1998).

Phillip Knightley, The First Casualty, *Harcourt, Brace Jovanovich, New York, 1976*, pp. 209-212.

Please Release Me (*http://releaseme.squarespace.com*)—a site with tips on how to write (and not write) press releases.

Randall, David. (2000), The Universal Journalist. *Sterling Virginia: Pluto Press*.

Reporter: Rove Told Him of Plame's CIA Tie.

Republic of the Philippines. "The Revised Penal Code." Chan Robles law Firm. Retrieved on 2006-11-24. "Art. 353. Definition of libel.—A libel is public and malicious imputation of a crime, or of a vice or defect, real or imaginary, or any act, omission, condition, status, or circumstance tending to cause the dishonor, discredit, or contempt of a natural or juridical person, or to blacken the memory of one who is dead."

Robert Taft, Photography and the American scene: A social history, 1839–1889 (New York: Dover, 1964), 446; and W. Joseph Campbell, *"1897: American journalism's exceptional year"*, Journalism History *29 (2004) (also here* et seq.*)*.

Rothstein, Documentary Photography.

Roy, Frank P., *Photojournalism: The Visual Approach* (Illus).

Ryan, C. (1991), *Prime Time Activism: Media Strategies for Grassroots Organizing*, Boston: South End Press.

Schlesinger P. (1987), Putting 'Reality' Together, 2nd edition London: Methuen.

Schudson, Michael (1978), Discovering the News: A Social History of American Newspapers. New York: Basic Books.

Schudson, Michael, *1997. "The Sociology of News Production." In* Social Meaning of News: A Text-Reader. *Dan Berkowitz, ed.* pp. 7-22. Thousand Oaks: Sage.

Sheila Reaves, *"Digital Retouching,"* News Photographer, January, 1987, pp. 23-41.

Shelagh Vainker in Anne Farrer (ed.), "Caves of the Thousand Buddhas", 1990, British Museum publications.

Shoemaker, P. and Reese, S.D. (1996), Mediating the Message. London: Longman.

Shook, Fredrick, *The Process of Electronic News* Gathering. Morton Publishers.

Simeon Edmunds, Spiritualism: A Critical Survey, *Aquarian Press, London, 1966*, pp. 114-115.

Société Radio-Canada c. Radio Sept-Îles inc., *[1994] R.J.Q. 1811 <http://www.canlii.org/fr/qc/qcca/doc/1994/1994canlii5883/1994canlii5883.html>.*

Sports Shooter Website (http://www.sportsshooter.com/), This Website is about *good* photography, not just sports photography. It contains many articles about breaking into the business, workshops and popular books about photojournalism and photography.

Steve Peha and Margot Carmichael Lester, Be a Writer: Your Guide to the Writing Life (2006).

Stone, Ejijah Melville (1921), Fifty Years a Journalist. New York: Doubleday, Page and Company. OCLC 1520155.

The Broadcast News Process (Third Edition)—By Frederick Shook/Dan Latimore, Morton Publishing.

The New Media Reader, *ed. Noah Wardrip-Fruin and Nick Nontfort. Cambridge, Mass.: MIT Press,* 2003.

The recent spat by the DBS bank is proof that the libel law in Singapore needs to be reformed.

Thompson, John B.: The Media and Modernity (Polity, 1995).

Times retracts Shakur story—Los Angeles Times.

Tsien, Tsuen-Hsuin (1985). "part one, Vol. 5", in Joseph Needham, Science and Civilisation in China,: *Paper and Printing*. Cambridge: Cambridge University Press.

USNPPA Code of Ethics.

Venables J. (2005), *Making Headlines: News Values and Risk Signals in Journalism; also (1993),* What is News? Huntingdon: ELM Publications.

W. Eugene Smith, *Aperture, Inc.,* New York, 1969.

Wood, William, Electronic Journalism. Columbia U. Press.

Woods, Donald (1981), Asking for Trouble: Autobiography of a Banned Journalist. *New York: Atheneum.*

World Press Photo; Best of Photojournalism; Pictures of the Year; The Press Photographer's Year.

Your World Cup: Join our pundit panels, BBC News, 2006-04-19.

Websites Links

209.47.161.50/articles/GlobeandMail/globe011017.htm Retrieved on 2007-06-07.

2theadvocate.com | Music | Combs denies '94 Tupac attack—Baton Rouge, LA.

50 Am.Jur.2d libel and slander 1-546.

archives.thedaily.washington.edu/1995/120495/wped.html Retrieved on 2007-06-07.

Collections.ic.gc.ca/heirloom_series/volume4/14-15.htm.

Dictionary.com: column.

Enforcement Policies Regarding Broadcast Indecency.

FCC Rules(CFR Title 47) On-Line at GPO.

FCC Website.

Federal Communications Commission Meeting Notices and Rule Changes from The Federal Register RSS Feed.

http://comunicaciones.udea.edu.co/index.php?option=com_content&task=view&id=9&Itemid=26.

http://en.wikipedia.org/wiki/Federal_Communications_Commission.

http://en.wikipedia.org/wiki/Mass_communication.

http://en.wikipedia.org/wiki/Printing

http://en.wikipedia.org/wiki/Printing_press

http://journalism.wlu.edu/Journalism.pdf.

http://www.chron.com/cs/CDA/ssistory.mpl/features/3176165)].

http://www.rtnda.org/ethics/CodeofEthics.pdf (PDF). Retrieved on 2007-06-07.

http://www.rtnda.org/ethics/CodeofEthics.pdf (PDF). Retrieved on 2007-06-07.

http://www.urosario.edu.co/FASE1/ciencias_humanas/pregrado_periodismo_opinion.htm.

Legal dictionary. findlaw.com. Retrieved on 2006-11-24.

Legal Terms. legal.org. Retrieved on 2004-10-22.

Net.au web site.

New Wave: The case for killing the FCC and selling off spectrum By Jack Shafer, 17 January 2007.

Online Etymology Dictionary. Retrieved on 2006-12-31.).

Photojournalism: The Professionals' Approach by Kenneth Kobre. This text covers the waterfront.

supct.law.cornell.edu/supct/cases/403us713.htm Retrieved on 2007-06-07.

www.rtnda.org/about/rtnda.shtml Retrieved on 2007-06-07.

www.spj.org/ethics_code.asp Retrieved on 2007-06-07.

Index